T0339924

# OLD TIMES IN OILDOM

METALMARK BOOKS

George W. Brown

# Old Times in Oildom

By

## Geo. W. Brown

---

Being a Series of Chapters in which are Related

the Writer's Many Personal Experien-

ces, During Fifty Years of Life

in the Oil Regions.

---

FOR SALE BY GEO. W. BROWN, YOUNGSVILLE, PA.

---

1911
THE DERRICK PUBLISHING COMPANY
OIL CITY, PA.

To my long time friend, a man of large heart and many friends and one of the original men in the oil trade,

### Hon. John L. McKinney,

#### Titusville, Penna.

Whose life has been lived for the good of mankind in general, this volume is respectfully dedicated by the author,

#### George W. Brown.

# Preface.

I wish to say to my readers that I have but two reasons for writing this little book. The first reason is that eleven articles were written to the Oil City Derrick, some years ago, in the way of correspondence. Then I was requested by the business manager of the Derrick Publishing Company, J. N. Perrine, to write more about "Old Times in Oildom." He explained that they would gladly publish it in book form.

My second reason is that I wish to enlighten the present generation regarding the many points of difference between the present time and fifty or seventy-five years ago.

It seems to me to be the duty of those who saw these great changes to hand them down to present and future generations —to those who can never know these things first hand. You will by reading this book learn that it is not a book of fiction, with a single thread running through all of it. Dozens and dozens of different little stories will be found in these brief touches on the history of the progress of our great country and state, and dozens of names of worthy but almost forgotten people will be found here.

The reader should thoroughly understand that the first eleven chapters of this book were written in 1896-1897. The additional chapters were written in 1909.

G. W. BROWN.

Youngsville, Pa., July, 1909.

## CHAPTER I.

## HAULING OIL ON SLEDS.

Coleman & Batchelor have just commenced a five years' lumber job at the "old Pennsylvania house," four miles below Irvineton. One peculiarity about this business is the fact that the saw mill is on the west side of the Allegheny river, and the shingle mill is on the east side of the river. A tramway is being built three miles back into the lumber woods, where all kinds of timber is found, that flourishes in this climate. They cut all, both hard and soft. The loaded tram cars are drawn by a steam locomotive, and run directly onto a ferry boat, which—by the aid of an inch wire—sails across to the mill, where the logs are tumbled into the river, being hitched to and drawn into the mill. This firm has leased the old Pennsylvania house, and a plot of land to pile their lumber on to dry. Speaking of this old house, reminds me of the early days of oil transportation. Before a railroad along the Allegheny was even talked of, the oil was transported from Tidioute to Irvineton in barrels. In the spring, summer and fall, large flat boats towed by two, three and four horses, in single file, were used to transport the oleaginous treasure from the wells at Tidioute to the P. & E. railroad at Irvineton. This was greasy work for the men, and killing work on the horses. In the fall and spring, when the shore ice was thick and sharp, the poor animals were pushed through the breaking ice, that would about half bear their weight, cutting their legs so severely that the generally clear waters of the Allegheny ran red with their blood. Many a noble horse laid down his life in this savage work. It was no uncommon sight to see the bloated carcasses of horses lodged along the shore. When a faithful equine would give up his life, the owner found it an easier way to dispose of his carcass by floating it off into the river than to bury it decently on the shore. But when the ice

got so solid, in the winter, that it could not be broken by the
horses' hoofs, the mode of transportation was on bobsleds,
drawn by horses that were not killed in the ice.   As the oil
wells about Tidioute, on Dennis run in particular, were considerably on the gusher order, it required a vast number of
teams to transport it.   One trip was a good day's work for a
team.   The loads ranged from six to twelve barrels each.
The reader can easily imagine the great necessity for hotels
and stabling under these circumstances.   The roads were completely lined with teams.   It was almost an impossibility for
the hosts of teamsters to find board and lodging for themselves and horses.   This was the situation of things when
"Jim" Conroe, an old farmer domiciled on the east bank of
the Allegheny, took it into his head to show his philanthropy
by building a four-story hotel on the narrow strip of land
between the wooded hillslope and the river.   He put on all
the masons and woodworkers that could find room to work
and soon the magnificent Pennsylvania house reared its tall
roof skyward, standing on an immense cut stone foundation,
and ornamented by huge wooden pillars in front.   People
were wont to say: "Now will Jim ever get his money back?"
Well, Jim did get his money back in about one year.   His
big hotel filled up every night, as if by magic, and some nights
more were turned away than were taken in, and Jim soon
found himself rolling in wealth.   But an end comes to all
good things.   Soon the cunning oil producer began to lay
pipe lines.   Then a railroad, now the W. N. Y. & P., then the
Warren and Franklin road, with its iron tank cars (brought
into use by the lamented Adna Neyhart), great iron tanks that
held the oil until convenient to move it to refineries, lightened
the weight of the crude on the ground where it was produced;
pump stations sent the oil through many arteries all over the
land, and James Conroe found his great hotel unoccupied by
guests.   He lived in this hotel with his family until it rotted
down over his head.   Then this lumber company came and
rented the property, rejuvenated the old hotel, and now three
families live under its hospitable roof, and "keep boarders."
Conroe, the builder, has moved out, and now contentedly
spends his waning years on the fine old farm above Dunn's
eddy, known as the "Dave Crull farm."   Such are a few of
the changes in the great oil business.   Oil cost something those

days. The fortunate owner of a gusher was obliged to pay
$2 each for his barrels, and $1 for hauling, a smart sum
for storage at the railroad depot, and high freights to the railroad corporations, which had not learned to respect this new
oil business.

If the eye of any of those old teamsters happens to fall on
this, they will recollect the late James Patterson, who checked
their loads of oil at Irvineton. Many a belated teamster
came after Mr. Patterson had "shut up shop" for the night.
The most urgent entreaties of these teamsters, asking Mr.
Patterson to check their loads, was invariably answered by, "I
cawn't do it," and the poor fellows—many of whom wished
to go elsewhere for the night—were obliged to linger until
morning.

---

## CHAPTER II.

## STAGING BEFORE RAILROADS WERE A BLESSING TO OIL CITY.

When the Atlantic & Great Western railway extended its
Oil City branch (or Franklin branch as it was called at that
time) to Franklin, the author, who, at that time, was helping
to supply Smith & Allison, the only lumber yard owners in
Oil City, with boards and shingles, was making almost weekly
trips to the "Hub of Oildom." On one of these trips he took
his wife along to let her see the beauties of oildom, as the
beauties shown forth at that time.

Well, one very cold winter's morning we took the P. & E.
accommodation to Corry. Here we changed "cars" for Meadville. A rather pleasant ride on the old Atlantic & Great
Western soon landed us in a great covered depot in Meadville.
After a first-class dinner at the McHenry house, that great
structure so well known to old-time oil men, where for $1 the
hungry traveler could be feasted as sumptuously as at any of
the great hotels of New York. Alas for all vanishing things.
How the greatness of the McHenry house has fallen, once the
white-aproned colored waiter flourished, now rats, and I was
on the point of saying, owls find a home. We took passage

on the "Franklin branch" for that "Nursery of Great Men"—
Franklin. No "Exchange hotel" at that time (in fact no
Mitchell lived there to build one.) We, wife and I, put up
at the United States hotel, Franklin's pride in the hotel line.
After partaking of a very palatable supper, we were consigned
to the only vacant room in the house; but after being piloted
in devious ways among cots by the dozen, placed in the parlor
and halls in every nook and corner by the accommodating
porter, we found that we were in a room without lock or
fastener of any kind. I did not feel safe, but my wife, the
courageous woman that she always was, said, "Let the door
go without fastening; no one will hurt us." With slight misgivings, I fell asleep that night to be awakened about three
o'clock in the morning by a man crawling around on the floor
of our sleeping apartment. (Don't get alarmed reader, nothing is going to happen.) I raised on my elbow and also raised
my voice in a courageous tone, and demanded of the intruder
his business in our room. The incoherent muttering of the
supposed culprit soon convinced us that the poor fellow was
a victim of old King Alcohol, and that he was on the verge
of the "jim jams." He was no criminal, simply in a dazed
condition. Several other men have been in the same condition
from the same cause. The next morning we took passage
on the stage for Oil City. Five dollars was the modest charge
for two of us. This would have been less burdensome if not
for the fact that the male passengers were obliged to jump out
many times and help extricate the wheels of the stage from
the deep, frozen "chuck holes." In fact, we not only helped
lift the wheels out of these holes, but many times we walked
along for quite a distance with our shoulders to the vehicle in
sometimes vain endeavor to keep the stage wheels clear of
those deep holes. After a short sojourn at the "Gibson house,"
which would not compare favorably with the pride of Oil
City, the Arlington, in size and accommodation, but in good
cheer its full equal, myself and wife concluded we would reach
railway accommodations by a different route than the one we
came. The route chosen was up Oil Creek "by stage" to the
Shaffer farm, where the "Oil Creek railroad" then had its
terminus. Profiting by my experience while getting from
Franklin to Oil City, I very gallantly paid $5 for my wife's
"stage fare" to the Shaffer farm, and "hoofed it" on terra

firma myself. You readers may think this is a sort of "buck-wheat,, arrangement to save $5. Nothing of the kind. This arrangement had a twofold advantage, in fact, a triplefold advantage. First, it was much easier for a man to walk from Oil City to Shaffer farm than to try to hang on to a "stage and ride"; second, my "better half" was much safer with her faithful husband walking by the side of the jostling, tipping, rattling "stage," ready with his strong arms to arrest the movement of the stage when it would be standing on two wheels, ready to fall on its side; and third, there was only room in the crowded thing called a "stage" for the female travelers. The ladies were afflicted with a harum-scarum boy for a driver, who would lash his horses into the numerous crossings of Oil Creek, without any regard to whether the ice was thick enough to hold them up or just thin enough to let them go through with a smash and a crash. Such driving I never witnessed before or since. It was really a relief to all concerned when the carriage, stage, wagon or whatever it might be called, broke down with a crash when two miles below Shaffer farm. I never saw a more willing set of travelers than those ladies. They never knew what a comfort it was to have a genuine breakdown before. When the cars were sighted, a happier set of ladies were not met with on Oil Creek than those who were just released from the perils of Oil Creek stage travel. All got to the train on time except one "smart" young man and his best girl. The young man had more confidence in his time piece than in others carried by experienced travelers and insisted on all taking a slower gate. All got on the train "just in time" except this "smarty," who had the fun of seeing the train move off, not to return for him and his girl until the next day. In this age of progress, let the passenger of those days answer whether there is an improvement when he now lies down in a luxurious berth of a Pullman sleeper and glides along the crooked, winding Oil Creek, without a jar.

## CHAPTER III.

### OIL CREEK POND "FRESH."

The young people don't know, and the older ones have nearly forgotten, when walking over the smooth, hard brick pavements of Oil City, what a change science and hard knocks have brought about. Let the reader look backward a few years—what do we see? We see a sea of thick mud in all the streets of Oil City, the depth of which could only be guessed at. The writer at one time stood on the corner near the First M. E. church (which was burned years ago) and saw, with his own eyes, three unfortunate horses floundering flat in the very deep mud, with as many gangs of men trying to tow the poor brutes to one side of the street, where the mud was not quite as deep as in the middle of this muddy canal. Now, mind, these horses were all down at the same time, in three different directions, all in plain sight of the corner spoken of above. One of the horses was owned and driven by the only Tom Hecker, who is known to every man, woman and child in Oil City, and who, from almost time immemorial, has raised chickens and took toll at the north end of the Suspension bridge. Tom can tell you about mud and Oil City pond freshets.

Fearing that the unsophisticated readers may not know what a pond freshet is, I will say that the mode of getting the oil from the big wells along Oil Creek to the Allegheny river was by towing boats and barges up Oil Creek to the wells along the banks on either side with horses, then running the oil from the wooden tanks into these boats, in bulk. Tube works were not heard of those days in this section, and the pipes that conveyed the oil from the tanks to the boat were generally made of boards, planks or anything that happened to be lying around loose. When all the owners of boats were ready, and they were legion, the chutes on all dams above Titusville would be cut. Then came the rushing waters, ropes that held the loaded boats to the shores would be cut and the mad race for the Allegheny would be on. No old pencil of mine can describe the scene. Little and big bulk boats would fight their way down the rushing waters, endways, sideways and in all shapes, these boats would heave in sight of the shanty town of Oil City. The old bridge across the mouth of the creek would be black with people who flocked from the rough board shanties, called houses, to see one of the sights of the world, such a sight as was never seen before and never will be seen again. I witnessed one of these runs which ended very disastrously. The first boat to reach the bridge was one carrying 400 barrels of oil, in bulk. The boat and oil was owned by an old Oil City citizen named Turner. He didn't turn that boat and cargo into money. The forward end of the boat struck a rock a few rods above the bridge, swung around and sailed up against the middle pier of the old bridge, the middle of the boat striking the pier. Turner's boat came around the pier in two pieces, and his oil painted the river green from shore to shore. But if the show had ended here a vast amount of money would have been saved. The first boat that cleared the old creek bridge safely stuck on the river bar, out in front of the mouth of the creek. The river was low, and the creek high, consequently the hundreds of boats piled up against each other until the creek was a great drift pile from the bar in the river, to quite a distance above the Lake Shore tunnel. As the oil was slashing around loose in all these boats it was as amusing to the observer as it was dangerous to the boatmen to see the oil, when the boat would smash into the jam, go surging from the rear to the front of the boat, there to pour into the waters of the Allegheny. As may be imagined, this general smashup was a great loss to the owners of the boats and oil. Tens of thousands of barrels of oil covered the surface of the river from shore to shore. This vast amount of oil, as it floated Pittsburgward, made the Allegheny one great river of green.

Old Oil City settlers will bear me out in saying that the young dudes and dudesses of the far-famed Hub missed one of the greatest sights that falls to the lot of mortals to behold by being born too late to see an Oil Creek oil pond freshet. And now here is where the irrepressible Tom Hecker comes in again. When Tom saw that so much beautiful green grease had got away from the owners he improvised a small dam near the old Moran house, gathered a lot of barrels on short notice and, as oil was about $10 a barrel at that time, he cleared about $900 on this afternoon's work.

One word about the price of real estate in those muddy times. The Hon. William Hasson offered to sell me one-quarter of an acre of land where the postoffice now stands for $200. I could have borrowed the money and paid for it, but my dim vision could see nothing in it. My neighbors, J. C. and D. Mead, took the venture and paid the $200, built the very substantial "Mead hotel," which cost them the sum of $500. They sold out in a year for $5,000. While they were building their hotel the Mead brothers urged me to take the quarter acre lot adjoining their hotel lot at $200, but my business capacity was not equal to the occasion, and I never became an Oil City lot owner.

---

## CHAPTER IV.

### PITHOLE HOTEL AND LIVERY CHARGES.

A few words about teaming. The word teaming meant something when Oil City was a shanty town. The soft alluvial soil on the Hasson flats was good material to form mortar beds of, when nothing could be moved without that faithful servant of man—the horse—and as business boomed to such an extent that thousands of horses were needed to keep things moving, the flats soon became, in a rainy time, one mammoth mudhole.

Now, to illustrate things, and to give the modern reader a slight idea of the cost of doing things at the time of which I write I will give an account of my first oil venture. I was taken in as a partner of J. C. & D. Mead, to operate a lease on Cherry run, about a half mile above Rouseville. I owned a quarter interest and unanimously elected superintendent. Well, to make a long story short, the first well was finished at a cost of about $9,000. The reader may think that there was mismanagement on the part of the superintendent in running up such a bill as that in putting down one well in "shallow territory." After an explanation, the reader will think different. The teaming was the great factor in the big expense account. In the first place, a boiler was drawn onto the ground by four span of horses at $18 a span. Then after trying to drill a few weeks, the fact leaked out that there were not enough flues inside the boiler and the old sawlog-shaped thing was hustled aside and a new $2,000 boiler put in its place. This last venture was satisfactory. That high priced boiler was equal to the task of making the steam to keep the unweildy old second-hand engine in motion. But now let us look again at the cost of this $9,000 job. Here is where the text "teaming" comes in again. This big boiler would not boil without heat, and to make heat wood or coal was required, and as wood was about $5 a cord delivered, we used coal, Cranberry coal. From the mines to our oil well was one great river of very stiff mud. This coal was hauled on wagons, to which was hitched three span of horses, and we paid the very modest little price of $1.25 per bushel. The owners of the coal were not unreasonable in charging what seems, in these days of railroads, a big steal. The sellers of this coal were fair dealers. They could not get the coal out of the crude Cranberry mines and haul it through this deep mud as fast as the green operators would take it at $1.25 per bushel. Well, the reader can see, without glasses, that this kind of work kept up for several weeks, with the little light tools of those days, could very easily reach the $9,000 mark. Scientific operators of today will wonder whether this company of Mead & Brown came off winners or losers. The answer is neither. Oil was $3.50 per barrel and the well panned out about 25 barrels a day, and kept up this production until the company sold out and were neither winners nor losers, from a financial standpoint. But in an educational point of view, the company were the gainers. They came off with a few hundred dollars' worth of experience.

Another leaf from my own experience will help along with this article with "teaming" for the text.

Mead & Co. (which means ourself and Nelson Mead, now of Corydon, Pa.,) leased a building lot on a back street at Pithole City and built a store house, of the rough order, on said lot. We were obliged to flatboat our lumber and material down the Allegheny from Irvineton to McCray's Landing, a noted commercial point at that time. From the landing to Pithole City, four miles, was found a typical oil country mudhole. We (Mead & Co.) paid $20 per thousand to have our lumber hauled and delivered on our speculative building lot. The store room went up with a rush, at a cost of $800. When completed we were offered $1,800 for the building. We wanted $2,000 for it. Our customer wanted us to give him three days to think about it. We gave the time. At the end of three days he had dropped $800 and offered us $1,000. After a hurried consultation, Mead & Co. concluded that at this rate of dropping off, it would not take a very long time to get below cost. So we closed the bargain, content with $200 profit on our venture. Our customer gave us $650 cash down and a bank note due in 30 days for $350. At the end of 30 days when Mead & Co. called at the then waning oil metropolis, our customer wanted to give us the property for the $350 note. As we were not anxious to buy Pithole City property on the declining valuation, we refused the generous offer, and called on the bank and drew our $350. Mead & Co. were not a grasping corporation and their kind hearts could not be brought to the point of taking a $1,000 property for $350.

To show the reader that horseback riding was a luxury those days, to be paid for as well as teaming, I will say I hired a little bit of horseflesh, with a saddle on, one day, during my business career in Pithole, for the purpose of riding four miles, to McCray's Landing and return. When the trip was finished, the liveryman, who was not stopping at Pithole for his health, charged me $5. I told the dealer in horses that I did not intend to buy the horse, but only to pay for the use of it about two hours. A glance at the man's face showed that he meant business and I handed over the fiver without further protest. When I took into consideration the fact that I had, that very morning, paid 75 cents to a hotel man for sleeping in a haymow in a barn, without even a blanket, I came to the conclusion that the liveryman was quite reasonable in his charges, and was only keeping abreast of the times.

----

## CHAPTER V.

### GEN. BURNSIDE'S RAILROAD.

The young citizens and part of the old of Oil City, while enjoying the blessings of four railroads, may not know the difficulty under which outside capitalists labored in bringing the present state of affairs about. I well remember that when the Atlantic & Great Western built a branch of their road from Meadville to Reno, the management found themselves "up a stump" when reaching the sacred precincts of the "Hub." The "city fathers" would not let a noisy and smoky railroad come into the golden "streets" of Oil City. The muddy streets and the creek and river were good enough for them. Besides, there was "no room on the narrow flats for railroad tracks." The city of Reno was not quite large enough for a great railroad terminus, so a railroad was built from Reno to Plumer. The city of Plumer was the terminus. Oil City, with its short sighted and high-toned council, was left out in the cold. I had the pleasure of riding from Franklin to Plumer several times on this picturesque and expensive railroad. I am not exactly sure as to the distance from Reno to Plumer, but I think it was about 16 miles. This is not as the crows fly, but as the surveyors laid out the road. The route ran toward Dempsey-town for several miles, when the top of the mountain was reached. Here a station was built, and a prospective town laid out in lots (Oil City speculators did not tumble over each other to buy lots); then down grade for a few more miles brought the road over dangerous looking trestles plump into McClintockville, then up through Rouseville and on up Cherry Run to Plumer, the terminus of the only railroad in this great oil region.

Coming down the mountain side from the direction of Dempseytown to McClintockville, a passenger could get a peep at a part of Oil City. ˙The part that could be seen seemed to almost hide its head in shame at the thought that Reno, Dempseytown, McClintockville, Rouseville, Cherry run, the Humboldt refinery and Plumer could have a railroad, but the greasy, busy Hub of Oildom could not have one . The city council and everybody else were obliged to get out of the city on a raft, flatboat, wagon, horseback or afoot, while Plum-erites could take a seat for New York or any city, on a soft cushion in a railway passenger coach. Of course the haughty citizen of Plumer was abliged to "change cars" at Reno, from the standard guage to the (then) six-foot guage of the Atlantic & Great Western. But what of that? Could they not glide down Cherry run and up through several townships over the mountain to Reno, with the serene satisfaction of knowing that poor little Oil City had no railroad connection with the outer world? Well, the reader may say, "Who was so short sighted as to build a road with such grades, when Oil City, with its commanding location, was sure to become quite a railroad center in no great length of time, regardless of near-sighted rulers?" I cannot answer that question—I can say that a man of great renown was president of the Plumer road.

The only time that I ever had the pleasure of seeing General Burnside was when he was seated on a pile of ties, on a flat car, or gondola, making strenuous efforts to get over the road, of which he was president. Two of these flat cars, partly loaded with ties, were hitched to a fine, new locomotive. Three times the start was made from Reno, and three times these two cars were backed down to the junction at Reno, for a new start, after having labored up the mountain side a mile or two. The fourth time the summit was gained, up among the Venago county farms, and the great general soon found himself and directors flying down over the dangerous look-ing gullies to the raging Oil Creek. I never heard the gen-eral's report after this patient ride, but very likely it was not very encouraging to the stockholders of his oil country rail-road.

Speaking of Plumer railroads reminds me of the old Pithole railroad. This was a six-foot guage, and it came to the very doors of Plumer. Little can be said of this road, only that it was built from the mouth of Pithole creek to the mushroom town of a few month's duration, Pithole City. When the city moved out the railroad moved out also. Plumer was tapped on both sides by new railroads, but they did not stick. Just imagine passenger trains running four trips a day from Pit-hole City to the mouth of Pithole creek. It is not likely that one passenger a day would pass over the road at the present time. The superintendent of the road, Blair, for many years superintendent of the Shenango road, kindly gave me a free pass over the four-mile road, but it ceased operation before I had an opportunity to use it, and the pass died on my hands. Before closing this No. 5 chapter, I wish to give the business youth of to-day a hint in regard to the cost of doing business in those days. I bought a quarter interest in one acre of oil land at Pithole, on which some men were trying to put down a well with a spring pole. In other words, they were trying to "kick it down." I did not know the exact location of my purchase, so I hied me away to Franklin to get a view of the docket. I found the clerk in the register and recorder's office and made known my business to him. I wished a copy of the lease. The clerk was driven with business. He was flying around in a great hurry. He said, "Can you give me the day of the month and the year when this lease was recorded?" I told him I could give the year but I had not the month and day. He said "I can't find it with that direction, but if you will give me $50 I will try to find it." As I had no $50 bill in my vest pocket at that certain time and as I had more time to fool away than the clerk seemed to have, I asked for a loan of his index for a short time. He rather reluctantly handed me the desired book and within the next 50 minutes I had a copy of the Pithole lease and felt somewhat as if I had done $50 worth of business in just 50 minutes. Court house tips those days were worth looking after.

---

## CHAPTER VI.

### JAMES S. McCRAY.

This article will treat upon Petroleum Center when it was a second Pithole City. You readers, who have not been an eye witness to the lively scenes that I am about to relate, have heard.more or less about ancient Petroleum Center. The wayfarer, in passing the quiet little hamlet now on a swift running W. N. Y. & P. train, don't see the surging, bustling, mixed-up masses of humanity that once thronged the streets. Your oldest readers will, perhaps, remember that about the time Pithole City made such a sudden fizzle, Petroleum Center dawned on the oil country scene like a meteor. The Maple Shade well and Coquette well, flowing their thousands of barrels per day of high priced oil, set the whole oil country wild, and soon the town of half a hundred had a population that ran into thousands, and what kind of a population was it? Well, that is a hard question to answer. It was composed of all classes, from the murderer to the minister of the gospel. The thugs, gamblers and soiled doves were in the majority. About 200 of the latter came down from the fast

waning Pithole City and took up their abode in Petroleum
Center's dance houses, of which there were about a half dozen,
free and easies and other "houses." The male population was
but little better than the female and Petroleum Center was a
"daisy town." Murder was among the crimes committed
here and the lesser felonies can never be enumerated. Still,
many good Christian people found themselves surrounded
by this wicked population. Three churches went up like
magic. Methodist Episcopal, Presbyterian and Catholic
churches; also a very creditable school building. I will speak
in particular of the Presbyterian church as I took the contract of building it. The late James S. McCray, who, when
alive, was known to every oil operator from Allegany, N. Y.,
to Lima, O., was chairman of the building committee. "Jim,"
as all called him, had a little income of $5 a minute, night
and day, Sundays and all, from his hillside farm, circulated a
subscription paper to raise $6,500, the cost of the church. Dr.
Egbert headed the list with $1,000 and "Jim" followed with
a like amount and two others, whose names have gone from
my memory, came down with four figures, and in less than a
day the whole amount was raised. McCray collected the
money as he went along, and took it home with him the same
night, put it under the pillow of his brother-in-law for safe
keeping, but one or more of Petroleum Center's crooks slipped a little chloroform in through the window and slipped the
great wad of greenbacks out, and in the morning nothing but
a strong smell of cholorform and a very sick brother-in-law
was found in the room.

The thieves had a gay time among the dance houses on
this church money, and "Jim" paid for the church from his
own pocket with as good grace as could be expected. His
time, at the period I speak of, was so much taken up in looking after his big income that he let the matter drop, after just
a little ineffectual scolding.

I mention just an incident or two that will show up the
oddities of this sometime millionaire. (This is the amount
that he could have placed his farm in a stock for at one time.)
During the period of two months while my carpenters were
building the church, Jim frequently invited me to accompany
him to his home, nearly a mile from town, on the mountain
slope. I often accepted his hospitality. (He was a second

cousin of mine and a very cheerful relative.) On a very dark night on one of these trips, as we wended our way up through the woods, we were a little alarmed by hearing a pistol shot a few rods ahead of us. We naturally thought that as there were but two of us and four of them that we would get the worst of it if that pistol shot meant war on us. We were somewhat relieved in mind when we met the four men, and they passed along without paying the least attention to the man of money. We never knew who the men were or what caused the pistol shot. When we were fairly away from the men and by the sound of their voices were convinced that they were at a safe distance Mr. McCray gave vent to his feelings in the following words: "I wish there had never been a drop of oil found on Oil Creek. I can't sleep nights. My dog makes a fearful fuss nearly every night, as if some prowlers were about. And I can't come up through these brush without expecting a club over my head, handled by some of these wretches who would murder me for my money." After we had safely reached his fireside I mentioned his big income from his 400-barrel wells, and oil at $3.00 per barrel. Jim took his pencil and figured a while, then he said: "My income is $5.00 a minute; if I had figured on this before we left town I would have hired a livery rig to bring us up." The next morning I was out of bed at quite an early hour. About sunrise—before breakfast—casting my eyes in the direction of one of Mr. McCray's many meadows, I saw a wagon load of hay coming toward the barn and Jim was walking along hebind the load with a pitchfork on his shoulder. He had glanced out of his sleeping room, at daybreak, and saw clouds gathering; then he hustled his hired man to the fields with a wagon and horses to save a load of hay that was liable to get spoiled if rain came. He pitched the load on the wagon himself. At another time I found him in one of his fields, in his shirt sleeves, digging green sprouts away from the oak stumps. He was covered with perspiration, and almost breathlessly, he told me that he had been "making fence and digging sprouts for two weeks, and was not quite done with the job yet." At this time he said; "I have 100,000 barrels of oil, and I am offered $4.50 per barrel. I have it in tanks, and I will hold it until it sweats through the iron before I take less than $5 a barrel for it." He afterward sold it for $1.12

a barrel, when much of it had been wasted by leakage and evaporation. There was only one James S. McCray. Of all the Oil Creek and other farm owners who were suddenly made rich by the oil business none were better known, and none were more honest and upright in their dealings with all. His word was as good as his bond.

And now, "one on myself" will not be out of place. When getting the lumber on the ground for this church I found much difficulty. No railroad passed through Petroleum Center at that time. The framing timber of the church had to be rafted and floated to Oil City, then towed with horses up Oil Creek to Petroleum Center. The lumber was billed to Pioneer, a mile above Petroleum Center. Then came the rub, to get this lumber down the creek through mud to the hubs of the wagon. A consrtuction train was at work building a side-track on the Boyd farm, across the creek opposite Petroleum Center. I slipped a $20 bill into the hand of the conductor of the construction train and bribed him to hitch three lumber cars to the rear of his gravel train and pull them down that mile. As there was no side-track at Boyd farm I got men enough to unload my lumber as quick as the railroad employees unloaded the gravel car. Thus, the conductor got his $20 and did not lose one minute of time. Twenty dollars was a "right smart" price for handling one coupling pin, but I saved about $50 by the transaction. But the reader has not seen the "one on myself" yet. Here it is: All this business kept me in this wicked town a part of the time. I stopped at the American hotel—a very good oil country hotel, that has long since disappeared. One night a dance was given for the benefit of the guests. The music was furnished by one of the dance house bands; three nice looking and very excellent musicians made the melody for the occasion. I was something of a violinist those days, and I played a few sets to rest these musicians, while they took a whirl at the "giddy mazes of the dance." Those three young men said they were not of the class that danced after their music, but they were far from home and were getting as much out of their accomplishments as possible, but that they would be sorry to let their mothers, away in the east, know the quality of their employers. I had no right to doubt their word and don't now. Now comes the joke. The next evening I was passing along the busy street and those melodious strains of music of the night before floated into my ears through the open door of a "dance house." I promised myself, when a boy, to never enter one of these places, and never had broken my promise. I could see my virtuous friends making music with piano, horn and violin and felt like speaking to them. I stood for a few moments undecided. Just two nights before that time a man had been shot and killed in a "dance hall" a little farther up the street. My thoughts told me that if I should go in there, and break my promise, if anybody would be shot it would be me. But for all this the music got the best of me, and I stepped in and greeted my newly-made musical friends. I was immediately asked to take the violin and "play a set." Well, I thought I could not get much lower, so I took the proffered instrument and lef off, and disgraced the best quadrille I knew. While the music of my violin floated on the air, very much scented, assisted by the skillful manipulations of the piano and cornet, my mind was busy. It was more troubled than ever was Dr. Parkhurst when visiting such places. Just as I was thing that if I should be shot and carried home to my wife a corpse the history of the occurrence in the newspapers would not be gratifying to my relatives, a big fight took place, and one man was knocked down and I could hear the blood spilling and gurgling from his wounds. The dancing girls came running back, dodging behind the piano, crying out," They will shoot! they will shoot!" Then I thought my time had come to atone for breaking my promise to myself. And as the piano legs were not large enough to protect the dancers and musicians, both, I opened a door behind the music stand, not knowing where it led to, and stepped out into God's pure air. By a flank movement I got around to the front street and to my hotel, with a new promise to myself, that as this was the first "dance hall' visited by me it would also be the last, and I have kept the promise.

## CHAPTER VII.

## THE GRANDINS AND J. B. WHITE.

I want to say something about the Grandins and J. B. White. The Grandins, aided by their immense amount of cash, always turned what at first promises to be a losing game into piles of money. Here is an instance: A few years ago they sent the Hon. J. B. White of Yougsville, into the state of Missouri to buy yellow pine timber land. Mr. White was as full of energy "as an egg is full of meat," and ere long he had a deed for about 70,000 acres of land nicely covered with a fine quality of yellow pine. Then, under the superintendency of Mr. White, an immense mill was built, and millions of feet of lumber manufactured. But this lumber had to be drawn on wagons over 10 miles to reach a railroad. Under the circumstances the cost almost kept pace with the income. And now comes the point where their capital came into good play. They took a large amount of stock in a projected railroad and insured the building of it. The road ran 27 miles through their pine timber. I was told by one of the brothers that now they make a profit of $8 per thousand on their timber, and each dollar counts $1,000,000 on the whole lot. In other words, $1 per thousand makes a million dollars on the estimated amount of their timber. They will make $8,000,000 on a transaction that would have broken 20 men without capital. The old saying that "it takes money to make money," is fully proved here. Another novelty in their way of doing business will no doubt be interesting to many of my readers. In their travels all over the United States they never kept an expense account. The late Adna Neyhart, their brother-in-law, the gentleman who first introduced the business of transporting oil in tank cars, was a partner of the three Grandin brothers. Neither of the quartette ever wasted ink and paper by keeping track of travelling expenses when abroad. Each had perfect confidence in all the others.

Now, I will finish this article by a couple of allusions of a couple of quite noted men. The first is ex-Senator James McMullen. I'll tell you how he commenced his career in oildom. "Jim," as he was familiarly called years ago, was quite an expert blacksmith at Warren, Pa. When the great oil strikes set the whole country nearly crazy Jim packed his kit of blacksmith tools and his household goods and made good time on a raft to Oil City. The author of this book was at that time second mate on a flat boat, which was propelled by very much jaded horses up and down the raging waters of Oil Creek. As there were no roads to speak of and mud galore the early pioneers in oildom were only too glad to avail themselves of this greasy mode of transportation. Jim McMullen was among the number that piled their "flittin" on the bottom of our greasy oil boat. We landed the goods safely, but not clean enough to brag on, at McClintockville, where Jim had built a rude blacksmith shop and dwelling house. About the first thing attended to was a "house warming." Then the musical ability of the "second mate" was brought into play. He, with the assistance of another music murderer, reeled off the "Opera Reel," "Money Musk," "Crooked S," "Chase the Squirrel," and other scientific pieces of music all night long for the lads and lassies of the then busy McClintockville, while putting in their biggest licks in the way of dancing "hoedowns." Music sailed around through the air in that hemlock shanty in great chunks. Music from Coleman's orchestra would dwindle down into nothing compared to ours. Well, all my Oil City readers will know that genuine genius cannot be kept in a hemlock blacksmith shop and "Jim" rose rapidly.

The first time I had the pleasure of looking at "Johnny" Steele was at Rouseville, after he had "blowed in" his million and a half dollars. He was seated on a high spring seat of an oil wagon, driving a black team of horses. The wagon was loaded with barrels filled with crude oil. Johnny was complacently smoking a cigar. At that time I was a correspondent of the Erie Morning Dispatch. I wrote him up. The item raised Johnny's "dander," but he did not know who to vent his wrath upon. A few months after that Johnny was the trusted baggagemaster of the Oil Creek railroad. One day Conductor "Pap" Richards said to me: "I wish you would interview John and set him right in the Dispatch. There are so many—exaggerated reports going the rounds of the newspapers that he is terribly annoyed. Tell him that I sent you to him." I called upon the baggagemaster, introduced myself according to Conductor Richard's instructions. Johnny opened up in dead earnest. His talk, as near as I can recollect, ran in this wise: "I will give you all the information that you ask, but it makes me mad to see the d—d fool reports in the papers. A d—d fool wrote me up last spring in the Erie Dispatch. He said I was hauling oil in a black greasy wagon, with a cigar in my mouth and a lot of other fool trash. D—n him, he was drunk all the time he was here—if ever I get sight of him I'll thrash him." I did not feel like telling Johnny that I never was drunk in my life, for the very good reason that I never took a drink of that which intoxicates. So I let him remain in ignorance as to who the Dispatch correspondent was. And now, to make this article not too lengthy, I will briefly give Steele's story:

"I will give you the correct statement for the Dispatch. The newspapers throughout the country have been saying that I hired a fine carriage in Philadelphia for a ride and when I returned to my hotel I bought the whole outfit and presented it to the driver. And on another occasion I rented the Continental hotel for one day—paying $10,000 as rental. The papers told too many other foolish stories about me to repeat here. I simply say that these reports are all false. The cause of the disappearance of my fortune in so short a time was sharpers taking advantage of my inexperience. They cleaned me out before I was aware of the fact. (At this point in his recital Johnny gave the names of some of the rogues that robbed him—I will omit their names.) After my large fortune was gone I made a solemn resolve, in my own mind, to be a frugal and industrious man the rest of my natural life. I have kept this self-made promise, and during the past few years I have paid for a home, paid for a team and outfit and I have a snug little bank account. I intend to reclaim a small part of my lost fortune and all of my good name."

While Mr. Steele was talking he impressed me favorably. His whole demeanor showed very plainly that he was no ordinary man. And his words and every action proved this. He was a faithful and favorite employee of the Oil Creek railroad when it required a good and competent man to attend to the business of baggagemaster at the then busy Rouseville depot. I was told that he had secured a more lucrative and important situation on some western railroad. There never was but one "Coal Oil Johnny" on the face of the earth. Who ever heard of a young man getting away with $1,500,000 in a couple of years, and then that same young man settling down immediately to the hard, solid knocks of a poor man's life and becoming an industrious, trusted model man of business and integrity? "Coal Oil Johnny" is both a novelty and an enigma. We may search the wide world over and we will not find his counterpart. Surely the "old times in oildom" developed some odd characters. Further on in this series of chapters I will mention more of them.

## CHAPTER VIII.

### NARROW ESCAPE FROM BEING A BLOATED BONDHOLDER.

I'll take a funny subject this time. I'll take my own experience. I'll tell how I did not make several fortunes. The first attempt was the leasing of about 3,000 acres of "dry territory." I was at Oil City at the time the dry territory excitement started north. When it reached Pleasantville I betook myself to my home in Youngsville, Pa., where I began to lease far ahead of the tidal wave. I wrote my contracts somewhat in this manner: "I agree to sell my farm to G. W. Brown, of Youngsville, Pa., for so many dollars per acre," and it was always a price quite low. (The land was worth fully the amount named for farming purposes.) "Provided said Brown pays the amount within three months from date." I picked up 3,000 acres within a couple of weeks, and rested on my laurels and waited for the wave to come. It came, and soon leasers were promising twice as much as I had promised for just as good land. I had some good offers, but as my time was not near up, and the price of dry territory was going up and up, I held on for the highest notch. I finally had an offer by which I could pocket a profit of about $40,000. I concluded to strike while the iron was hot; but the iron did not stay hot quite long enough. I'll tell why. When I made the sale, I found that I must locate each separate lot on the Warren county map. I had about ten days to drive around and make my locations. During these ten days, Sherman took Atlanta, and capitalists made up their minds that greenbacks were better than dry "territory," and the bottom fell out of this kind of business. I paid a big price for learning that "a bird in the hand is worth two in the bush."

My second lesson was somewhat connected with the first. While contracting the 3,000 acres of land, spoken of above, my good old friend, Alden Marsh, came to me and said: "George, let me put my 100 acres of pine land into your deal. I will let you have an option on it for $1,600." As this land was worth double this amount, I wrote a contract immediately. A month later Mr. Marsh came to me with another remark, which ran in this wise: "George, I let you have the option on my land too soon. Now, I will tell you what I will do. I will give you 100 acres in Cherry Grove. It did not cost me much. I bid it in at a few cents an acre for taxes due, and it is not worth anything. I will give it to you if you will give up my contract for the 100 acres of pine land." Mr. Marsh bless his—memory—being my best friend in a business way, had only to ask this favor to get it. And now I will tell you where the trouble came in. I thought, with Mr. Marsh that Cherry Grove land was worth nothing, and did not take the trouble to get a deed made out. Years after Mr. Marsh died and about that time the oil excitement began to creep toward Cherry Grove. Then it was that I asked Mr. Marsh's widow about this land of mine. Of course, Mrs. Marsh knew nothing whatever about this very careless land trade, and had sold the land for $3 an acre. Not very long after this, the great "mystery," or "646," was struck, and upon close inquiry I found that the great well was located less than a half mile from my 100 acres. And the 100 acres that I didn't own was worth about $50,000 in the market. This time I paid a big price for my negligence.

Now comes another close call. A short time before Edenburg became a great oil town, a citizen of rather shaky repute, living near the old hamlet, discovered large quantities of white mica on his land. He soon took into collusion with him a man living near Youngsville, Pa., and samples of "melted silver" were exhibited about Youngsville and vicinity. Men who had accumulated money by shrewdness and good investments, grabbed at this bait voraciously and paid big bonuses for leases in this silver belt. After several thousand dollars had been invested by Youngsville citizens Chapin Siggins (an old California miner,) D. Mead and myself made a visit to this new Eldorado. It was a two-day jaunt, on horseback, under a broiling sun. When we reached the neighborhood of the "mines" we boarded for a day or two with an old farmer, who charged us the princely sum of six cents a meal, and six cents a feed for our horses. As we expected to soon make a great fortune in silver mines, we did not kick at this "extortion." Our California expert soon pronounced this shining silver white mica. As we were then in the confines of Clarion county, and as the weather was too hot for comfortable traveling, and as our finances seemed to be ample to pay our "bed and board," we concluded to rusticate a day or two. Before leaving this enchanted spot where fortunes had not been made and lost, but simply lost, our silver company took an option on 100 acres of quite good farm land. We paid a large amount down "to bind the contract." This sum was one dollar, cash. This contract was gotten up in fun, and ran quite a long time. It read, that if we paid $4,000 within two years, the farm was ours. Here is just where the fun did not come in. If we had made the time four years (which we could have done, with the full consent of the owner), we would have had an option on a $100,000 farm, for $4,000. This same farm was one of the best in the Edenburg oil field. When the Edenburg oil excitement was at its height our silver syndicate was not sure of the time of our option, and hastened to look up the contract, not knowing at that time whether our contract ran one or ten years. We found the limit about six months short at one end.

---

## CHAPTER IX.

### THE LUMBER BUSINESS IN PARKER CITY.

In this ninth chapter I will give a little attention to the once famous Parker City.

When this oil town was just getting a good start, your humble author was crossing the Allegheny river on the old chain ferry, owned by McLaughlin and Fullerton. And right here let me say that each of those men made a nice little fortune before the Iron bridge was built spanning the river at that, point, and connecting Clarion and Armstrong counties by this old ferry. Day and night, it was loaded with teams and passengers.

I heard "Jim" Lambing say: "My, I wish I knew where I could get two carloads of lumber." I offered to deliver the lumber within three days. Mr. Lambing was delighted with my offer, and thus I commenced quite an extensive lumber business. When the two loads were delivered to Mr. L., (Mr. Lambing was afterwards mayor of the city of Corry, Pa.), I contracted to deliver two carloads more to another party. When this last lot reached Parker City I found that my man was not a "gilt-edged" operator, and I refused to let him have the lumber without the "cash down." He failed to come to time, and I left the lumber with "Doc" Harmon, to be sold by him, he to have half the profits for his trouble. Doc then began to fire orders at me as fast as I could fill them. Then a base of operations became necessary and I leased a few square rods of swamp land of "Old Fullerton Parker," as he was familiarly called, paying $600 a year rental. After renting the ground I was obliged to haul in about 100 loads of gravel before I could pile lumber on the soft land. Then an office appeared on the scene, and G. W. Brown ran the first lumber yard in the greasy city of Parker. For about two years my luck was the very best. I had for customers the best operators in the (then) new field. They paid their bills at the end of each month. But "it's a long lane that has no turn." If any man did owe me during the first two years of my yard business in Parker's Landing, and happened to go into bankruptcy, he had just paid me off in full. This was rather a pleasant experience for me. But the trouble came in the turn of the lane. At the end of two years, when my individual profits had been about $15,000, oil took a downward plunge, and fell from about $3 a barrel to about 60 cents. Then it was that my heretofore good customers went into bankruptcy by the dozen, and I was kept busy for a few months going to Pittsburg to adjust claims with the register in bankruptcy. I became quite well acquainted with this genial gentleman. And this genial gentleman made more money out of this kind of business than I did. In the end I found that I had been throwing good money after poor money I never received one dollar on my adjusted claims. I learned that when a Parker City oil operator went into bankruptcy he went in to stay. What money he had in his pockets when the crash came, stayed there. I never heard of an assignee, register in bankruptcy, or any other officer of the law getting his hands on any of it. The creditor always paid his own railroad fare, hotel bills, and register's bills without aid from the debtor. The debtor generally started a little business of his own, as soon as he got his discharge from all his former obligations. This was my experience, at least, and I have yet to hear of a creditor who came out any better than I did. "Old Times in Oildom" were indeed slippery times. Of about 40 lumber yard men, who ran lumber yards in these "old times" but two, to my knowledge, came out unscathed.

I'll give a couple of items now to prove the "slipperyness" of these times. One of my customers at that time, a carpenter, imbued with the spirit of the times, took the job of building an addition to the Phillips hotel, owned by James E. Brown, the millionaire of Kittanning. The thirfty carpenter gave me the privilege of furnishing all the lumber for this addition, amounting to about $800. When the job was finished, said carpenter collected the money from James E. Brown for the whole job and forgot to pay G. W. Brown for the lumber.

My only hold was to take a mechanic's lien on the building for my claim. I employed a young lawyer, of Parker City, whose mind—at that time—was pretty well taken up in writing a novel, entitled "Platonic Love," to attend to the legal part of the transaction. This young lawyer wrote out a lien, and left out the township, county, state, and the United States from the document. The young lawyer engaged an old lawyer, of standing, in Clarion, to help him along with the case. The old member of the Clarion bar, copied the lien, and added nothing to it. He did not commit any sin of "commission," but, with his young colleague, "committed the sin of ommission." When the week of the court came around, I took a wagon load of witnesses to Clarion, to prove that the lumber all went into the Phillips house improvement, and boarded them at the "Jones House" all week, and when Saturday came my suit was put over until the next term of court. When the next court came I had my wagon load of witnesses back, for another week's visit in the stilly streets of the sacred precincts of the old-fashioned town of Clarion. After each witness helping himself to well cooked viands spread out before him on Jones' table for a week, my suit came on Saturday. It required less than half a day to prove my claim all right, but after my brilliant lawyers had made a strong speech in my favor, the opposing lawyer—Judge Campbell—arose in his majesty and pointed out the fact to my lawyers that they had presented a blank to the august court. Judge Jenks took the case from the jury before they left the box and they were deprived of their little visit in the jury room. My old Clarion lawyer jumped to his feet (said feet had been resting on a writing table) and applied for a new trial. The judge promptly refused and that was the last of that lumber bill. I suppose the judge though a lien that failed to state whether the hotel was located in England, America, or any other place, was not worthy of his attention. I learned one fact, though not worth $800 and other expenses, by this experience, and it is this: That I, as a Warern county man, failed to cope with Clarion county lawyers and judges.

My second item is one showing luck, and no luck. One Saturday evening I took the paltry sum of $2,000 insurance on my lumber yard, worth about $7,000. Sunday about half of the city burned, taking in my lumber yard. When the news was telegraphed to me Monday morning, to my Youngsville home, I thought I had been lucky in getting the $2,000 insurance placed before the fire took place—but now comes the sequel. The company failed to come to time, and I got a tip from a reliable fire insurance agent that my company was a little "shaky." Then I hied me away to Philadelphia, the headquarters of the concern, where I found the president of the company, and parleying for half a day, I received $540, which I considered a good thing for a company to do that would not be slated by the commissioner of insurance, who considered the company insolvent. Some people think there is no place of punishment after death. I am not going to argue that question, but simply say that it is my belief, and hope, that there is some place, for some folks, called in the Bible—hell. I'll give my readers one of my reasons for thinking so. A man, (I will not say a gentleman), had just finished a new hotel, before this fire spoken of here. He owed me $400 for windows, doors, etc., used in the construction of his hotel. He had $1,800 insurance on the building. I had a lien on the hotel and if the fire had held off one day the hotel would have been sold to satisfy the claim (if not in the meantime.) But the fire settled the lien business. Then the man told me that he would certainly pay me when he received his $1,800 insurance. I saw him a short time afterwards, and he told me that he had received his insurance money, but had invested it in junk, and that he would have returns in one month. He asked me to draw on him at expiration of one month for $50. I did so with not the least expectation of having the draft honored and in a few days the draft came to the Youngsville Savings Bank, with these words written on the back: "Give Brown my love, and tell him to draw again." As I had, in the meantime, learned this man had smuggled his property out of his hands, I pocketed both the insult and loss. Now, dear reader, do you wonder that I desire a place of future punishment. Many, many men like this were inhabitants of the old regions, and helped to make "old times in oildom" miserable.

---

## CHAPTER X.

## JOHN GALEY AND THE ROBINSONS.

A few items from the book of memory concerning "down at Parker" will help to make up this tenth article.

When the lumber business had become a little slow on Oil Creek the author of this book transferred his rambling tread to the busy, busy precincts of Parker's Landing. There the oil business brought together a most motely crowd. No oil town produced a more mixed crowd. No oil town produced so many rich oil farmers as did Parker. The Parkers, Robinsons, Foxes, and scores upon scores of families were rich enough to live without oil, but when the oleaginous wealth was forced upon them they very meekly accepted it. Among the richest, both after and before striking oil, were the Robinsons. There were three brothers, and each had a good, large farm, and every acre was good oil territory. The piling of riches on these good natured and contented men did not set them up above poor folks. They always dressed well and had a gentlemanly air about them not often found among ordinary farmers, and the striking of dozens of big wells on their farms, when oil was worth $3.00 a barrel, made not the least difference in their dress and actions. It was always a comfort for the author to visit with any of the brothers, before and after the finding of oil on their farms. Nearly everybody has their hobby, and one of these brothers had this for his hobby. When he bought lumber of me he paid at the end of every month just as regular as the end of the month came. But the odd cents on the bill he would never pay. If the bill was $500.01 he would pay $500, and if the bill was $1.99 he would pay $1. He always drew the line on cents. He would never pay only even dollars, but would never find any fault with any bill, either large or small. He was one of my best customers while I kept a lumber yard at Parker City. While operating his large oil farm his monthly lumber bills ran very high, and in my four years' business I never was obliged to present a bill for payment. On the first day of each month he would call for his bill and write his check for even dollars. If all my customers in Parker had been Robinsons I would have been just about $10,000 ahead when I quit the lumber yard business. What a blessed world this would be if all the people were Robinsons.

John H. Galey was one of the many business men of Parker at the time I speak of. John's history from that time to the present is well worth a brief mention. He was an active boy, as the run of boys go, generally. He had his eyes open for some kind of an oil trade. For a while he did not have his mind made up as to what kind of a trade it would be. Finally an operator put a well down on Stump Creek island, a mile above Parker. The operator struck a very good paying well and offered the island to Galey for $10,000. John thought the matter over and made up his mind that $10,000 and more than that amount, could be pumped from that well, but to use his own words: "I had not the $10,000, but went to Pittsburg and borrowed it and paid for the property, and I have taken from that and another well which I put down on the same island $125,000, and I have run the wells only 18 months. They are producing nearly as much as ever and they make a nice little property. John went on making money hand over hand for a time, then he went far toward the setting sun and built a large, thriving town. One day, when he was away on business, the Indians came and wiped out his town. But John Galey was not the man to sit down and mourn over the loss of his wealth. The next time I heard of him he plunged into the wilderness at Haymaker, McKean county, Pa., and leased a large amount of land farther north than any oil company had thought of going. He took that well known and moneyed firm, the McKinney Bros., in to the deal with him, and ere long Galey was sailing over financial seas as gaily as ever before. The next time I met John was several years afterwards at one of his boarding houses, or houses where he boarded, near Oakdale, Pa. This is the very strange story he told me on that occasion: "I came to McDonald a couple of years ago to lease gas territory for Guffey, Galey & Co. No oil had been found in this section at that time. But thinking that this was gas territory I commenced at McDonald and made leases along this ridge for a distance of nearly three miles. Our strip is a little over a mile wide, on an average. Now every acre of it is the best oil territory in the McDonald field. I happened to keep right on the belt as near as if I had known just where the oil lay. A little side belt struck us occasionally but run out just as soon as it crossed us. We have the largest wells in this field, one of them producing 16,000 barrels a day when first struck (this is the old Matthews well). One flowed 30,000 barrels before we could control it. The oil rushed down the creek through Nobletown, but luckily did not take fire. It is the most strange thing to me imaginable to think how I followed this belt so far, and then stopped at the end of it, when I was leasing gas territory with no thoughts of oil. I cannot but think it almost a miracle."

I'll give a few more items concerning the once famous Parker territory in chapter 11.

## CHAPTER XI.

### PARKER CITY.

I take for my subject, in this eleventh chapter, Parker City. Who has not heard of Parker City? Certainly every oil man has become familiar with the name.

This little city is one of the "has beens." It never will be the great oil center that it once was, but it might have been one of the best of its size in Western Pennsylvania, if not for the short sightedness of the original landholders. This remark applies particularly to "the flats," or First Ward.

When Mr. Fullerton Parker began to rent his land holdings along the river front, the oil business was so great that he could get nearly any price he put on it as rental. If one man did not give $10 a foot front as rent per year, another man would, and Mr. Parker did just what most any other man would in the same situation—put on a big price per year. He could get it, and it was worth a big price. His mistake was in not selling the lots and letting somebody beside himself pay part of the city taxes. This plan would have tied many business men to the young city, and they would have been residents today, instead of helping boom some other city. The selling of the lots would have been the best plan, as, with the united efforts of the many owners, the city would have had a steady growth, thereby gradually increasing the value of city property.

This is no guess work. All travelers know that large towns are not found in bunches. As the traveler passes through the country at intervals of 40 or 50 miles, he sees large towns. The shadow of a large town keeps the little towns weak and spindling. A little town don't grow much with a large town just close by to take all the trade away from the small town. This is one of the uncontradicted facts. Kittanning is far enough down the river and Franklin is far enough up the river to give Parker City an open field. No shadows from any direction would dwarf the growth of "pretty little Parker City," with its magnificent view of the swift running old Allegheny. Coal, oil, gas, timber and good soil are found all around the city. What more could be desired in the way of building up a large city? It is a fact, known to every Parkerite, that when rents were up to fever pitch and business booming, there was no grumbling, but when business began to adjust itself to the decreasing output of the oil wells of the vicinity, rents were not adjusted.

The author speaks from personal experience. He paid $600 a year rent, for several years, on a few rods square of swamp land, as a spot to pile lumber on. The land was made usable by said author hauling many loads of gravel into the swamp. By the application of this gravel, the land was made firm enough to hold up lumber. This expense was borne by the renter. But, as I said before, Mr. Parker was not considered an extortioner at this time, as he could get the high rent from other parties, if your scribe had not frozen to the lot. But the trouble came when business fell off nine-tenths, and your humble servant plucked up courage enough to approach W. C. Mobley, the superintendent and son-in-law of Mr. Parker, and asked him, in view of the fact that the profits on sales of lumber would not pay the rent, to lower the rent a trifle. Mr. Mobley's answer was, "Not a cent." The result is easy to see. The lumber yard was obliged to close out business.

This was the case with many other branches of business. Instead of the motto being carried out. "Live and Let Live," thereby holding the population, the motto, "Die and Let Die," was carried out, and Parker City missed its great opportunity. I'll mention a few points that will not be new to the old residents of the city.

Before the bridge was built, John McLaughlin and 'Squire Fullerton bought a chain ferry, paying $8,000. It paid for itself in a few months, and made a handsome fortune for the firm before the bridge took away their business. But with business foresight, McLaughlin and Fullerton took a good slice of the bridge stock, and again piled up money. 'Squire Fullerton is now dead, but his widow lives on the "Bluff," where she can overlook the place of her late husband's victories. John McLaughlin built the Globe hotel and conducted it for several years, then sold it to his two sons, George and Will. Their father is connected with the natural gas business and lives at Murraysville, Pa.

Who of the old operators but knew Fin Frisbee. "Fin" together with "Doc" Book, built the Central hotel. Oh, but that hotel did a great business. Just one little incident will

prove this. I was a lodger one night, and by the noise below
my slumbering place, I took it that the bar was doing quite
a business. As I was used to noise, it did not deprive me of
"nature's sweet restorer"—sleep. But "Curt" McKinney. of
Titusville, did not fare so well. I stood in the office the next
morning after the noise, when "Curt," (as he was called then,
but now he is called Mr. McKinney,) came down stairs and
approached "Fin," who stood in the office, wearing one of his
contented smiles, and adderessed him in this manner: "Mr.
Frisbee, if you allow so much noise about your bar every night,
as you did last night, I will not stop over night with you
again." "Curt" said this with his usual earnestness. "Fin"
looked up very much unconcerned, and replied: "I took in at
the bar last night $500. I will not trade a noisy $500 at the
bar for a quiet 70-cent lodging. Poor Frisbee. After becoming proprietor of the great Kent House at Lakewood, he sold
out, and removed to Duluth, where he added very materially
to his wealth, and bid a long farewell to his dollars and crossed
over the river of death, to try an unknown existence. If
there are no hotels to be run in that other life, "Fin" will be
unhappy.

I met Elisha Robinson on the street this morning. He is
the same unassuming man of money that he was when his oil
wells were forcing him to go to Pittsburg every few days to
deposit his piles of cash. He is the same true Christian
gentleman yet that he was when, 33 years ago, he would come
as regular as a clock into my lumber office to pay his bills. If
all my customers had been Elisha Robinsons I would have
$10,000 more money today than I have. And his brother,
"Sam," still clings to this terrestrial ball, which means that
another good, honest, rich man still lives. Both brothers are
tilling the soil the same as before that same soil poured forth
rivers of oil. Elisha has his affections fixed, this spring, on
a piece of hoarded land that he will clear up this coming
summer and put in a state of cultivation.

Fullerton Parker, who was monarch of all he surveyed in
this city in its palmy day has, with many other pioneers, been
gathered "to his fathers," but his mansion on the "Bluff," still
overlooks the city which bears his name. There are Parkers
and Parkers here yet, but they are not of the old settlers.
There is one in Oil City (William Parker, who is remembered

here as the owner of the old "Rob Roy" well at Karns City, which produced nearly 150,000 barrels of oil and put nearly as many dollars into the pockets of its owner.) There were very few "Rob Roys." None ever came and stopped with me. The "Rob Roy" spoken of above, gave Oil City an ornament, in the great brick mansion of "Bill" Parker. It is lucky for noted Oil City that such men as Mr. Parker gravitated in its direction, when they became too rich to stay anywhere else.

And now, let me close this article by saying that if Parker is not the Parker of old it bears unmistakable signs of former prosperity, in its five good churches, fine brick school building, water works, bank and many substantial buildings that were paid for when money was no object. For this and many other blessings the Parker of today has reason to be thankful So mote it be.

---

## CHAPTER XII.

### OIL CITY SIXTY YEARS AGO.

Talk about old times! Why, the inhabitants, the younger ones, know very little of the growth, from the beginning, to the present. I was born within 10 miles of the Drake well, or the first well drilled, 80 years ago, in Centerville, Crawford county, Pa., and had the pleasure of seeing its production for the first two days, and the same with the second well, right across the creek from the Drake well, on the John Watson farm. This second well, known as the Williams well, made more of a splurge than the Drake well. It sent the oily fluid many feet skyward, with a vim which the natives of this corner of God's footstool never dreamed of. The natives, your humble servant not excepted, were nearly dumb. The inhabitants of that period had never seen oil in all its glory before. The inhabitants along Oil Creek had smelled it, inasmuch as a few drops of it would occasionally ooze through the ground. I, myself, at that time lived here at Youngsville, Warren county, Pa., on the banks of the Brokenstraw creek. For many years, before the time of striking the first oil well, I had made trips down the Allegheny river, on lumber rafts,

nearly every time the water came to a rafting stage. Always
when passing the mouth of Oil Creek, a strong "Seneca oil"
smell came floating on the air. That was all there was to it—
just a smell. Compare that smell with the present oil business,
if you can. I leave it to any living man or woman to make the
comparison. I will not attempt it.

Oil City, at that time, consisted of a grist mill, hotel, one
little store and two dwelling houses. The hotel was the most
pretentious building of the town. It lacked "a small trifle"
of bieng a mate to the Arlington of today, in size and equipment, but bore the same name of the "best hotel" in town.
The old, and indeed most of the young inhabitants of the
"Hub of Oildom," have seen the old Moran house, at the
lower end of the city. That one hotel was the real money-
maker of the town. When a good rafting stage was on, the
man that got a good bed to sleep in had to be on hand early
in the afternoon, as quite a while before dark the Allegheny
fleets—or rafts—would begin to tie up for the night, in Oil
Creek eddy. Before dark the river would be filled nearly to
the opposite shore with rafts from almost every place on the
Allegheny river from Oil City to Coudersport. The main
points from which these rafts came were Tionesta, Irvineton,
Warren, Jamestown, N. Y., Kinzua, Pa., Corydon, Pa., Sala-
manca, N. Y., Tuningwant, Pa., Olean, N. Y., Port Alle-
ghany, Pa., and Coudersport, Pa. The reader will see that the
Keystone and Empire states divided the honor of furnishing
this great river trade. This was caused by the river starting
in Pennsylvania, and straying off into the state of New York,
but finding the Yankees no better than the Dutch Pennsylvanians, the waters strayed back into the parent state, and
commingling with the waters of the Monongahela, slowly and
peacefully wended their way through the slave country of the
south, to the sea.

Speaking of rivers, let me say, fearing it may slip from my
memory, that years ago I sat in the office of a hotel, on Keat-
ing Summit, Potter county, Pa., and gazed on the drops of
rain falling on one inch of ground, where it divided, a part
going into the Atlantic and a part into the Gulf of Mexico.
The question in my mind was, which part will reach the salt
water first? But I am getting off the subject of "Old Times in
Oildom." To make it plain to the readers of this article, I will

say that the old Moran house was not supposed to hold all the hardy men that manned the oars which guided this large number of rafts. The "hands" which did the work at the end of those oar stems, generally rested after their hard day's work, in a raft shanty, which was anything but a shield against rain and snow, being constructed of green boards, roof and all. This shanty was built for but a short period of service. Only for a place, for perhaps a dozen men to sleep in, for a week or two, according to the distance floated. There was one man to watch the raft until sold and delivered. Only the owner of the raft and the pilot indulged in the luxury of a bed in the far-famed Moran hotel. Sometimes a "hand" leaning a little toward dudishness, would mix in with the above named owners and pilots, and invest a quarter of a dollar in a "downy" bed. I don't speak from experience regarding "downy beds," because in my youthful days, I considered myself as belonging to "the Brotherhood of man," and I always slept, spoon fashion, in a board bunk, partly filled with straw in the shanty.

Before leaving this subject, I wish to mention the fact, that old-time raftsmen seemed to be in the old fogy class, in regard to inventions. Speaking within reasonable bounds, the lumber men of the days gone by, for 50 years at least, practiced the most foolish methods of landing their rafts. As the evening began to appear, the raft was rowed into the first eddy approached, and tied to a nearby tree or stump, or anything that would hold the raft quietly until morning, and until the "hands" had got out from the straw, in the shanty bunks, and appeased their keen appetites on potatoes, meat, (generally salt pork) and bread. Then the pilot would exclaim in a sort of commanding voice, "untie that cable," and away Pittsburg-ward would go the raft and crew.

And now comes in the foolishness, practiced for a half century. The rope or cable used for tying up the raft was from one and one-half inches to two inches in diameter, perhaps from 100 to 300 feet long. The raft was pulled to the shore and a strong hand would pick up the tremendously heavy rope, which lay coiled up like a great anaconda, and would struggle up a generally steep bank, run to the nearest tree with all of the rope that had not been pulled away from him by the downward movement of the raft. One end of the rope was

tied tight to the raft. By the time that the out-of-breath man
on shore could get a good "half-hitch" on that tree, two-thirds
or more of the rope was usually dragging in the water. Then
the man ashore would let go of the cable, and a man on the
raft would pull it on the raft, and throw one end to the man on
shore and the same foolish work would be repeated over and
over until all hands were completely exhausted, and the lower
end of the eddy reached, if the eddy was long enough. But
many times, in a short eddy, the raft defied all efforts to land
it, and it ploughed the water all night.

After about a half century of this kind of work, the so-
called "Kendulltuckyans" taught the so-called sharp Yankees
how to land a raft. Those Kentuckians would take a 1,000
foot inch and a half rope, and coil it up on the rear end of
their acre raft of logs, put in a snubbing post, near the rope,
and when they wished to land, they would paddle the raft
ashore with their great long oars; then one of the "hands"
would jump ashore, and the man on the raft would quietly
hand him one end of that light, long rope. The man ashore
would then take a "half-hitch," and sit down and hold onto
the end of the rope until the raft was stopped. Many times
not half the rope was used at the first hitch. After the "lapse
of years," the "Yanks" caught on and we have enjoyed the
work of landing lumber rafts ever since. Why, it is one of the
wonders of the world that those early day raftsmen did not dis-
cover this simply, easy way of landing a swift running raft.
The shover of this pencil belonged to those slow learners. The
first time I ever saw the new way of landing, I took the lesson
from my Kentucky brother raftsman. At that time I saw
those men land about one acre of logs at the first hitch, on the
Ohio river.

Of course I am talking about almost a thing of the past.
But little lumber has been rafted to the markets since the "iron
horse" made his appearance. Of course, said iron horse don't
reach every lumber mill in the country even now, and once in
a while when he fails to make his appearance, the water transportation takes his place.

## CHAPTER XIII.

## JACK McCRAY.

I'll commence my 13th article by saying a few words about "Jack" McCray, one of the pioneers of the oil country. He owned a farm, the south line of which came within a few rods of the Drake well. When the Drake well was struck, leasers came to him by the dozen. His was a large farm, lying between the John Watson farm the Drake well. "Jack" laid out his land in acre leases, on which he charged $100 bonus and a royalty of one-fourth the oil. The writer of this secured two of these leases at these figures, and soon found himself out of pocket $200. As the wells were kicked down by the aid of a spring pole those days, there were more leasers than operators. Many more men planked down their money and signed contracts than put down wells. After many weeks of kicking by stalwart men, dry holes would turn up in disagreeable numbers, discouraging the many would-be operators, myself among the number, and in the course of time, "Jack" had more copies of leases than interests in oil wells. The oil belt seemed to follow Oil Creek down toward the "mouth of the creek," instead of going up Pine Creek, over McCray's land, as the old wells of Captain Funk, Noble & Delamater, Phillips and many others testified. But "Jack," with his bonus in his pocket, became the owner of the famous McCray hotel, where speculators from the east, west, north and south, were wont to assemble to talk over what was a business of that time, to them, of an unknown quantity. "Jack" was soon known all over this country by his attempt at a laugh composed of two syllables—or the same sound given twice—"Chacha." The two sounds came often, as he was of a very jovial disposition. No one, either by seeing or hearing, would know that this noise was meant for a laugh, as not a muscle of his face moved. Yet these indescribable sounds did duty as a sign of merriment on his part.

"Jack" kept spanking good race horses and driving teams, and made the most of life for many years, then struck into the wilds of Forest county, as general manager of a large lumber company and pioneered the pine lumber business for many, many years. He "grew up with the country." He was

elected and served one term as associate judge of the Forest
county court. His name will be handed down to all future
generations. During his residence in this wild county of Forest, a postoffice which was located in his township, which is
named McCray, and when the B. & O. railroad was built,
the station was named McCray in honor of the judge. When
all the nice timber was cut into lumber and shipped away
from his jurisdiction, it became too quiet for a man of his
ambition and he hied himself back to his old stamping grounds
—Titusville—and soon bid farewell to al mundane things,
and crossed over the unknown river where, perhaps, there are
no oil wells or lumber mills.

Pithole comes vividly to my mind just now. My first visit
to this mushroom city was an experience. I found a daily
newspaper, railroad, telegraph office, opera house, many hotels
and boarding houses and everything that goes to make a
modern city. The people of the village said the population
was about 25,000. I did not believe it then and I do not
believe it now. But there was a "right smart" of people there
for a three months old city in the woods. I put up at the most
tony hotel in the city, and had water biscuits, half baked, for
supper. Although I registered about 3 o'clock p. m., all the
beds were engaged for the night. But the obliging clerk told
me he would provide a place for me to sleep. When bed time
came this smiling clerk took a lantern, and by its dim light, I
was led to the barn and handed a blanket, by the said clerk,
who told me to "climb that ladder" and I would find plenty
of hay at the top of the mow to make a bed of. I did as
directed and about 40 feet skyward I found plenty of hay,
and also men that had preceded me to the roosting place as
patrons of this hotel. I found a vacant place among the snor-
ing crowd. Mingled with the unmistakable smell of bad
whiskey. But morning came at last, and also a dose of the
hot biscuit. When the bill was paid I found the modest
charge of $1.00 for each meal and 75 cents for lodging.
After breakfast I hired a little bunty saddle horse, to ride to
McCray's Landing—four miles distant. When I returned the
obliging liveryman charged me only $5 for the use of the
little animal, about three hours. There was never but one Pithole. Just think of six-foot guage railroad being built four
miles to Oleopolis and then dismantled in a few short months.

The last time that I passed through Pithole I saw but two occupied houses. As that was 20 years ago, it is dollars to cents, if
there is one house there now. In the palmy days of Pithole
considerable oil was put in barerls and towed up the river to
the P. & E. railroad at Irvineton.

I loaded a boat with shingles for the mouth of Pithole creek
and accompanied the crew of five down to the place of delivery. After we got the shingles off the boat was loaded
with barrels of oil. The five men rolled barrels nearly all
day. Two young coopers were tightening the hoops on the
barrels on shore. The five brawny boatmen kept nagging the
coopers and poking fun at them all day. One was an Irishman and the other a Dutchman. I stood on the high bank of
the river late in the afternoon. I heard the young Irishman
say, "You have made fun of us all day and now we are
going to pay you for it." With this exclamation on his lips,
both coopers jumped and ran onto the boat and in five minutes
the two coopers had five big boatmen badly whipped. Two of
them ran, but they were soon overtaken and knocked down.
A part of the boatmen called themselves great fighters before
the coopers got their "dander up." We did not hear anything
more about pugilistic achievements after this battle. The boatmen did not dare to let their boat lie at the landing that night,
but hitched on their horses and towed it two miles up the river
and spent the night out of range of the coopers. All this was
an object lesson—showing what can be done by courage, displayed by the weaker party. And this reminds me of a similar
case that came under my observation at Reno, at the time
General Burnside was building his railroad over the hills and
through the valley to Plumer. The railroad workers were
gathered in a crowd at the junction of the wildcat road with
the junction of the Atlantic & Great Western road. A lively
discussion arose on some question among them and one stalwart young Irishman took it into his head to whip the whole
crowd, and he did just what he undertook to do. He just
walked around among those laborers and knocked down every
one that came within reach of him. After this generel knock-
down business had gone about five minutes, the boss, a big
finely developed man, belonging to the same country of the
fighter, with a big plug hat on, stepped up to the pugilistic
gentleman and commanded him to desist from his dangerous

pastime. The fighter struck out, square from the shoulder, and sent the boss down among the other victims of this young man's rage, his plug hat rolling and tumbling another rod ahead of him. The boss struggled to his feet and stood as a quiet witness, until the fight ended for lack of more men to knock down, and the whole circus ended right there and then, with the young Hercules standing peacefully in the crowd— with a victorious smile on his face and no one to question his title to the name of boss knocker. He was another exemplification of the power of one man, energetically applied, that is fresh in my mind to the present day.

---

## CHAPTER XIV.

### A GREEDY LANDLORD.

What shall I say in this chapter? The reader may think I have run out of material by this time, but let the reader consider that a man who was born before such things as railroads, telegraph lines, trolley lines, steamboats, telephone, ocean cables, mail delivery routes, flying machines, sewing machines, oil, gas, automobiles, electric power and many other things that I could mention came into use, ought to know more than would fill a small book. The young men and women of the present time may well wonder how human beings could get along without the things above mentioned. But they did get along 6,000 years before these conveniences came to help mankind in general.

When I was a boy a party of young men and young ladies would get into big box filled with straw, on a pair of wooden bob sleds, drawn by old "Buck and Jerry," a faithful yoke of oxen, and go on a snail's gallup miles upon miles to a dance, in zero weather, with as light hearts and as much—or more— merriment than is now shown in automobile loads of young heirs to millions of dollars. A man worth $10,000 was considered as great a man as a multi-millionaire is at the present time. I think as to happiness, perhaps these old-time young people had the best of it. The ox teams never killed anybody. As much cannot be said in the favor of automobiles.

Many people of great wealth have passed to the other life on account of their wealth. A poor man or woman cannot own one of these man-killers. Human life is much safer behind an ox team than behind an automobile. Of course a certain few, and very few, owned horses and buggies, but they stood no higher in society than ox team people. There were no distinctions or classes, at that time. All stood on the same level. There was not wealth enough in the country to make it worth while to draw a distinction. There are so many cliques and classes, nowadays, that when either class gets up any kind of an entertainment it is a puzzle to the "committee" to know who to invite. This troublesome puzzle did not come in at the time of which I write, consequently they had more room for unalloyed happiness.

Where the hilarity came in, in the old times, was at the country corn husking or apple paring bees. The patent apple dryer was not invented and the main dependence was a pocket knife. The unsophisticated young man was right at home, and perfectly contented, when, sitting beside his best girl, with a pan of apples on his knees, pocket knife in hand, removing the skin from the luscious apples, and his intended life partner busily engaged in stringing the nicely quartered apples as they came from the nimble knives. Whole evenings would be spent in perfect contentment on the part of both. In fact, the longer the apples lasted the better. When bushels of apples were nicely pared and strung ready for hanging all around the fire place—no stoves then to take up the room in a house—a nail would be driven into a wall, to hang the strings of apples on to dry—then a halt would be called and refreshments served by the good lady of the farm house. After devouring the "nick-nacks" the time, generally running into the morning hours, would be spent in dancing, or playing "snap and catch 'em," "the mill goes round," "chase the squirrel," and dozens of these innocent plays. If I am a good judge, more harmony existed then than now. A good and substantial reason for this is easy to be seen. The people never had heard or dreamed of these luxuries or conveniences of the present time, therefore they did not quarrel and wrangle over these things.

I have been writing so far in these articles, about older times, not oil times, as no oil was dreamed of then. I will now come down to oil times. Speaking of dancing, I should have said in the right place, that no quadrille had been invented when I first kept time to Arthur McKinney's single fiddle—that was what we called it then. It is now called a violin. We had no caller either. The dancers bossed themselves. We had learned to get through the "Opera Reel," "Money Musk," "French Four" and many other "country" dances. Each dancer was a self-taught scholar. All good dancers had learned their pieces "by heart," and but few mistakes were made. The writer remembers his first venture on the dancing floor. He selected one of the best looking and smartest girls in the room for a partner. She knew her business to a "t" and so did all the rest except the writer. But, grabbing every hand extended to him, hopping back and forth, as the other seven in the set did, turning every corner in the imitation of my partner, and keeping not very good time to McKinney's fiddle, I came off victorious. I had won my first ball room battle. But I was not a real independent dancer yet. I had followed the motions of others and had before me the many figures to learn before becoming a full fledged dancing beaux. But, as in most of the undertakings of this life, perseverance won, and ere many moons I knew where to go without being directed.

I must mention one dance given in Parker City, soon after oil was struck. I was in the lumber business and occasionally visited the place before it was a city. At each visit I stopped at the same hotel. One evening I registered as usual and soon learned that a big ball was to come off that night. The proprietor of the hotel offered to find lodging for me outside the noise of his dance. I told him not to take the trouble, as the noise would not disturb my slumbers in the least. This landlord had engaged two violinists from Brady's Bend. There was not a violinist at Parker City at that time. The musicians were promptly on hand; also a big crowd of dancers. About 11 p. m. one of the musicians received a telegram calling him home immediately on account of the death of a relative. He lost no time in catching the Pittsburg train that was just ready to leave the Parker depot. As the absent violinist was caller of the quadrilles his partner was left in a bad shape. The band was also left in a bad fix, with two violins and but one player, and the player could not call one quadrille. I had played and called quadrilles for 25 years, but nobody in Parker City knew it. The landlord told me that he would be obliged to pay a part of the money back to that large crowd if he stopped the program half finished. The milk of human kindness began to flow in my veins, and to save this clever landlord from making such a sacrifice, I told him that I could fill the place of the absent musician. To say that he was pleased would be putting it lightly. He smiled all over his face and I took up the absent man's work, and saved a break-up of the ball. I lost my full night's sleep. I got a couple of hours sleep in the morning, and that landlord charged me 50 cents for supper, 50 cents for lodging and 50 cents for break-fast, and I paid it without a word—just the same as he always had charged me when I had not saved $100 for him. However this fiddler never stayed another night at that hotel after paying for the privilege of saving the collapse of the big ball.

Now, for the purpose of showing the hardships and trials of the early settlers in this part of the country, I recite one circumstance which came to my own family. Many years before the Philadelphia & Erie railroad was built through Garland, my folks lived there, when I was a boy 8 years old, 73 years ago. Flour of all kinds became scare. There was none to be found in the valley of the Brokenstraw; none of the stores the whole length of the valley had any meal of any kind. Our folks had used the last in the house and starvation stared us in the face. We had kind neighbors, but they were nearly as bad off as we were, so we could not rely upon borrowing. The morning after the last flour had been used my father, very much discouraged, started out from home to see his neighbors and talk with them. The first neighbor he met told him that a man from Titusville was coming that day to the valley of the Brokenstraw with a wagon load of flour. The man was to take the shortest route through Enterprise and over Cole Hill, leaving about four miles to be traveled to reach the route of the "bread line." My faithful father took the tramp with an empty bag on his arm and reached a place on the Titusville road called the "Birch Springs" before the eagerly looked for wagon came along. When it did arrive father purchased, at a high price, 100 ponnds of nice wheat flour and carried it on his shoulder the four miles to his anxiously waiting wife and three children. We—the children—looked upon our father as a sort of savior, and our exclamations of joy must have been to him part pay for his labor of love. You, of the present age of all kinds of vehicles, can form but a faint conception of the labor and suffering of the early pioneers of this country. Long before the discovery of oil or gas, O, what a change! In the days spoken of above in order to have a light at night the housewife would melt a cake of tallow, saved from butchering time, and pour it into tin molds—let it harden in a cool place—warm it by the wood fire, and pull them out of the molds. Rather a nice looking candle but a poor light giver. In place of matches, which were unknown then, a sliver would be lighted in the stone chimney fireplace and applied to the wick of the candle, and an alleged light, which would burn a little while, would be produced. Every now and then the tallow would burn too far below the top of the wick. The light would be too dim for weak eyes, then a pair of iron nippers would be used in clipping off the burnt wick surplus. I can almost see the change now that would take place in the light as I sat reading, when someone would say "Snuff the candle." Another way of making candles was to tie cotton wicks about two inches apart on sticks and dip a dozen at a time in the hot tallow, and after the tallow cooled dip again, and continue to dip and cool until the candle was large enough to suit the taste of the dipper, then lay them away for use. This last mentioned was named "a tallow dip." One of these made about as much light as a full grown lightning bug. Compare this manner of lighting with the present manner. Now you strike a friction match and touch to the wick of your gas fixture and instantaneously your room is as light as day. And if you are too lazy to turn it off when you retire let it burn—it needs no snuffing if it burns a month or a year. The difference between "the light of other days" 'and the present is beyond my ability to describe.

And there is still more difference in the heating of a house. Then, no matter how deep the snow, the oxen were yoked up and driven to the nearby woods. A hardwood tree, maple. beech, birch, hickory, oak, ash, or any hardwood that encumbered the ground was used. The driver of the oxen would chop a tree down, trim the limbs off from the bottom to top. hitch the ox chain to it and take the whole tree to the house and "the man of the house" would chop it up to the desired length (generally about four feet, owing to the size of the open fireplace). You begin to think now that these fire logs would have a little snow on them. Well, you make a good guess. When you put those logs upon the live coals you could hardly distinguish those logs from snow balls, but by adding a little dry kindling wood to this snow-fire a warm room would soon be the result. The half is not told yet. No stoves were in use then. The danger of sparks flying out of that open fireplace at night was a sleep destroyer for nervous people, but custom will do great things and as all were accustomed to this danger a great majority of the people gave it but little thought. They got used to it like the people of Etna and Vesuvius, who build the villages on the courses of the dry lava streams. I never lost a moment's sleep by reason of the thought that a spark might come sailing across the room at any time and make a bonfire of my bed. Many is the time that I have heard the snap of the red hot log and saw the burning coal light on the floor without any nervousness on my part. Each chimney had a stone hearth from two to four feet wide for the sparks and coals to fall upon, trusting to the Great Ruler of All Things to arrest the flight of sparks or coals before it passed over these flat stone protectors. But as all old settlers are aware, the coal was governed by the force that sent it. As many passed beyond this imaginary line as stopped on the hearth, but as there were no carpets the danger of firing the house was much lessened. I have many and many a time seen a parlor floor covered with black spots caused by hot coals not hot enough to burn clear through an inch board and set the house on fire. And strange to say, there were but few of those log dwellings burned from the cause mentioned above. This statement is hardly believeable under the circumstances. How could any one of the present day, go off up stairs and quietly lie down and go to sleep to the music of popping logs and flying coals down stairs? Although familiarized when young it would disturb my nervous system now when old.

Before leaving this firewood question, I will just tell "one" on the old settlers. They never, except a very small number, cut their firewood a few months in advance and let it dry before using. They cut their wood—a tree at a time—as described above, all winter long, instead of cutting it about a third of a year before burning and letting it dry and then putting it under a roof where no snow could reach it, thus saving the trouble of compelling green wood to burn, and saving dollars and dollars. I'll explain. With green wood when you want a little fire you must build a big fire. You must put in lots of kindling, then pile on many sticks of green wood before you can possibly get a fire hot enough to boil a teakettle. In the summer time you have a hot fire, in a hot house, and must wait until it burns itself out when you have no use for it. On the other hand, you can lay one stick on a few remaining coals and it will blaze up immediately and boil your teakettle, and one stick of wood is soon consumed and you have a cool house. No one can afford to burn green wood. The cost is more than double, to say nothing about the convenience of the dry wood. As in nearly everything, there has been a great change in the wood business. Now a large majority of the farmers cut their wood, dry it, and house it as carefully as they do their hay for their stock, thus keeping pace with the improvements of the age. Now and then a farmer sticks to the old wasteful way of "from hand to mouth." What I have been saying does not, of course, apply to us lucky ones who live along natural gas lines. All we have to do is to touch a match to our gas burner in a stove and instantly we have a fire that will burn without touching again for a day, week, month, year or five years. How is it possible to appreciate natural gas for cooking, lighting or heating? Our minds are not capable of measuring the distance between 80 years ago and today in the question of light and heat. I have left out a part of this article. But it is not too late yet to make amends. I mentioned the fact of no matches being invented, in the old times, but failed to describe the substitute. We took a piece of hard stone called a flint, then struck the flint with the back of a knife, or any piece of steel, a slanting blow and the fire would fly, dropping onto a piece of punk held under the flint. How often have I seen men "striking fire" when not a live coal could be found about the house! Everybody depended upon the flint as we now depend upon matches. The punk that was used to catch the fire from the sparks was but rotten knots taken from old hardwood logs and dried and kept as carefuly as we now keep matches. Hunters in the woods were never without the punk and flint. In fact, anyone who ever expected to need a fire carried these two things. I cannot say where the flint came from, but they were made of very hard stone, as clear and resembling common glass. The flint in flintlock guns was made of the same material.

## CHAPTER XV.

## WHEN OIL CITY WAS A SHANTY TOWN.

When I was younger than I am now, and when Oil City was younger than it is now, I helped "Smith & Allison" in their lumber business all one summer. The manner of handling lumber at that time was crude in the extreme. A raft would be run down the river and tied up below the old grist mill. As no such a thing as a brick house was thought of at that time, a large number of boards were used in building what passed for a dwelling place. These houses were constructed by putting up a frame of hewed pine timbers—no scantling balloon frames were in vogue at that time—then nailing rough boards on the outside, after which "battens," about three inches wide, were nailed over the cracks. Lathing and plastering were not a part of the make-up of an ordinary dwelling house at that time. When the mercury fell to zero, accompanied by a north wind, Jack Frost found it easy to penetrate the best abodes of the few people living within the limits of the present Oil City of fine, warm homes. Store rooms and all business places were constructed in the manner described above. When nothing but Cranberry coal and wood were used for heating purposes, the reader has only to guess at the discomforts of the pioneers. No anthracite coal—no railroad to bring it in—no electric light, no gas lights, and none but oil lamps, fashioned in a crude state, was the fate of the founders of Oil City. Many old people are alive today who can appreciate what is printed here, but the young folks of the present will simply have to guess at the hardships and inconveniences of "Old Times in, Oildom." It is not possible for me to guide my awkward pencil in giving a description of all the hardships endured by the founders of this tremendous and present great oil business. Just let the rising generation look at the Oil City of today, and then let them try to imagine how the people got along without a bridge of any kind across the river—only one little chain ferry, nearly up to Siverly-ville; an island in the middle of the river, about where the covered bridge now stands; an island covered with a crop of corn, accessible by skiffs. One could row a skiff from the north side of the river to this island, then lead it through the eddy at the lower end of the cornfield, then from there to the south side of the river, thus getting across the Allegheny without paying a chain ferry fee. But what would anyone go across for? They would only see one farm, with one old house, and barn to match, on that side of the river. But few people crossed the river, owing to the fact that there were but few people to cross. Well, I'm wandering again; I'll get back to the early lumber business.

"Smith & Allison's" lumber yard was located where the Arlington hotel now stands. Not all the lumber they handled was piled there. The largest share of it was sold on the river beach. A teamster would back his wagon down into the water, against the raft, and load the lumber on the wagon, and drive directly to the spot where it was used, thereby saving a double handling. My business was to measure the lumber as fast as loaded, and report at the office. The office was located just about where the obliging clerk of the Arlington now rakes in the sheckles. One teamster, in particular deserves "special mention" here. He was familiarly called "Nigger Jim." He was a well-to-do colored man. He owned the team of horses that he drove, and a house and lot, about half way to Siverly. Jim worked like a man of business. When he was wanted he was always there. He had a black skin but a white heart. It was necessary to wade in the water while getting the bottom course of each raft, and float the boards to shore, so that a teamster would keep his feet dry. This wetting of feet came to the measurer as an offset to the easy work that was his. For several days I was "rather under the weather" and hardly able to work. This came to Jim's ears, and he, unasked, jumped into the water and for a week he would not let me get my feet wet. I never met Jim after that without giving him the warm hand of fellowship. For many years I have not met Jim. I don't know whether he is alive or not, but I hope he is alive and prospering as of old. Perhaps there are teamsters with a white skin that would be just as kind under the circumstances, but I never happended to find them. The kind deeds of "Nigger Jim" will never vanish from my memory.

Ballard's barrel piles were one of the many wonders of the oil business. Empty oil barrels were made up the river somewhere, in "York State"—and tied together, in great rafts, and floated to Oil City. One "barrel yard" was located just across the street in front of where the Arlington now stands. I will not try to give the height of the pile of barrels, generally on hand, but will say that the tiptop of the pile pointed skyward, to about the same degree as the present Chambers block. Mr. Ballard's barrels found a ready sale, until the advent of tank cars and pipe lines. Then the great pile melted away and gave place to large business blocks, which are an honor to the city and a source of income to the owners.

To return to Smith & Allison. Mr. Smith built the first dwelling house on Cottage hill. The people called him a "fool for building up in that cornfield," where he would be compelled to walk—or climb to his rather imposing looking home. Years, and years ago, Mr. Smith crossed over the divide—passed through St. Peter's gate. He was the very personification of honesty and uprightness. Mr. Allison is still in the land of the living, and seems to be enjoying himself. He lives off west, somewhere, but came back to Franklin a couple of years ago, and made one of the best speeches on the occasion or Old Home week. Thousands of his hearers will bear me out in saying this. I had the pleasure of meeting him at the house of a relative of his, at Salina, Pa., when he was making that eastern visit. I was surprised to find him the same "Doc" Allison of old. Some men never get old, and "Doc" is one of them. The Derrick published his "Old Home week speech" at the time, as doubtless its readers remember the speech. It was full of good things from first to last.

Before leaving the lumber question I will mention a little transaction that does not savor of square dealing.

I landed a river "fleet" of square pine building timber in Oil Creek eddy, or rather in the mouth of Oil Creek. It was for sale. A man came up from Franklin, who owned a lumber yard in the "Nursery of Great Men," and looking all over the raft, made an offer for it which I accepted. I agreed to run the timber to Franklin, the next day, which I did, and landed it at the junction of the river and French creek as directed by

the man—I will not call him a gentleman—paid off the men
who helped me run the raft, walked over French creek to this
man's lumber yard and notified him of the arrival of his timber. "All right, I will go right over with you," was his
answer. When we arrived on the raft he made this most un-
expected speech "This timber is too old. It must have been
cut last winter. I will not accept it." I told him the timber
was cut in the winter but it was not quite a day older than
when he bought it. I told the man I was below the market
now, as I could have sold it at Oil City, where they were
using such timber in large quantities. The man still refused
of take it. I thought I was completely "hoodooed." I started
for town using language for the benefit of my timber customer
that I would not like to see in print. He started with me to
return to town, but I would not be seen in his company going
into Franklin. I walked faster than he and with a "Benediction" left him far in the rear, but fortune favored me after
all this treachery. I sold my raft to the city of Franklin the
same day for crosswalks for $50 more than the rascally lum-
ber yard man agreed to give me. Now, dear reader, what
do you think of that for a display of cheek?

------

## CHAPTER XVI.

## HIGH STANDARD OFFICIALS WHO ARE NATIVES OF BROKENSTRAW VALLEY.

Perhaps it will be news to many readers to mention the fact
that the Brokenstraw valley is the only valley along the Allegheny river from Kittanning to Coudersport that has not produced oil in paying quantities. It has produced oil operators.
John L. McKinney, J. C. McKinney and "Cal" Payne are
Brokenstraw productions. All three were reared about three
miles from Youngsville. "Curt" McKinney and "Cal." were
considered good average little boys, but John L. McKinney
was somewhat different from the common run of boys. He
always was a little on the dude order. Other boys who were
not inclined to put on airs like John poked fun at him. Little
they dreamed of him outstripping them all. No doubt but

that he could now buy and sell the whole batch of those boys
who at that time tried to hold their heads higher. In fact, he
could buy the Brokenstraw valley and have a good wad of
pocket change left. This is a changeable world. From boyhood to old age makes changes that are hardly believable.
John was always on hand at the balls that were very numerous in his boyhood days and on account of fine dressing and
pleasant manners he was a great favorite among the fair sex.
The writer of this has helped to make music (such as it was)
for John to trip the light fantastic toe many and many a
night. No one thought at that time that he had a business
streak running through him that in after years would make
him a power in the financial world. And "Curt" McKinney,
although a more sedate boy than some of his young companions, has "surprised the natives." Both of these brothers belong to an oil family. This family of James McKinney, one
of the pioneers of the Brokenstraw and Warren county, I
might say, are a family of oil workers and have done more
than their share to make the oil business what it is today.
The family consisted of six boys and one girl, and the girl
married an oil man of Meadville. Colonel Drake did not
know the opportunity he was giving to develop some energetic
intelligent families when he opened up this world-wide business near the city of Titusville. If Mr. Drake had lived to
the present time he could not help feeling proud to think
of the growth of the business that his busy brain laid the
foundation for. If any one had told of what the oil business
would come to, the morning after the Drake well was struck,
they would have been pronounced fit subjects for an insane
asylum. I must not leave out the boy "Cal" Payne. He always had an old head on his shoulders and was always doing
something that boys in general could not do. He first surprised the denizens of the Brokenstraw valley by getting an
appointment as passenger conductor on the Philadelphia &
Erie railroad. That was out of the ordinary for a farmer boy
to take charge of a passenger (or any other) train on a great
railroad. Well, reader, "Cal" was not content to punch
tickets and be looked up to as a great man by his outstripped
companions and resigned and started into the oil business.
Nearly everyone who was acquainted with the young conductor thought him very foolish to leave his position on the rail-

road for the then uncertain oil business, but "Cal" knew what
he was about and he came up, up and up until his name as
one of the high officers in the Standard Oil Company is a
household word everywhere an oil derrick is to be seen in
this broad land of ours.

I began this article by telling the readers about the barren
oil territory of the Brokenstraw valley. The valley is not
entirely barren of oil and gas. About 30 years ago Mr.
Nevans, of Titusville, leased a lot of land in Youngsville
and put down a well on the John Siggins farm, between the
P. & E. and the D., A. V. & P. railroad stations. When about
900 feet down he struck some gas and got a one barrel well.
As this was not much of a well in the days of 1,000 and 2,000
barrelers, he moved his tools about 15 rods from the location and drilled another well. This was a mate to the first
and Mr. Nevans left for richer fields, continuing to operate
until called to the life beyond. Before leaving Youngsville he
told your humble servant that there was oil in the Brokenstraw valley. His theory was this: The rock, about 40 feet
of it, was too hard for much oil to come through, but that
more open rock was not far distant, else there would be no
oil or gas seeping through. He said that if he knew which
way to go for this loose sand he would put down another
well, but it was impossible for him or anybody else to tell
which direction to take. Several wells have been drilled
since Mr. Nevans left. All got both oil and gas, but not
enough to convince the owners that it would pay to pump
them. Through all these years some of these wells have been
producing lightly, the oil being taken out with a sand pump.
No well has been tested yet in a scientific manner. Those
interested in oil matters are in hopes the new methods of
operating oil wells will soon be tried here. A Pittsburg company has secured several leases lately and will commence operations very soon. It is to be hoped that the mile-wide
valley of the Brokenstraw will not be left out in the cold many
moons longer. I think that the good Lord would not place
oil in paying quantities in the valleys of Mahoning, Red-
bank, Bear creek, Clarion, Scrubgrass, French creek, Two
mile run, Oil creek, Horse creek, Pithole, Hemlock, Tionesta, West Hickory, East Hickory, Big Sandy, East Sandy,
Tidioute, Dennis run, Kinzua, Sugar run, Corydon, Sala-

manca, Olean, Portville, Eldred, Port Allegany, Coudersport, and all the smaller streams, tributary to the Allegheny river, from Kittanning to the headwaters, and leave the widest and most beautiful, the Brokenstraw valley, minus this rich blessing of oil and gas.

I see I have omitted in the enumeration of valleys the most prolific of any—Tunungwant. Excuse me, ye dwellers among the never failing oil and gas wells of McKean county. And even if the days of one barrel wells ever come, Youngsville and vicinity will be oil producing territory, even if Mr. Nevan should be mistaken in his loose sand prediction. A few years ago a well was drilled inside the borough line to a depth of 800 feet, when oil and gas were struck. The gas blazed 40 or 50 feet high, with a roar that could be heard at a distance of a mile. Several barrels of oil were thrown out. The driller, Mr. Meeley, had great hopes of a good paying well. The well was shot and the flow of gas was by some means shut off. Mr. Meeley commenced to clean the well. Each night 40 feet of quicksand would run into the hole, which required a whole day with the sand pumps to remove. This kept up for a week, when the superintendent abandoned the well with 40 feet of quicksand in the hole. Mr. Meeley was so much chagrined by this order of the superintendent that he (Mr. Meeley) said he once had a similar quicksand job on his hands and it required three weeks to exhaust the quicksand. When exhausted they had a 25-barrel well. A then resident of Yougsville, a very successful Cherry run operator, and afterwards a Tiona and Clarendon operator, pronounced this well good for heating and lighting half the borough of Youngsville. But for some reason the superintendent abandoned this best prospect in Youngsville and the north and west side of the borough is an uncertainty up to the present time. A line of wells had been drilled—four in number—along the Brokenstraw creek, each prospect nearly as good as the last mentioned, but none has had a scientific test, and it is an open question, which could soon be solved, whether this valley of the Brokenstraw will remain small territory, or take its place among the many productive valleys along the Allegheny river.

## CHAPTER XVII.

## BIG THINGS WHICH STARTED IN WESTERN PENNSYLVANIA.

I wonder how many of my readers ever thought of how very important a part of the country is this section of Western Pennsylvania. The writer of this was born in Centerville, Crawford county, Pa. Several great things had a beginning within a radius of 18 miles of this rather unpretentious country borough.

First—The A. O. U. W., a beneficiary order, was organized a few miles south of Centerville. Jefferson lodge, No. 1, was the first fraternal insurance lodge organized in the United States. Now lodges are found in every nook and corner of this great country. They are numbered by the thousands and hundreds of thousands of members have died, leaving their beneficiaries—widows and children—provided for, who, if not for that first organization of the Ancient Order of United Workmen, would have been left destitute. One hundred and seventy millions of dollars have been paid by this order to stricken families where the Great Reaper has entered the homes. Reader, just try for a moment to estimate how many little children would have been ragged and hungry, who have been clothed and fed, today if it had not been for the A. O. U. W. And not only this but other fraternal orders, taking the cue from this pioneer order, have multiplied until now over 200 different associations, of different names, flourish in America, with over 7,000,000 members, paying about $80,-000,000 yearly. All from that little start of eight men, led by John J. Upchurch, of Meadville, 40 years ago.

Second—The first fraternal dollar was paid 18 miles north of Centerville, at Corry, Erie county, Pa. Lodge No. 1 at Meadville was the first lodge organized, but it did not have the first death. Lodge No. 2 was located at Corry and had the first death. At that time the two lodges had 260 members. The assessment on the death of a member was $1 for each member. This assessment was always paid in advance. So, you can see, that there was $250 lying in the treasury at Meadville, awaiting a death to take place. At that time the plans of the order were in a very crude state. Members joined

for the first three years existence of the society without a
medical examination.  People by the hundreds were saying
that after the first death and the first assessment had been
paid out, no more money would be paid in.  So, after due
consideration, so the story runs, the Corry lodge agreed to
make a test.  They initiated an old fellow who was nearly
gone with consumption.  He died in about three weeks, and
the recorder of the lodge, Mr. Fenton, of Jamestown, N. Y.,
who runs a pail factory at the place, but who lived at Corry
at that time, took the $250 to the home of the widow.  The
"smarties" lost their guess.  Not a member of the 250 failed
to pay in their dollar assessment, and, beyond the most ardent
dreams of the members, the income of the order, in place of
$250, is now nearly a million dollars a month.

Third—The first oil well was found at Titusville, Pa., 10
miles from Centerville, on the edge of Venango county, Pa.
I need not say that from one little Drake well blessings far
beyond description have come to the world.  And right here
let me call your attention to the point that the hand of Providence must have guided the hand of Mr. Drake.  He drilled
his well on the only spot where he, with his limited means,
could have secured oil in paying quantities.  Had he drilled
his well on any other spot, we poor mortals would now be
warmed by coal and wood, and we would be writing at night,
by the light of a pitch pine knot or an old glass lamp covered
with soot or grease, or by the light of tallow candles, or some
other kind of an arrangement.  Mr. Drake had only enough
money, by being helped, to put a well down 70 feet.  Where
would he have been if he had been obliged to go thrice that
distance?  The answer is: He would have quit before another
70 feet was drilled.  Compare the tools that Mr. Drake was
obliged to use with the improved tools of the present, and
what is your conclusion?  I claim to know something of what
I am talking about.  Just after the Drake well was struck the
quiet but energetic John B. Duncan, of East Titusville, a
cousin of mine, took it into his head to kick down a well on
Pine creek.  I helped him six weeks with his laudable undertaking at the princely wages of 75 cents per day.  You had
better believe that during that six weeks John and I did some
kicking and twisting of sucker rods.  I left John at the end
of six weeks to work out his own salvation, and with a few

weeks more of hard kicking he was rewarded with a five barrel well. Oil was at a good price at that time, and John made a little money as a reward for his perseverance. John was almost a brother of mine. When he was born his mother died. I was only 11 months old at the time and my mother, who was a sister to John's mother, took care of us both. Good woman that she was, she managed to bring us both to the six-foot notch. I always felt as though John was my half-brother. I think every man, woman and child in Titusville knew and respected him. He was a walking encyclopedia. He would take the time any day to impart information concerning the old settlers in Oil Creek. Several years ago he passed away.

When we sum it all up, where can we find another part of the United States where such godsends have taken root within a radius of 35 miles? Meadville, Corry (Corry paid the first fraternal insurance dollar in the United States) and Titusville are names to be emblazoned on the pages of fame. Do you blame me for feeling a trifle proud of being born at Centerville, about the middle of this triangle of little cities? Right close to Titusville lived Henry R. Rouse, at Enterprise, Pa., four miles from the Drake well. The lively suburb of Oil City—Rouseville—took his name. But to go back a little. Young Rouse came to Enterprise, Pa., when but a school boy He soon pitched into the lumber business and turned the tall pine trees into money. He displayed great aptitude, and the people of Warren county sent him—the boy representative—to the state assembly. He soon made himself felt in legislative affairs. About the time his term of law-making in Harrisburg expired, the oil business electrified the world. Young Rouse took a lease of the Buchanan farm, on which Rouseville now stands, and commenced successful operations. When nothing but brightness and prosperity stared him in the face one of his wells caught fire, and he, with many others— Willis Benedict, one of Titusville's prominent men was among the number—was fearfully burned. Mr. Rouse lived but two hours after the accident, but in that short space of time he made a will that could not be improved if he had given it a month's study. He was a single man with no relatives but his old father. After providing for his parent, he bequeathed to Warren county the remainder of his lumber and oil property. Half the interest of his fortune he wanted used for the benefit of the poor and the other half to be used for building a court house, and for building iron bridges and other road improvements in Warren county. The voters of the county were amply rewarded for sending him to the legislature when he was but a boy. Warren county has had no poor tax to pay and but few iron bridges to build since the flames burned out the life of that noble, enterprising young man—Henry R. Rouse. Passengers passing through Youngsville on either the Lake Shore or Philadelphia & Erie roads can see from the train the county poor farm and the Rouse hospital, erected by the bequests of this man. A marble monument stands on the lawn in front of the hospital to commemorate his memory. Although of a respectable size, it is not half as large as it should be, when compared with the princely fortune left for generations yet unborn.

---

## CHAPTER XVIII.

### COULD NOT GIVE HIS ROCKY HILLSIDE AWAY.

In this chapter I will mention the "on to Buffalo" business. When the Dunkirk, Allegheny Valley & Pittsburg railroad was being built, the Buffalo and Titusville people were very eager for the road. They expected that a competing line would be built from Titusville to Oil City, connecting with the Lake Shore branch to Ashtabula, O. If this could have been carried out to the Lake Shore, as it is now called, it would probably have been a better paying road today. This route would have given a traveler from the east to the west a trunk line ride through the oil region instead of going up the lake, where not a derrick is to be seen. But the managers of the old W. N. Y. P. put up the bars by laying down a track on the east side of Oil Creek to hold the right of way against all comers. I write this to show the moves on the railroad checker board. I never saw in my limited travels a railroad built such a distance and lie unused until the ties rotted under the rails except in this one case. Perhaps the embargo will be lifted some day and that link in the line of 17 miles will be put in. But even with this drawback, the D., A. V. & P.

road was needed between Titusville and Dunkirk to take care
of the Chautauqua Lake and Lily Dale travel, the local business all along a good farming country, including Warren and
Youngsville, and the oil and lumber trade of Grand Valley.
The smoke has ceased to pour forth from the stacks at the
lumber mills, as is always the case at all lumber camps in the
course of time, when the timber is all sawed, and the production of oil and gas has fallen off to a certain extent. But it
will be many days before all the oil and gas is gone. Two of
the men familiar to the lumber operators have handled their
last carload of lumber and the last barrel of oil. I allude to
L. B. Wood and Judge C. C. Merritt. The Judge left for
the untried land a few years ago. And let me say the Judge
was the first to die of a most remarkable family of brothers.
The Judge had 11 brothers. There were 12, counting himself,
in that family. All lived to be old men, and not one of the
12 ever used tobacco or whiskey in any form. L. B. Wood
was a man who is missed. Indeed he was in "Grand Valley."
When he was gone the whole valley seemed almost deserted.
He did a vast amount of business and was a leader indeed.
Wood left a son (Williston), who has the father's traits about
him to such an extent that the immense business of his father
will not suffer. L. B. also left a brother, Frank, and the
large business built up by the lamented L. B. Wood will
move along without much change. But the pleasant and business face of L. B. Wood has been missed in his office, store
and on the streets of Grand Valley.

The first man of Youngsville who made money at the oil
business was John Davis, a shoemaker for years before oil
was thought of. He was born and reared on a farm near
Youngsville. He, by hard work, could only make "both
ends meet." He had but little money but a good supply of
courage. At the very first of the developments at Tidioute he
moved his family to that town and took a lease, set up a
spring pole and pegged away until he struck one of those
shallow wells that was the fashion, those days, and sold it for
$6,000. John worked away until he got money enough ahead
to live in Meadville. Then he took the opportunity and
migrated to the county seat of Crawford county, Pa., and
thereafter rather dropped out of the ranks of the numerous
Davis family in Youngsville. His interesting family received

an education in that college city that they never could have had if they had remained in Youngsville. The members of the Davis family remaining here have always been noted for their musical abilities, the M. E. choir at one time being entirely composed of Davises. It was named "the Davis choir." John's family was not an exception in that respect, one of his daughters being the organist in Miller and Sibley's Baptist church choir at Franklin for many years. It may naturally be supposed that a lady who can play a pipe organ and give perfect satisfaction in the far-famed church and Sunday school patronized and financially sustained by those world-wide Christian workers, Miller and Sibley, is pretty well up in the music line. Well, the genial John came from his Meadville home, about two years ago, to visit his numerous relatives at Youngsville, at the "ripe old age" of 92 years. One of his relatives was his "Aunt Prudence," but two years his junior. He told her that he feared it would be their last visit. His fears were well founded, as within the next year both were "sleeping the sleep that knows no waking."

Reading a few days ago, concerning R. K. Hissam, the bank president, reminded me of a conversation that I had with Rev. Mr. Hissam, who owned an oil farm straight across the river from Sistersville, in the state of Ohio. He gave me a short history of his oil career. He was a Methodist Episcopal minister and years ago was a "circuit rider" on both sides of the Ohio river. The country stands on edge in that section, and as Rev. Mr. Hissam weighs over 300 pounds, riding up and down these mountains was very laborious for both himself and his horse, the horse in particular, and he concluded to make a change. He bought 200 acres of sidehill land, a mile from the river, on the Ohio side, and became a Buckeye farmer. A year or two convinced him that he was not intended for a farmer—certainly not for a farmer with land that stood edgeways. He then tried to sell his farm. Now came "the tug of war." By hunting high and low he could find no man anxious enough for farming such a hillside willing to give half the amount he gave for it. In other words he could not give it away. He was in for a farmer's life, and he settled down to his fate. Then oil was found at Sistersville, W. Va., and oil operators found that the oil belt did not run with the windings of the Ohio river, but that it

ran straight across the river, through Mr. Robison's 600 acre
farm about a mile and then through Rev. Mr. Hissam's 200
acre farm. The reverend gentleman did not have to look
after buyers for his farm after that. He leased it to an oil
company at a good royalty, and when I talked to him his income was about $500 a day, with oil at 60 cents per barrel,
and no wells drilled except protection wells half way around
the 200 acres. I don't know what his income was when the
rest of the protection wells were drilled and all the center of
the 200 acres, and oil at $1.75 per barrel. James McCray
had nearly such an experience. Just before Petroleum Center,
Pa., became a prolific oil town, "Jim" owned a farm there
of about 200 acres. About 50 acres was a very rocky sidehill. He did not value it enough to pay taxes on it. He paid a
surveyor for the work of surveying off this 50 acre piece,
made out the papers and went to Franklin and put it on the
"unseated list." The county treasurer learned that there was
an error in the transaction, and he refused to sell it as "unseated" land, and dropped it from his list and it fell back into
"Jim's" hands again. Soon after the "Maple Shade" well,
with its 1,000 barrels a day, was struck. When J. S. McCray
related this circumstance to me he had leased this rocky sidehill, in one acre leases, at $3,000 bonus and half the oil. Oil
at that time was bringing $3.00 a barrel. His income from
this 50 acres of "unseated land," not sold for taxes, was $5 a
minute—night and day, Sundays included, all the year around.
Here the old saying comes in play, "It is better to be born
lucky than rich."

In these articles I spoke of working for Smith & Allison in
their lumber yard in Oil City, one summer. I have told of
Mr McCray's streak of luck. In a very small way, I had a
little streak of luck in the early winter of that year. Now this
little sketch will look insignificant compared to the one just
related above, but it was luck all the same. After I finished
up my summer's work among the board shanties of Oil City
I came home to Youngsville and bought a couple of "creek
pieces" of boards and a boat, such as was used to run oil out
of Oil Creek, in bulk, at that time. When ready to start
from Brokenstraw eddy I made common cause with J. C. and
D. Mead, two brothers who had been in the lumber business
as partners for many years, but at the time mentioned above

were operating for oil at McClintockville, a mile above Oil City.

I hitched onto their raft and was accompanied by one of the brothers to Oil City. We sold out our lumber and oil boat. Then one of the brothers went on to Pittsburg and sent me back after a few creek rafts that I had formerly engaged and had come out of the Brokenstraw creek on a sudden rise of water. We were to be partners in this last mentioned deal. When I arrived at the Brokenstraw eddy I found the other brother in possession of the lumber I had engaged. Of course he knew nothing of my claims to the promise of this lumber and ignored my claim of it. The fault was with the former owner of the lumber in not telling this brother up here what he had done. I finally said, "Am I out of this deal?" The answer was, "You were never in." Well, as rough oil country lumber was nearly as scarce as hen's teeth that year, and I had promised Smith & Allison the lumber that I had engaged, and that had slipped out of my hands as slick as oil, I felt somewhat blue—not the "blue" that the raftsmen in general were afflicted with, but the real sober kind. As I stood on the bank of the old Allegheny, with no pleasant thoughts passing through my mind, I cast my eyes in the direction of the upper end of the Brokenstraw eddy. There I saw a vision that roused my drooping spirits. A half dozen little creek rafts were tied to the bank. I soon found the owner. I traveled five miles the next morning and soon became the proprietor of those rafts, which were loaded with nice pine shingles. One day's run put this lumber safely into Oil City. It was the night before Christmas and the river was covered with slush a foot deep from shore to shore Christmas morning. If I had been one day later I would not have got that much needed lumber into market that winter—perhaps never—as the ice in the spring might have swept it away. I settled with Smith & Allison in the evening after I landed the lumber and started for Youngsville at 4 a. m. Christmas morning, my route being up Oil Creek, creeping along the shore of the creek in places between the high mountain and the water's edge. When daylight came I had reached "Tar farm," and had enjoyed a warm and well cooked breakfast at the hotel. Was not that rather a ticklish job—travel-ing up along the fearfully rough bank—part of the time through woods and darkness all alone, and liable to a holdup any minute by footpads? A man had been murdered a few nights before on this path, within the limits of Oil City, for the few dollars in cash he carried in his pockets. The spot was near the tunnel of the Lake Shore railroad and several holdups had taken place in different parts of the new oil country a short time before my Christmas morning's walk. As there were no policemen to protect the lone traveler in those early days, I confess I felt slight misgivings concerning my personal safety, as I was carrying the price of my raft and shingles in paper money in my pockets—not, as it would be nowadays, in a check which no thief could use. After breakfast I made my way up, up, and to the Shaffer farm, where the terminal of the railroad was located at that time, and took a glad seat in a comfortable coach, and I found myself enjoying my Christmas dinner under my own rooftree. Now, reader, can you see any good luck about this trip. Perhaps you can better understand the buoyancy of my feelings if I tell you I doubled my money by that one day's run on the raging Allegheny. The reason is apparent. Winter was so near at hand that the man that I bought the lumber of feared to run the lumber when such slush as I have been writing about was liable to tie up navigation for the winter at any hour. Consequently, he gave me a low price for taking the risk of rafting so far out of season. Now, what do you think of my luck?

---

## CHAPTER XIX.

### A PUBLIC SPIRITED AND SUCCESSFUL EDITOR.

These chapters would not be complete without a reference to one of the most lively, energetic and public spirited men to be found in the oil regions. This man commenced in his younger days as a writer from the oil towns. A visit to a dozen towns a day, and a letter sent from each town, to the lucky paper that had him for a correspondent, was just a play spell for him. He soon developed into an oil scout—a very important part of the oil business in the early days of oildom—and the new well that came in without a diagnosis from his eagle eyes, was far away, indeed, and had a good dark hiding place in some swamp, or far-off section. This man, to make a long story short, kept on rising until he owns and edits the only paper on earth that gives a complete account of the oil business. About the first literature to meet the eye of the writer of "Old Times in Oildom" as he has stepped into hundreds and hundreds of oil derricks, is this man's newspaper. In the oil business it is regarded as indespensible, all the way from the millionaire owner of many wells to the poorest pumper.

As showing the enterprise of this man it is only necessary to mention that he bought and placed in his large establishment one of the first linotypes ever used out of the great cities of New York and Chicago. To show how he is regarded by his fellow workers in the newspaper field it is only necessary to mention that he was one of the first presidents of the International League of Press clubs. With all this he is a model of modesty. If he was aware of my writing this he would soon draw his blue pencil through this scribble of mine. Well, reader, you already know the name of the paper, and the editor. But fearing that this may fall into the hands of some backwoods reader, in this wide world of ours—some one who knows little or nothing of journalism and the wide, wide world, I'll proceed to give the name. The name of the paper is the Oil City Derrick, and the name of the editor is P. C. Boyle. My first acquaintance with Mr. Boyle was at the hanging of young Tracy, at Smetheport, Pa. Tracy had made a lengthy statement, and left it with his lawyer—not to be read until after the hanging. Mr. Boyle was then a correspondent of the Titusville Herald. Many other correspondents were there from the New York Herald. New York Tribune, New York World and other papers. Their fingers were itching for this statement. Immediately after the execution Mr. Boyle hurried to Tracy's lawyer and borrowed the document, telling the lawyer that he wanted to copy it. The last train for the day was ready to leave. Mr. Boyle made all haste to the depot, and sent the story by express to the Titusville Herald, which had column after column of this "confession" the next morning, and the big New York correspondents were obliged to go to the Herald for their "news," one day late.

Venango county people have all heard of Judge Cross, of Clintonville. I am now going to tell about something that happened long before the Drake well was thought of. I tell this to show what a wonderful memory some people have. About 50 years ago I traveled all one summer with a concert company. In the meanderings of our musical aggregation we struck Franklin—that "Nursery of Great Men." Our show held forth two nights in the old Presbyterian church. And, by the way, I engaged the use of that church of "Plumb" McCalmont, the then brilliant young lawyer and afterwards the greatest temperance advocate in Western Pennsylvania. Mr. McCalmont was a genial gentleman. Even then he made the green young fiddler and showman feel right at home as he tramped along with him to a back street to show him the capacity of the old red clap-boarded church. Judge Cross was one of the associate judges of Venango county at that time. Accompanied by his daughter he was attending court that week. They stopped at the same hotel with our famous concert troupe of two violins, two singers and one melodeon. Both nights the judge and his daughter attended our musical entertainments. Twenty years after that I went down to Pittsburg as an oar puller on a lumber raft and came back by stage. The route led through Clintonville. When nearing the little town I asked the stage driver if Judge Cross lived there. He said: "Yes, he is now postmaster." I made this remark in the hearing of the stage full of passengers: "I saw the Judge 20 years ago at Franklin and have not seen him since." The stage driver replied in this wise: "If he saw you 20 years ago he will know you now." I told the driver that could not be as when I saw the judge I was dressed fit for a showman—a great contrast between my clothes then and now. "I am returning from 'a trip down the river' with old dirty clothes and have slept in a raft shanty bunk with nothing but straw for a bed for the last eight nights and I am 20 years older, 20 years dirtier and 20 years raggeder." The driver said: "That makes no difference. If Judge Cross ever sees any man, woman or child once he will know them if he ever sees them again. Come in and wait while he changes the mail and when he sees you he will know you." When the stage drew up to the door of the judge's store in which was the postoffice I walked into the store and took a seat on the farthest end of the counter. The whole stage load of passengers had become so much interested that all followed me into the store and stood around as very much interested spectators awaiting the result. The judge sat behind the boxes busily sorting the mail. He inadvertently cast his eyes in my direction and immediately exclaimed: "Isn't your name Brown?" Then a big roar of laughter came from the stage load of passengers, and the stage driver claimed a victory.

I will say a few words about the old Noble & Delamater well, near Pioneer, on Oil Creek. What I am going to relate many old people already know, some middle-aged people know about it, but not many young people have heard of it. When the well was drilled in it flowed at an average of nearly 1,500 barrels a day for the first year. The price of oil was $14 per barrel—no wonder the proprietors started two banks, one in Erie and another in Meadville. The well was drilled on the very edge of the lease. The adjoining lease holder thought he could plainly see a "scoop" and lost no time in putting up a derrick, nearly touching the Noble & Delamater rig. He soon had a neighboring well in close proximity to the big gusher. The theory is that the Noble & Delamater well struck a crevice in the rock. In other words, the crevice was composed of one crack in a solid rock, with the oil flowing through it. Be that as it may, the cute business man that tried to tap the source of the Noble & Delamater fortune did not even grease his drilling rope. This shows the uncertainty of the oil business. And about a mile from this great money maker occurred an exemplification of the uncertainty of keeping money when once in your possession. Mr. Benninghoff, whose farm was second to none in the production of oil, bought a safe to store his immense piles of greenbacks in, thereby saving him many long trips to town to deposit the burden of cash, which poured in upon him daily. While quietly seated at his farmhouse table, surrounded by his wife and happy farmer sons and daughters, a gang of ruffian robbers entered, and at the point of many revolvers, they were obliged to watch and see their honest cash carried off—by the $100,000—by the lowest pieces of humanity that God ever permitted to walk the earth.

## CHAPTER XX.

### SOMETHING ABOUT GAS.

In these chapters I have said but little about gas. In fact I tell little in these chapter that would permit being called "Old Times in Gasdom," instead of "Old Times in Oildom." Just think a moment—those of our readers who were on earth when the first big flow of gas was struck at Titusville on the Jonathan Watson farm. The first big flow of gas was not worth ten cents; not good for anything in fact but to scatter the nice flowing yellow oil to the four points of the compass For years after that the gas from the many wells in the oil region was more of a nuisance than a benefit. It caused considerable expense. The owners of the wells were obliged to buy iron pipes to carry the gas to a safe distance from the well, where it was burned, to prevent the mischief it might do. And mischief it did do in hundreds of cases. It killed the lamented Henry R. Rouse, and several others with him at the same time, besides disfiguring for life a score or more. Many lives have been lost and much property destroyed before this vapor was finally bridled by the ingenuity of man. The operators in Butler and other sections soon found a safe way to destroy this terror. They laid a pipe, as described, touched a match to the gas, thereby destroying its power to kill. I stood on a high eminence in Butler county one night, and counted 63 great gas torches high up in the air. It was a grand sight. But oh! the millions of money that was vanishing, all unawares to mankind. Even "Cal" Payne, who at that time lived in his big new house, at the city of Butler, was doing his full share in destroying one of the best servants of mankind ever known. I guess he knows something about it now, as he sits on the throne and gives directions in regard to this vapor, as it lights millions of homes with a brighter light than oil, and softer light than electricity. And more than that—it cooks millions of meals, and good housewives have only to strike a match, and one match may even suffice for all winter. My own little town of Youngsville would be in comparative darkness if not for this mischievous gas. Instead of a dim flickering street lamp, as in nights of old, we now have street lamps on nearly every corner and one bright light greets another all over the borough. The Forest Gas Company leads this once uncontrollable stuff, in iron pipes, from away over the Allegheny river, in the wilds of Forest county, to nearly every room in nearly every house in Youngsville. All stores and public places are a bright blaze of light. Did you ever think of the triple benefit of this excellent illuminant. First, it saves you from straining your eyes while reading at night; second, it saves much hard work in cleaning lamps; and third, it saves a vast amount of wood chopping and whittling shavings every time a little fire is started. People within range of the gas are apt to forget to be thankful every day that gas was struck in their time and that it was not postponed until another generation. And I must not forget to say that another great benefit is derived from this source. The young timber, instead of being cut up for fire wood, is allowed to grow up into high priced lumber all over the gas producing region.

The great ruler of the universe—God—will provide for future generations. This is only one of the many benefits that will be vouchsafed to the millions of people who will come to fill our tracks after we have traveled that unreturnable journey. Great is gas, and it came from small beginnings.

When oil was stored in large iron tanks to a greater extent that it is since the Standard Oil Company commenced the business of transporting it directly from the wells to the refineries, lightning played a conspicuous part in depleting the producer's bank account. Now and then, a tank is struck by lightning, even yet, but a good share runs to the refineries or to the seacoast safely under ground in iron pipes, free from danger from lightning. I have seen a great many tanks burning after being struck by lightning and the most dangerous one of the lot that I have seen was one at Monterey, Clarion county, Pa., about 28 years ago. Near a half dozen large tanks, of about 28,000 barrels capacity, stood on the left bank of the Allegheny river at Monterey. They stood on a sidehill, about 40 rods from the railroad tracks and the river. One morning during a heavy thunder storm lightning struck one of the tanks and there was a wicked blaze immediately. It burned all day and in the evening a carload of us traveled five miles in a chartered car on the Allegheny Valley railroad to see the tremendous big black blaze. At this time I was a reporter for the Erie Daily Dispatch, and I went with the crowd for the purpose of reporting this oil fire. A couple of hundred people, both men and women, had gathered about this great blaze and about 3 o'clock in the afternoon, the overflow that always comes when a full tank of oil burns about half way down, came, and rivers of burning oil started down the sidehill. The volume before spreading was about four feet high. For some unaccountable reason, I happened to be below, right in the way of this burning oil. All the others happened to be off at one side, where they easily got out of the range of the burning fluid. I was the only one who had a nip-and-tuck race with the flames. I ran slantingly across the sidehill towards a piece of woods. I came to a rail fence which I climbed on the double quick and dodged into the woods. As I went under the trees the blaze from the burning oil struck the tops of the trees over my head with an ugly roar. As I ran the heat struck my back with great force and I was quite strong in the belief that there would soon be one less reporter for the Erie Daily Dispatch. But as was my luck, when I struck the edge of the woods, I found a rise in the ground that turned the oil straight down the sidehill, leaving a breathless correspondent sitting on a log, thanking God for a deliverance from sudden death. This was a fire to be remembered, as it cleared a couple of acres of woodland between the oil tanks and the railroad. The burning oil poured down the hill, devouring green trees and everything it came to. It swept the Allegheny Valley railroad tracks, stopping trains for a day or two, burned a planing mill, a lumber yard, several dwelling houses and a barn—then poured a great buring stream into the river—a stream which spread from shore to shore and floated Pittsburgward. It was a strange sight indeed to see that broad expanse of fire towering high and moving down the old Allegheny on top of the water

I began this chapter by speaking of gas. I am reminded by this Monterey fire of the Wilcox (Pa.) burning well. Here was another gas freak. I and three others drove four miles from the Wilcox hotel to see the famous burning well. We were amply rewarded for the trip. When we arrived it was dark. Every seven minutes, without fail, the gas would throw the oil and water nearly twice as high as the derrick. Each time when the flow would come, a man with a long pole, having an oiled rag on the end of it, would reach out the full length of this pole and set fire to the oil and gas. The gas would throw an eight-inch stream far up into the air. The water would form itself into a barrel shape, and the gas and oil would go straight up this round tunnel, all ablaze, entirely encircled by the water. Then the water would spread and fall in beautiful spray, forming all colors of the rainbow. Such a sight taking place every seven minutes cannot be described by my weak pen. This free show has long since gone into "innocuous desuetude." It is doubtful if ever a counterpart of this wonderful Wilcox well will ever be seen again. This is an age of wonders, and perhaps something will turn up in this picturesque line that will excel the wonders of the burning well at Wilcox. But, I say again, it is doubtful.

---

## CHAPTER XXI.

### YOUNGSVILLE'S PROSPECTS OF OIL AND GAS.

It is rumored that parties from Oil City are quietly leasing land around the Allegheny sulphur springs, about one mile south of Youngsville, with the intention of giving this territory a thorough test. I have already mentioned the small wells about Youngsville. I left off a description of the work that has been done along the Brokenstraw creek, between Youngsville and Irvineton. Twenty years ago five wells were drilled within a distance of two miles. All produced more or less oil, but not quite enough in the minds of the different owners to justify the expense of pumping them. It takes quite a good well to pay the expense of pumping one well, but when a dozen small wells are pumped by one engine the case is different. No two wells have ever been hitched together in Youngsville and vicinity, although there are about a dozen of them. A "second crop" operator could probably make money by getting control of a half dozen or more of these and harnessing them together. The owners of a majority of these wells contented themselves by sand-pumping the well until they got a wagon load. Then they would drive to Warren refinery and sell it. But I am wandering from my subject —the five wells along the Brokenstraw creek. One of the five was owned by A. McKinney and others. It produced about two barrels a day by flowing. The owners put up a 250-barrel tank to receive the oil. The well flowed at intervals until there was about 150 barrels of oil in the tank—a wooden one. Then came the great flood when so many lost their lives at Oil City and Titusville. The Brokenstraw creek went over its bank doing about $200,000 damage in the Brokenstraw valley. The tremendous rush of water swept everything off this lease—tank of oil, and all. That was the last work done on that lease to this day. But the well flows occasionally—up to the present date. The oil is not saved, however. Some day the well may be cleaned and tested. This same company drilled a well about 200 rods above the one just spoken of and it was nearly a mate for it. I, with my own eyes, saw the above mentioned well flow about three barrels of oil into a wooden tank in the space of 15 minutes after being "shut in" two days. Although this was the time of the great flood this last named well has continued to flow and many a wagon load has been drawn to the Warren refineries from it. Now we come along up the creek a few dozen rods and another well has about the same history, only the oil that it flows has not been saved. Then we come along up about 60 rods and we find the most abused well in the lot. It tried to be something but the superintendent "shut up shop" when it did not prove to be a great gusher without cleaning out the quicksand that gathered with oil and gas in fair quantities in the hole. At the west end of this two miles of wells, with not a dry hole, is a vast expanse of territory which has never been tested.

I recently read a communication in the Oil City Derrick from the Rev. P. S. G. Bissell, concerning his father's claim to the honor of drilling the first oil well. Then I read in the Derrick the editorial comment on the letter. I saw the Drake well the second day after oil was struck. I have seen George H. Bissell many times at Titusville. I have stopped at the same hotel with him, conversed with him, and I always found him to be a very agreeable gentleman and a strong believer in the great future of the oil business, but I never heard his name mentioned as the discoverer of the first oil well. It was Drake, Drake, Drake, on all sides there at Titusville, but never once Bissell—so far as I ever heard. The name of Colonel E. L. Drake has been a fireside word the whole world over. How many of the young people at the present time, have ever heard of George H. Bissell? The intelligent business men who furnished the money to pay for the fine memorial in Titusville cemetery are not likely to make a mistake and put the momument over the wrong man. If George Washington's monument had been named Thomas Jefferson's, it would have looked funny. To my mind, the editorial in the Derrick relating to Queen Isabella and Mr. Bissell did not go far enough There was quite a difference between the two. Queen Isabella did not drop Christopher, but continued to furnish the "dingbats" until the discovery was made. She did not let the burden fall on a Fletcher or a Wilson, as did men who are now trying to take the honors away from Drake.

How things have changed since I was a boy! I saw this country when it was, you might say, "a howling wilderness." Tall pine trees darkened the country in places, as far as the eye could reach. A large part of it belonged to the Huidekopers, of Meadville, Pa. Each quarter sessions of court at Warren two of the brothers would drive in a covered carriage to Warren on Monday and write contracts and deeds all the week. All the people in this section of the country thought the Huidekopers "some punkins." Everybody tipped their hats when they met the Huidekopers driving their fine team of matched horses hitched to a shiny covered carriage. A man in a covered buggy those days, looked bigger than a man in an automobile does nowadays. And the price—there was but little difference between giving the timberland away as at present and selling it at only $1.50 an acre. Think of good soil for farming, covered with the finest of pine timber, bringing the magnificent price of $1.50 per acre! I myself borrowed $150 of that kind-hearted and wealthy gentleman, John McKinney, often called the "Uncle to Standard Oil," and paid Huidekopers for one hundred (100) acres of good land, covered with the best of pine timber, and one year from the time of borrowing the money had paid back the money. And the Good Samaritan that he always was, would not take one cent of interest. Was not that getting land on easy terms?

The Huidekopers had their own troubles, as "all the sons of men" have in this business world. Timber thieves were numerous. Nearly every man that made shaved shingles helped himself to all the pine timber that he manufactured into shingles the year around. The Huidekopers tried to guard against this wholesale robbery by engaging men who lived in the vicinity to watch their property. This plan did not even retard the shingle making business. The many shingle makers never lost a day's work after the appointment of the watchers. The watchers seemed to have enough of business of their own on hand, without meddling with the shingle making of their neighbors—at least not according to my best recollection, was a man ever arrested for stealing timber. The woods were full of shingle makers. There were no shingles sawed in those days. Shingle mills were unknown. The shingles were all split out with a frow and maul, then shaved on a "shaving horse" and packed into half-thousand bunches, and they were ready for the Pittsburg market. Nearly the whole output of shingles in this then vast lumber country was hauled to Brokenstraw eddy on bobsleds in the winter time, and then piled on board rafts in the spring and run to Pittsburg and sold to the farmers all around the Iron City, and far into the Buckeye State. Not all stopped in Pittsburg, as many of these rafts ran the whole length of the Ohio river. Cincinnati got quite a share of this shingle trade. But I am wandering from this stealing trade subject. This cutting Huidekopers' pine timber became so respectable and safe that a man was thought just as much of when working up stolen timber as if it was his own. It was a common occurrence for a couple of men to go into the woods, build a shanty on Huidekoper land, and live in the shanty all summer and pick out the best pine trees and make them into shingles, without even a thought of wrong doing or of being arrested for theft. In fact, these men often stole the timber from each other, after the first man had cut the timber lengths, ready for the frow. In one case amusement comes in. A certain man living about a mile from Youngsville hired another man to help him saw and split into bolts a goodly pile of this timber, for his own use when he would get the time to work it up. A short time after a neighbor came to him and asked the loan of this ready cut timber for a short time, or until he could get time to steal and cut enough to pay it back. The man that owned the timber refused to lend it to his neighbor, as he was ready to commence the job of manufacturing the stuff into shingles. Then it was that the would-be borrower, without a blush, made this remark: "I have already made that timber into shingles and

sold them, but I will cut more on the same lot and pay you
back soon." He never make his promise good, and as it would
be a delicate and dangerous business for one thief to arrest
another, the transaction dropped right here. All the satisfaction ever gotten out of it was that the thief of the first
part seemed to enjoy himself in telling his neighbors what a
mean man the thief of the second part was. The writer of this
got this unbelievable story from the man who stole and sawed
the timber. Both men have long since gone to put in their
claims to heavenly mansions not covered with pine shingles.

This stealing timber business is not guess work with me. I
once bought two tall and large pine trees from Judge William
Siggins. This was a legitimate transaction. The stealing
comes right in as soon as I can get this pencil to it. I hired
a neighbor to help me cut the trees down, saw them into
"double lengths," and pile them up, ready for hauling to our
shingle shanty to be manufactured into shingles. When the
time came I yoked up "Buck" and "Bright," the very faithful
old ox team belonging to my father and hitched them to the
woodenshod sled and drove two miles in to the forest where
I expected to get a load of my timber, but I din't. Not a
bolt was to be seen. Then I began to look for tracks. I
found sled tracks in abundance, but a lack of timber. I followed
the sled tracks about a mile and found my timber snugly piled
up by the side of another man's shanty. The man was contentedly smoking a pipe and shaving shingles. He looked up
—without any appearance of embarrassment—with a smile
and a hearty "good morning." I soon broached the subject
nearest my heart and inquired the cause of my timber being
piled at the wrong shanty. He answered in these words: "I
got in a hurry for some shingles and took yours; I will cut it
on the Huidekopers' land and pay it back to your right way."
I told him that I must have those shingles and as he had made
4,000 already and a large hill would have to be climbed before
reaching my shanty, I would give him the "going price" for
making up the balance of the timber, about 16,000 shingles,
and delivering them at Brokenstraw creek raft landing. He
readily agreed to my proposition. But when I came around
for a settlement, he had worked up all the timber and sold all
the shingles, and pocketed all the money. In place of putting
the sheriff on him immediately, I took his promise to replace

them in a fixed time. He never paid me a dollar, and I was green enough to let it stand until he, too, crossed over where no sheriff annoys.

---

## CHAPTER XXII.

### BAD OIL SPECULATION.

My experiences were not extensive as an oil operator. My first, last and only venture in drilling a well was on Cherry run, in Rouseville. When the oil business was yet in a very crude state, J. C. and D. Mead and I, formed a co-partnership, and leased one acre of the old Smith farm, at Cherry run, so close to Rouseville that it was really a part of the village. Having a majority vote of "the company," I was elected as superintendent. This was making a superintendent out of raw material. But no more raw than a majority of the bosses in that early day of the oil business. Superintendents that had learned the business were not to be found, as the business had not been learned by any living man. It was "cut and try" with the best of operators at that time. I am very sure it was "cut and try" with my company. I am quite certain as I was the "cutter and tryer." And there is no use in postponing the acknowledgement that I was not a howling success at the oil business. My first work requried more muscle than brains. The work consisted of chopping down a big white oak tree, on the sidehill above Rouseville, and hewing out a sampson post. I did about half the work on all the timber framing for our derrick and engine house. But now comes in the brain work. After consultation with my partners who knew as little about the business as I did, I bought an old boiler and a new engine. The boiler was somewhat antiquated, and in shape and size it would compare favorably with a 12-foot average saw log. One little "lackage" about this boiler was the fact that it did not have a single flue in it, and it showed weakness from the very start. After much tribulation and vexation, and consultation with my partners in the venture, I concluded to sell the old cylinder and replace it with an up-to-date boiler. I forget the price of this new fangled boiler, full of flues, but it took quite a little pile of notes on the "State

Bank of Ohio" to pay for it, and commence operations. The cost of coal was an item that bore down hard on oil operators. We used Cranberry coal, at $1.25 per bushel, delivered at the well. This seems funny now when all around us millions of feet of gas are being piped away from the wells. It compares favorably with work that I helped my father do when I was a boy. When clearing land for farming we would girdle nice, green, pine trees, killing them, so that they would not shade the crops, or cut beautiful clear stuff, red oak, into logs, hitch oxen to them, haul them and roll them up into "log heaps," with much hard lifting, and burn them. And this burning was no "fool of a job," as the timber was very green and soggy. It needed punching up while burning, at very short intervals. It required much attention for two or three days and nights before the last embers were consumed. This same red oak timber—if standing on the ground today, would bring $30 per thousand feet, without the owner touching it. We have two large furniture factories in Youngsville which consume 20,000 or 30,000 feet of just such lumber daily. A part of it is now brought by rail from West Virginia.

But let me get back to my oil business again. When this Cherry run well was finished, it had cost about $3,000. It was a fair producer, about 10 barrels a day. Oil at that time was brining $3 per barrel. But in the course of a year the output commenced falling off, and as the Roberts torperdoes were beginning to make a stir in the oil region, my partners asked me to go to Rouseville and have a shot put in our well. I told them that I would go down and attend to that shooting in 10 days. The Warren County Agricultural Fair, of which I was chairman, was on hand, and I did not propose to put "business before pleasure," but stayed by the agriculturists until the end of that year's exhibition. One of the Mead brothers became impatient with this delay, and went down to Rouseville and sold out our lease at a ridiculously low figure to Mr. Nelson, a Philadelphia operator. This purchaser immediately did what I should have done—had a shot of glycerine put in it. This shot brought the well up to 40 barrels a day, and convinced Mr. Mead that he acted a little hastily in the premises. If he had waited until the close of the county fair that glycerine shot would have put quite a sum of money in our pockets, instead of passing into Mr. Nelson's. We were having another

6

well drilled on the other end of this acre which came in as good a producer. But my being so slow and Mead so fast deprived our company of doing much in the way of oil operations.

The old times in the oil country were frequently enlivened by fire getting started in the tinder-box houses forming all new oil towns. I was running a lumber yard at Karns City at the time that that quite noted town went up in smoke. I owned an opera house, a building for a lumber office and Western Union telegraph office, lumber yard and hotel, all located in the lower end of the town. Fire companies came from Millerstown, Petrolia, and Parker City just in time to stop the fire before it reached any of my property. In fact, nearly every building in town was burned except mine. I scored good luck for once. The fire started in a little store. The proprietor was away from home. The story flew fast that the man, a Hebrew, by the way, had been burned out three times and had been insured every time. When the man came home the next day an angry crowd met him on the street and accused him of being the cause of their homes being in ashes. The man turned white with fear in a moment and pro- tested his innocence. But his hearers were crazy mad and threatened him with lynching. A rope was procured and pre- parations made to hang him to the nearest tree. Just then the constable arrested him and started with his prisoner for the lock-up. On the way to the lock-up an amateur cowboy sent a rope whirling through the air three times, but each time it failed to coil around the man's neck. I never saw a lynch- ing bee, but I might have seen one if that rope had caught on around the man's neck, as lots of men were ready to grab the end of the rope and run for the nearest tree. That night a trial was had before 'Squire Stewart and the store proprietor was sent to the Butler jail for safe keeping. He remained in jail a few days and then caused the arrest of his captors for false imprisonment. He proved that he was in Clarion all day on the day of the fire. He also proved that his wife's gold watch and chain and all of his best clothes were burned, and that one child, through fright, ran and concealed itself under a bed and was accidentally discovered just in time to save it from a horrible death. The would-be lynchers had to pay quite dearly for their cowboy play.

Although this fire swept the most of Karns City from the

face of Butler county, no lives were lost. But after all this, when a hotel had been built near the depot of the Parker & Karns City railroad, a terrible loss of life took place when the hotel burned—seven perishing. The hotel people and two transient lodgers were burned. But this was not as bad as the hotel fire at Chicora a short time before that, when eight people were cremated in one hotel, and many more injured. I was an eye witness to this holocaust.

If all the sudden and tragic deaths that have taken place in the oil region since the Drake well was drilled, were mentioned, it would fill a large sized book. Of the hundreds and hundreds of lives lost by glycerine I will mention just one that took place over on Bear creek when the stuff let go with a jar that broke plate glass windows in Parker City, two miles away over a hill. I accepted an inviation from a Mr. Stephenson to ride with him in his buggy to the place indicated by the sound. When we reached the spot we found a great hole in the ground, about eight feet deep and eight feet in diameter. About one-half of a horse lay in the road unscathed, cut as clean as it could be done with a knife. It was the forward part of the animal that lay in the road cut through the middle about half way between the fore legs and the hind legs. The hind quarters were nowhere to be seen. Only a little of the wagon could be found. Not a vestige of the well-shooter could be discovered except a portion of the skin of his face. That was found hanging on a bush about 20 rods away. One wagon tire was driven through a hemlock tree a foot in diameter.

I might describe many other scenes that I have observed in the torpedo line. I have stood in three different towns, and have seen plate glass breaking, and falling onto the sidewalks, all caused by glycerine magazines exploding—Butler, Willow Grove and Parker City. Death followed in the wake of all these explosions.

## CHAPTER XXIII.

### H. P. KINNEAR AND THE I. O. O. F.

What changes come with time! As I, with my mind's eye, look back through the years, many things come to me that, to say the least, are surprising. A few remarks about Youngsville lodge, No. 500, I. O. O. F., will not be amiss. There were about 50 members when I joined, a half century ago. Only one, besides myself, is a member today—David McKee, of Corry, Pa. I am the only one living within the vicinity of the lodge room. The Kinnears, Meads, Siggins, Johnsons, Blodgetts and others—all gone—either dropped out of the order, left the town or have passed to the Grand Lodge beyond. Reader, try and put yourself in my place. Think of stepping into lodge with over 200 members all initiated since I was shown the secret workings of the order. Is it any wonder that a gentleman living in this town recently published the alleged fact that I had "long since passed the age of imbecility." The gentleman himself is no "spring chicken," and if God lets him live as long as he has let me live, he will not be one day younger than I am now.

Several items are worth mentioning in "Old Times in Oildom" concerning this lodge. Mr. Kinnear, who was the originator of this lodge nearly 60 years ago, was the moving spirit in the business of the lodge and all other movements for the upbuilding of Youngsville. He was the representative of the lodge at the Grand Lodge of Pennsylvania every year of its existence, from its organization until he passed beyond all earthly things. He voted on the destiny of No. 500 about 45 years. Mr. Kinnear was one of the go-ahead men of his day. He held the office of sheriff of Warren county for two terms; represented the county in the legislature two terms; was one of the founders of Point Chautauqua; held the triple position of chairman of the commmittee on Grand hotel, superintendent of the grounds of the association and treasurer from the time of the starting of this association up to the time of the destruction of the great summer resort by fire. To enumerate all the achievements of this public spirited man for the interest of Youngsville would take more space than can be spared. Suffice it to say that he "builded better than he knew," for upon the foundation that he laid the liveliest and best town of its size in Western Pennsylvania stands today. Mr. Kinnear was president of the Youngsville Savings Bank at the time of his death, 22 years ago. His picture hangs on the wall of the lodge room and is a smiling reminder of the founder of the second lodge organized in Warren county. The three-story building, constructed of wood, is owned by the lodge, and next year it will be replaced by a fine brick building of modern design. Youngsville is proud of another man who has been a credit to the place—the Hon. William H. Short, who is 86 years of age and who steps along the streets without the aid of a cane. He has been a man of ability and business, a resident of Youngsville since a boy. He has filled the offices of everything that the borough of Youngsville could bestow upon him, besides being president of Sugar Grove Savings Bank for many years. He was one of the directors of the far-famed Chautauqua founded by the great Vincent, a member of the State Legislature, two terms, and, last but not least, Mr. Short has filled the office of United States consul of Cardiff, Wales.

Youngsville has many excellent business men of a younger generation, but I am writing of "old-timers" and the younger men must be left out for the present.

A little incident that came near being a big incident is this: I, in partnership with William Davis, built a boat for the purpose of sending out of Oil Creek, oil by the barrel, into Oil City. When finished we floated it out into the river, preparatory to going to the Hub of Oildom. When we were about to cut loose from Youngsville 40 ladies came on board for a ride of three miles to Irvineton. As it was a flat bottomed boat, with no seating capacity, the ladies were obliged to stand up during their ride. When nearing the Irvineton mill dam, your humble servant, who had the distinction of being pilot of the craft, discovered the disagreeable fact that the water pouring over the dam was hardly deep enough to run the boat over lengthwise; so to make sure of not sticking on the high dam, I plied my oar with much vigor until the boat was lengthwise of the dam, thereby catching all the water in the creek from shore to shore. The boat obeyed the rudder to perfection and the water was found to be deep enough to carry the boat over. But now comes the sequel. The pilot never had this experience before, always finding the water deep enough to run the boat endways. I did not have forethought enough to let the ladies disembark, walk past the dam, then run the light boat over the dam and land, taking them on again and out into the river eddy, but instead rushed into danger. The boat alighted on the roaring and swirling water on one edge coming up nearly full of water. The ladies all stood in water knee deep, with a chance of the boat sinking any moment. The weight of the

ladies caused the boat to sink so deep that an inch more would
have let the water pour over the top. One inch more and 40
ladies and 10 gentlemen would have been floundering in 16
feet of water. As it was, by order of the pilot, they all stood
perfectly still until the water logged boat, loaded with feminine
humanity, slowly floated to more shallow water, where the
boatload of fair ones waded ashore and were happily saved.
The pilot would have had many lives to answer for if that boat
had been a trifle more shallow, but a "miss is as good as a
mile."

I never was troubled by ladies asking me for a boat ride
after that trip. Bad management has been the cause of many
ships, and many lives being lost. Bad management would have
had the same effect in this case, only on a smaller scale. And I
may as well tell it all when I am about it. I am now living,
and have been for many years, in partnership with the best
one of that lot of ladies, but she has never invited me to take
her boat riding since that particular occasion.

Years ago, when I was at Smethport, Pa., I witnessed the
only hanging of my lifetime. The readers of this will no
doubt call to mind the taking off by the rope route of Young
Tracy, for the murder of his sweetheart. The night before
the hanging, I spent an hour with W. Ed Marsh, a young
lawyer of Corry, Pa., but who had an office in Smethport.
The sheriff chanced to call on the young Blackstone. We both
tackled him for a ticket admitting us to the jail, where the
hanging was to take place. The sheriff was a very kindly
man, and told us that his tickets were all gone—to 12 witnesses, 12 jurymen, several deputies, about 30 newspaper re-
porters and a few friends, but if we would come to the front
steps of the court house at 2 p. m., he would come and open
the door and let us in. My only excuse for asking
admisison was that I was a correspondent of the Titusville
Herald, but as P. C. Boyle was the regular traveling oil
region correspondent for the same paper, and had traveled in
ahead of me, my chances seemed slim, for awhile. Well, 2 p. m.
next day found us eagerly awaiting the appearance of the
sheriff at the door. Ticket holders by the dozen—P. C. Boyle
among the number—came rushing along, and handed their
pasteboard to the guardian at the door, and passed on to the
death chamber. The limb of the law and myself stood on the

stone steps of the court house, with a battery of 3,000 pairs of eyes fixed upon us, acting like a couple of little boys trying in some manner to gain entrance to a show, "without money, and without price."

The situation seemed to work on Mr. Marsh's nerves and he said, "Let us go. The sheriff has forgotten his promise to us and will not be likely to open this door for us. It is now 10 minutes past 2." My answer was: "We have not forgotten our promise. We are here as agreed upon. If we leave and he comes, we have broken our promise. Let us do as we have agreed. That agreement was to stay at this door until he comes to let us in." Every few minutes my lawyer friend would renew his request and I would get up new arguments why we should stay. After quite a delay the sheriff, true to his word, opened the door and polietly escorted us to an advantageous standing place near the scaffold. We saw a double hanging. Tracy passed within a few feet of us, with a complacent face, and a priest on either side of him, trying to give him spiritual comfort. And, indeed, he did not seem to harbor any fears although death was staring him in the face. He stepped boldly onto the scaffold and when the black cap was drawn over his face and the trap was sprung his body shot down through the opening, the rope became untied from his neck, and he fell nearly on his coffin, which sat beneath the scaffold. Then he was pushed back through the opening and another rope was adjusted by ex-Sheriff King and the trap was sprung the second time, and in a few minutes he was pronounced by the physician as dead. It did not require a very long time to get the second rope around his neck, as the sheriff had foresight enough to have the second rope, in case the first one would not hold. A professional hangman, of Buffalo, tied the knots on both ropes; one held and the other did not. Not very complimentary to his "profession." When the second rope was being adjusted Tracy made the remark, "Jesus, Joseph and Mary, save me." I was told by an old citizen of the town that only one man had been hanged in McKean county before this and this man showed exceeding coolness. When he was led onto the scaffold he put one foot on the edge and let his weight on by degrees, before he would trust his whole weight upon it.

## *CHAPTER XXIV.*

## OIL REGION INHABITANTS.

In writing of "Old Times in Oildom" I have left off until the 24th chapter what should have come in the first article. I have, within the last 31 years, organized 475 lodges (158 Good Templar lodges and 317 insurance lodges) in New York, Pennsylvania, Ohio, West Virginia and Canada. More than half of these lodges were organized in the oil region, and let me say that no better people are found anywhere than in the oil towns. The towns are made up in general of the best heart ed people in the world. They are intelligent, industrious, kind and good, and a majority are skilled workmen. Go into any oil town and look at a crowd of greasy, dirty men. The crowd is principally composed of pumpers, drillers, pipe line men, telegraph operators, rig builders and representatives of other occupations.

Skill of the first order is required. The oil regions are principally made of educated and go-ahead people. The old drones are not apt to dig out, and move into, and take up the activities of an oil country life. They leave that life to the most energetic of their children. True, there are people living in oil towns who are getting old that commenced an oil country life many years ago. They were young when they took up the business. As to the men making provision for their families, but few die in the oil region leaving their families destitute.

Many men die and leave more than enough money to bridge over necessities. Many belong to several insurance lodges. It is a common thing to find men carrying from $5,000 to $10,000 insurance. Not only the married, but the single men, are insured. About five years ago I organized three lodges in succession in Butler county—at West Sunbury, Middletown and Butler. While I was at work in each town a single man was brought home dead and one mother got $3,000, another got $5,000, and another got $1,000. Each young man had named his mother, with the understanding that if he should ever get married the benefit certificate should be changed in favor of his wife. One of those mothers that I speak of came within a day of losing $3,000. Her son was killed at an oil well just one day before he was to have been married. I write this to show that many young men carry protection. A young man who promises to shield and protect a young wife and then dies and leaves her over a washtub to keep starvation away, is looked upon as failing to do a duty towards a loved one, when he could have protected her by putting a few cents into some lodge treasury once a month. But I am getting away from what I started out to tell. I wish to say to the readers that although some bad characters inhabit the oil towns, that their number is surprisingly small, considering the heterogen-- eous crowds which naturally drift into a new oil town from all points of the compass and from nearly all nationalities. It is a remarkable fact that there are towns and towns where there never was a drop of oil found that will outstrip the oil towns, two to one, in all kinds of rascality and meanness. I think I have had an opportunity to judge of this matter. Dur-- ing my 31 years' rambling over the states mentioned above, I never felt unsafe many times.

The first time was between Linesville, Venango county, Pa., and Edenburg, Clarion county, Pa., near 30 years ago. It was on a bright, shiny Sabbath morning, that I left Linesville and took the nearest road for Edenburg. I traveled along about two miles, by pleasant farm houses, where all, to a lone traveler, looked happy and serene. Birds were singing their best Sunday tunes, and all nature seemed to be at rest. Then came a sudden change. The pretty farms gave way to a dense thicket of oak and chestnut underbrush. The road led down quite a steep hill, at the foot of which stood an old, very old, two-story log house. Where there had been long ago glass in the windows, old hats, and any old thing that could take the place of a light of window glass, did duty in the way of keeping the wind and rain out. Right opposite the old castle was a cool crystal stream of spring water rippling into a horse trough. So inviting did this look to me that, although not very thirsty, I could not pass such a clear cold stream of water untasted. So I leaned over the rippling waterfall and had just absorbed a couple of swallows of water, when bedlam seemed to have been let loose across the road in the old house. Although it was the holy Sabbath day, profanity poured forth in its rankest form, and a sound came to my ears resembling pots, kettles, chairs and household furniture in general being hurled through the house. I cut out the water drinking very suddenly, and took a glance across the road, and there at a front window sat a man with a long black mustache. He had an expresison on his face that was anything but reassuring to me. The man sat with his elbows on the window sill, his face resting on his hands, and his eyes steadily fixed on the lone traveler. I had on my "Sunday-go-to-meeting" clothes, a gold watch and chain, and a new handbag. It did not take very long for the following reasoning to slip through my mind: People that would get up a Sunday morning's battle of both words and fists, might take a notion to inspect my pockets and handbag. Lodge organizers are very seldom worth robbing. But these people did not know that, and I could not tell but what they might take a notion into their heads to find out for themselves, so I put a very unconcerned expression on my face, picked up my satchel and started on my way without a parting look or word. The road led up hill from this habitation, in the little narrow valley in the woods, with dense brush on both sides of the road. I expected very moment to see an investigating party step from this thick underbrush into the road ahead of me. I did some pretty tall Sunday walking up that mile long hill through the woods. And how glad I was to reach the top of that hill, and see a beautiful farm and farmhouse, and hear beautiful strains of music floating out from a quartette of two brothers and two sisters, accompanied by an organ. What a transformation—from the valley a mile below, to a mile above. I called at this Christian home, and for an excuse asked for a drink of water. The reader will remember that I did not finish my last drink. The young people played and sang their best hymns for the benefit of the lone organizer, and after a pleasant hour, I resumed my lonely Sunday walk, and reached that busy oil town of Edenburg in due time. I said nothing to my new found friends on the nice farm at the top of the hill about their neighbors a mile below, and I am in ignorance to this day as to who, or what kind of a family occupied that old two-story log house in the deep hollow, two miles on the road from Linesville to Edenburg.

The second rather alarming place that I struck was between Frostburg and Byrom Station, in Forest county, Pa. The distance is a little over a mile, and, like the last woods described, lined by dense underbrush on both sides of the road. When I was nearly half way through this piece of woods I saw at quite a distance ahead of me a large man come from the brush into the middle of the road and take a good look at me, and then step back out of my sight into the brush. I put my watch and chain into my inside coat pocket, so that no inducement in that line would be held out, if the big fellow turned out to be a robber. I put on as bold a front as could be expected under the circumstances and trudged along. When opposite to the place where I had seen him reconnoitering I turned my eye around and beheld this giant, with a cowboy mustache, standing in a path about two rods from the main road, looking me square in the eye. As I did not want to form an intimate acquaintance with a stranger adopting those tactics, I did not even pass the time of day with him, and he proved to be as "short on courtesy" as I, so I walked along, not showing any sign of alarm, and, of course, I did not look around to show that I was interested in him, and I never saw him again. He may be there yet, as far as I know. I was perfectly safe all the time, but I did not know it until I was safely out of that luxuriant underbrush. The same God that has guided me in those hundreds of strange places was with me then, but, with my dim vision, I could not see this until distance proved it to me. I have often wondered why this last man was there. I have thought that he was evading the officers of the law and was keeping an eye out, but the fact that he remained so near the road, instead of going a little farther back, would disprove this theory. Then again, if he was there for the purpose of robbery, why did he not pitch into me?

And now I come to the third fright. About 16 years ago I was walking down the Lake Shore railroad track, between Ashtabula and Ashtabula harbor. As night came on I overtook four men walking leisurely. As soon as I came up to them and spoke, I made up my mind that they were common tramps. My pleasant "good evening" was answered in a very surly manner. My fears got the better of me and I quickened my gait. There was a deep cut in the road at that place, and the only way to get out of that company was to outwalk the big lubberly fellows and reach a street crossing, where steps could be found leading up to the wagon road. The faster I would walk the faster the tramps would walk. When I reached the wagon road there happened to be two or three teams crossing at that time, and I skipped up the bank and mixed in with the crowd and I was safe from the tramps. Two weeks after that time I read of a gang of tramps killing a man for his money at that identical spot. I really think that this quartette of tramps expected me to travel down the railroad and that they would "go for me." I "showed the white feather," but I would rather show "white feathers" while alive than have an undertaker show black feathers at my funeral.

Anyhow, I think I have proved my original assertion that, after having worked up and organized 475 lodges, over half of them in the oil regions, with only three little "scares" and no real attacks, the oil country is not a very dangerous place in which to live. I have a very warm spot in my heart for the oil country and its inhabitants. When I say this, I praise a great many people, and they are getting more and more numerous every day. Just think of it! From a little spot here in Western Pennsylvania, this business has spread to New York, Ohio, West Virginia, Kentucky, Illinois, Texas, Oklahoma, Indian Territory, California and Canada. Truly, oil is a wonderful thing!

## CHAPTER XXV.

### PICKPOCKETS.

These chapters would not be complete without a mention of my experiences in the pickpocket line. The first greenbacks that I ever saw, when they were first issued, were stolen by a light-fingered and low-lived rascal in Pittsburg, Pa. I, in partnership with Nelson Mead and Hiram Belnap, floated a raft to Pittsburg and sold it and received $425 to bind the bargain. My partners trusted me to carry that package of new and bright bills home, while they agreed to stay until the raft of boards was delivered on the south side, when the balance of the money would be paid to them. I was obliged to sit in the Union depot until 1:30 a. m. before a train left for up the river. I bought a ticket and took my seat in the waiting room, and, like the greenhorn that I was, fell asleep, and waked up when the starting of the train was announced. I took my seat in the coach and when I felt for my pocketbook it had disappeared, together with the $425 of the handsomest paper

I had seen up to that date. I was unsophisticated enough to think that possibly the book had fallen into honest hands and I quit the train and returned to my hotel and took one of my partners with me at the break of day to look about the depot. This was a sign of imbecility on my part, but I was not as old then as now. We looked around the depot a short time, but did not find any pocketbook lying around loose filled with brand-new greenbacks. I then went and called on "Bob" Ford, the well-known Pittsburg detective. He told me that this kind of business was of almost nightly occurrence at that depot and that three nights before I called upon him a man had $1,300 stolen. Mr. Ford told me that he offered to pay every dollar stolen from that depot in one year if the city would pay him $1,000, but the city fathers refused and the traveling public was suffering the consequences daily.

I felt a little bit green over this transaction and told the partner that went to the depot in the morning to not let the other partner know anything about it and I would stand the loss. I didn't want to tell anyone—not even my wife—until I struck oil. In about two years I struck a little oil and then told the story on myself.

The second time that I was robbed was at Warren, Pa., at the time of the Cherry Grove excitement when "The Mystery." or "Six Forty-Six," was struck. The price of oil depreciated at this time to such an extent that small operators suffered greatly. If the Standard Oil Company had never done anything but steady the price and stop such fluctuations, the Standard would have proved a godsend to the country. Well, as I was saying, a great rush was caused by this strike. Warren was full of all kinds of people, with a sprinkling of pickpockets to boot. And as I stepped on the P. & E. train at Warren in a great jam and took my seat in a coach I missed my pocketbook. When I missed that I immediately felt for my watch and was really surprised to find it in my vest pocket untouched. However, pickpockets at that time generally let time pieces alone for they were very much more easily identified than the money. I had one satisfaction in this. I had only about $10 to lose at that time, although it did happen that I lost some valuable papers. The third call by this class of visitors was in my own town of Youngsville. I was returning from attending Buffalo Bill's Wild West show. There was a gang of those miserable blots on the face of the earth following Buffalo Bill's Wild West show on that trip and two of them took the same train west on the P. & E. that I did. In getting off the train I was considerably crowded by two young, good-looking men, who pretended to be in a great hurry to get to vacant seats. They were crowding from both sides of the aisle. I though that I recognized them as pickpockets and as I stepped out of the coach door I felt for my pocketbook, but as I expected, it was not there I stepped off the train and told the conductor that he had pickpockets on board his train. He asked me if I could point them out to him. I told him that I could not, as they were lost in the crowd, and consequently they escaped arrest. But this time the joke was on the thieves, as they got only about $2—hardly worth the risk. I suppose the rascals must have let off some cuss-words when they opened the book. But I was inconvenienced somewhat by the loss of papers which could do the thieves no good.

Three days after this I attended the grand lodge I. O. O. F., of New York, at Jamestown, N. Y. In the afternoon a little party concluded to take a ride on the lake, and as I thought I might not have money enough to carry me through, I asked a friend if he had $5 that he would not need until he reached Youngsville. He answered, "I don't know, but will look." I said: "Don't look at your money in this crowd. There may be pickpockets here—go into the writing room." He complied with my request and soon came back with the remark, "Yes, I can let you have it." I stepped into the writing room of the Sherman House and wrote a check for five dollars, came out and into the public room, handed my friend the check and he handed me the money, in the presence of a hundred men. I put the money in my book, and—reader—give a guess as to the length of time that I had possession of that money. Being well aware that you will make the time too long, I'll tell you—just about three minutes. A street car came to the door of the hotel, and a party rushed for seats, or pretended to, and my pocketbook. They got the book, but not the seats. They preferred to stay in Jamestown, and pick up other easy marks, like myself. I was quite certain before I got into the car—by the actions of this crowd of New York City excursionists—that they belonged to the fraternity that always had a liking for me, and I found my prognostications to be correct when I felt for my pocketbook and found that it had very recently changed owners. When I made my predicament known a friend loaned me a sufficiency of cash to enable me to stick to my crowd of "Brother Odd Fellows" until my arrival in Youngsville. And let me say, that although sixteen years have come and gone, I have not lost a pocketbook since that time, for the good reason that I have not had a book in my pockets since. I don't know how many times those meanest of things in the shape of men have had their hands in my pockets since the Jamestown donation, but I do know that they have gone without their regular meals if they depended on me to pay their bills. It is a little more safe to keep your money in the bank, and fill blank checks when you wish to use it than to carry your money in your pockets.

This reminds me of a funny little incident. Away up in the mountains of the "Mountain State," West Virginia, I gave a check for 75 cents on the Youngsville Savings Bank, 400 miles away, to a hotel man in payment of my hotel bill. I happened that way again six months afterwards. He was still the owner of the check. He said it was too small an amount to send to his bank. I remained under the hospitable roof on this second visit until my check was large enough for him to "bother with," but I am not taking any chances with pickpockets. I cannot account for the fact that I am "a shining mark" for this class of miscreants that I have mentioned, when my neighbors all escape. I know I have reached the point of intense hatred of the people who make their living that way. They have nothing to lose and everything to gain. They don't risk one cent. It is all income and no outgo. Nothing would please me more than to see the whole crowd—no, I could not see them all at the same time, there are too many of them—hanging by their necks.

## CHAPTER XXVI.

### OLD TIME LUMBERMEN.

In writing this chapter there comes to my mind old rafting times. Years ago, when I was a pilot of lumber rafts on the Allegheny and Ohio rivers, when the spring flood came, us young fellows, and many of the old fellows, would begin to look around for work at rafting. Even before the water came deep enough for rafts, we would begin to build our "creek pieces" on the ice at the mills. We had no steam mills then. Water power made all the lumber then. The logs were hauled to the streams, for the sawing into boards. And oh! what boards. The logs were rolled onto carriages, and set to the right thickness with crowbars—by guess. Sometimes a board would be a quarter or half inch thicker at one end than at the other end. The saw was hung in a sash, made for one single saw, and played up and down with an uncertain speed, owing to the height of the water in the dam above the mill. And after a log had a slab taken off of both sides—sometimes a board or two would be sawed, thus flattening a log, these boards would be piled on the flat side of the log to be edged. The sawyer would sit on these boards in front of the saw, and as the saw would near him he would hitch away from it, but must keep his weight upon the boards, to keep them down, so that a single saw could do its double duty of sawing the board under and edging the board on top, at one and the same time. When I was a young, green mill hand I came the nearest to passing into the life beyond that I ever did, through this very method of edging boards. I was sitting in front of the saw, hitching away at intervals. The skirt of my coat dragging behind, I like the fool boy that I was, took the notion that I would let the saw clip a little notch in my coat, so I let the saw creep up to it. But instead of clipping a little notch, the coat was jerked down into the log with such violence that the skirt was nearly torn off, with a dozen holes in it. As the saw came up out of the log for another stroke I jumped with the agility of a cat, or any other smart animal. If not for that quick motion I would have been mincemeat in a second. I never again tried such an experiment. But to the subject.

When the snow melted and raised the creek to a rafting stage then the fun began. The Brokenstraw creek would be full of rafts passing through Youngsville from morning until night. One might stand on the bridge spanning the Brokenstraw creek all day long and not be out of sight of a floating raft, either up the creek, down the creek, or passing through town. At that time sawmills were strung along the creek from Irvineton to the headwaters in Chautauqua county, N. Y. And as no railroads were even contemplated all the lumber was floated. Even the tributaries, Little Brokenstray, Garland, Spring creek and Hare creek, put out their share of this lumber. But the show came when these hundreds of "creek pieces" were landing in the Brokenstraw eddy. They must be coupled up preparatory to starting for Pittsburg. At times the Brokenstraw eddy was not large enough and a share of the coupling up into river rafts of about a dozen creek rafts, put into one river raft, went to Dunn's eddy and to Thompson's eddy. It required a considerable fishing and figuring for each of perhaps 50 owners to get their different creek pieces out of the general mixup and coupled into river rafts. Well, I guess there was a hurrying time among the men that did this work when the water was falling in the river. Men have been known to work all night with only the light of pitch pine knots. No electric, gas or acetylene lights were dreamed of those days. And when the "Allegheny fleets" were all coupled up a shanty was built of boards, a stove put in and some hard "bunks" for the "hands" to sleep in. A supply of salt pork, potatoes and bread was put abroad and the raft was ready to "pull out." The pilot would say "Left forward" and the fleet would be propelled from the shore where it had been tied by a long cable since the work of "coupling up" commenced by the most willing set of workers that ever left friends and foes behind for an outing down the river to Pittsburg, Wheeling, Cincinnati, Louisville and many times to the falls of the Ohio river and New Orleans. These robust raftsmen were the most jovial, rollicking fellows to be met with anywhere. None but the stoutest men undertook that work. It required being out of doors in all kinds of weather. The men had to be near their oars every moment as when the pilot gave orders to right or left each oar was expected to be dipped in the next few seconds. Rain, snow and sometimes a mixture of both had to be endured. Weakly, consumptive fellows were very seldom seen on a raft. Only young men full of warm blood and deviltry were right at home on a raft in the old times. These latter named would pull into a river eddy in any kind of a storm, take their hurried meal and after all kinds of jokes and pranks would crawl into the bunks filled with straw, with their clothes on and sometimes frozen stiff, lie down, spoon fashion, go to sleep, and not wake up until the break of day when the pilot would jump out and yell "Tie loose." In about a minute

7

the raft would be gently floating towards the "Smoky City." If those early pioneers had been obliged to adjust their cuffs, collars, neckties and see that the seams in their pants had the desired appearance it would have taken more than one minute to get afloat each morning. And the air would be filled with cusswords. The pilots, in general, were men who used steamboat language when they got in a hurry. And the wages for hard work and fare, we, "the hands," got the magnificent sum of $10 a trip and pay our own way back.

If a man walked back home he could clear $1 a day, if he did not "tie up" for high water or walk too slow in coming back. The average walker would clear about $1 a day if he was a total abstainer. If not, he would fall short, as those who indulge in strong drink will testify to, even at the present time. Since the world began strong drink has been a great absorber of money, and the saddest of all sad things is that all the money spent for strong drink vanished into the air. No good ever came from it—all bad, bad, and no good. Since Adam and Eve's time it has a poor record. If our legislators would wait before passing laws to protect the sale of intoxicating liquors until they see the benefit derived from a drink of whiskey, taken as a beverage, they never would pass another law of that kind until doomsday. And now arises the question, why cannot our lawmakers make good laws just as easy as bad laws? No doubt but what the people, one hundred years hence, will look back upon us and call us barbarians for making laws for the protection of the greatest evil on the face of God's green earth. I said the greatest evil; I'll make it stronger—I"l say it outweights all other evils combined. It is time that the north quits looking down upon the south. We ought to begin to look up to them on the temperance question. Why, God bless them! they are nearly half prohibition now, and if Pennsylvania and New Jersey don't wake up soon the south will be all prohibition before they begin the good work.

Now I'll get back to my subject again. When those footsore travelers got back to their homes along the upper waters of the Allegheny river a large majority would swear off going down the river on a raft again. But when the next "rafting fresh" came there would be more begging for trips down the river than could be used. And now, about the price of lumber. Good pine boards have been sold in Pittsburg for $4 per thousand feet and nearly a fourth of it "clear stuff." Compare this price with the present price and you are almost staggered. The same quality of lumber today would bring eight times as much in the same market.

Among the old-time lumbermen in Warren county, was "Joe" Hall, L. F. Watson, Boon Mead, Erastus Barnes, Orris Hall, Guy Irvine, John McKinney, James McKinney, Eben Mead, John Mead, J. C. and D. Mead, John Garner, Amasa Ransom, James Durlin, John Durlin, Robert Andrews, Dr. Wm. A. Irvine, Samuel Grandin, H. P. Kinnear, a Mr. Funk, Joseph Green, James Eddy, Charles Whitney, J. B. Phillips, Alonzo Patch, Joseph Mead, Hardin Hazeltine, William Siggins, Daniel Horn, William Demming, Alden Marsh, James Donaldson, Sterling Holcomb, John Brown, William White, William Frese, Philip Mead, L. B. Wood, Chapin Hall and many more that I could name. In fact, there were more lumbermen than farmers. Farming was not the picnic those days that it is now. Where farms were cleared up the stumps were comparatively green. The trees had been but recently cut, and the stumps were green with tough roots, extending out in all directions, a rod or two, making anything but pleasant work in ploughing and making land ready for the crops. The main crops were hay, oats, corn, wheat, potatoes, rye and buckwheat. What a difference between now and then. Now the most of the stumps are rotted, or pulled out with a machine! Many of the fences are made of pine stumps.

These fences were not beautiful to look at, but theye were very durable. The pine roots were filled with pitch, and never would rot. A few of the fences can be seen at the present time scattered over the country. If these fences had not gone out of fashion, they would be here yet, sound and in good order. But a new-fangled way of farming sprang up and no fences, or but a few, are needed. In the early days, cattle, sheep and horses ran all over the country at random, where now the farmers only make fences around their pasture fields and keep all their stock shut in, so that few fences are found in the country, and where boards and rails were used then, now posts and wire are used.

When I finished writing the names of the old time lumbermen the thought struck me that I would look over the list and see how many of those old time lumbermen were alive today. And, dear reader, how many do you think are alive out of the 40 named? To my utter surprise, I found not one alive. Now, do you believe that I am writing of "old timers?"

---

## CHAPTER XXVII.

### NEW TIMES IN OILDOM.

This chapter begins with what might be named "New Times in Oildom," at it is a mention of the latest in oil in Youngsville. Recently a Pittsburg company commenced drilling a well in the row of small wells below town, or on the very edge of the borough. And a well a little farther west of that will be put down in the town by local parties and another four miles north of town will be put down by a foreign company. This seems like a revival of the oil business here, two commenced and two talked of. If it can be arranged to hitch the two dozen wells that have been drilled in Youngsville and vicinity together and run them with one power the production would pay nicely. If oil ever gets scarce and rises in price Youngsville will be an oil town. If all the wells put down in Youngsville and vicinity, say a distance of three miles in diameter, were hitched together it would make a nice thing for the owner or owners. Of course it would not be a big income, but it would help some.

I will mention a change in the oil business in our nearby neighbor—Garand, seven miles west of Youngsville. Before the pipe line days, the oil came from Enterprise, Pleasantville and that section of the country by teams and wagons to Garland, and there the P. & E. railroad was reached and the oil was loaded on the cars for market. It came in barrels. Six or eight barrels made a wagonload, according to the size of the team. Eight barrels were a heavy tug for even the stoutest of teams. The roads were anything but smooth when the oil business struck the country. But when this array of teams began their tramping of the mud, a mortar bed was soon formed that was something awful to behold and much more awful to navigate. When this mud became frozen, but still not quite hard enough to hold a horses's weight and not quite soft enough for easy wading, it was killing on the poor brutes, and not easy on the drivers. I one day met "Bob" McMillen, of Garland, driving a big "team of grays" with an eight barrel load.

"Bob's" face looked as though it had been through a threshing machine. In crossing one of those corduroy bridges, he had been tossed from his slippery seat on an oil barrel, alighting face downward on a rock. He was a sight, but he kept his place in that long line of teams until he reached the railroad and also helped unload his wagon. Garland was a lively little town in those days. A heavy lumber business was carried on.

The D., A. V. & P. was not built then and the P. & E. had all the railroad business. Garland is not as large as it was at that time, but is a town more solid and permanent. The people have to a large extent pursued farming and depend on agriculture. Oil may come and oil may go, lumber may come and lumber may go, but the good soil will always be with them. Garland has soil that is rather above the average Warren county soil and the inhabitants are of the thrifty kind, and they will not starve. The writer was a citizen of that town when he first began attending school and will make mention of the first and only punishment that he ever received at any school. This was the way of it: An old Scotchman was the teacher. His rules were ironclad. One day when he "let the boys go out," one boy—a sort of an Ananias—said the schoolmaster asked him "to tell the other boys" to wade into the "West Run," a nice little stream that invitingly passed close to the school house—and wash their feet. All attended school barefooted in those days, and, of course, our feet could bear considerable washing, and then not be any too clean. Well, believeing this to be a reasonable request, we all pitched in, doing some lively kicking and splashing. When we were called in the teacher took a look at our drabbled pants. He called us out on the floor and lined us up in a row. Then he took his ferule—a great wide ruler—and grabbed each boy in rotation by the fingers, holding the palm of the hand upward. He then gave each one five heavy strokes, applying his whole pedagogical strength. That long, wide and heavy ferule had its effect on that line of a dozen boys in different ways. Some would quietly cry, some would cry with a loud voice, some would smile, and others hop and yell. I took my medicine with quiet heroism. The old bachelor teacher then permitted us to take our seats, and we put in the rest of the afternoon in considerable unhappiness, caused by wet pants and tingling fingers. And thus ended my first and only punishment, brought on by my faith in our Ananias.

Before leaving the subject of this school house I wish to enlighten the present generation in regard to pioneer Sunday Schools. My first Sunday School training was in this old Garland school house. The services consisted principally of committing Bible verses to memory and reciting them to the teacher of the class. We had no leaflets, gotten out by the best Bible schools of the age, as we have now. The exercises were indeed crude. But we worked the best we could considering the tools we had to work with. The class that I belonged to had a scholar, a boy by the name of David Moore. He had a good memory, but I had conceit enough about me to think that I could equal if not exceed him in that line. Well, I bantered him for a test. We agreed each to do our very best for one week and, for our own enlightenment, find out which could commit to memory the largest number of verses and recite to our teacher at the end of the week. The result was: Moore, 145; and Brown, 105. David died many years ago after living an exemplary Christian life.

And now before I leave this old school house, let me tell a little fish story: I fished for the beautiful and palatable speckled trout in the streams about Garland in those long ago days that I have been talking about. One day not satisfied with the Garland fishing streams I hied me away a couple of miles to "Blueye" and fished all day, and failed to get a nibble at the hook. When on my way home I stopped on a bridge, right in front of the old school house, and as I had quite often discovered an immense trout, lying quietly in quite deep water, under this bridge, I took a peep through the cracks of the floor of the bridge, and there lay the big spekcled trout. I immediately set myself about preparations for his capture. I took my hook and line from my pocket, tied the line to a long stick, dug up a fish worm from the ground nearby, baited the hook with the worm, and slipped up noiselessly and dropped the bait down through a convenient crack in the bridge, and watched the result. The bait landed on the gravel, on the bottom of the stream, about 10 inches in front of the trout's nose. I watched a moment but no motion of the fish. Just as I had made up my mind that the big fish was not hungry I noticed a very slight motion of its tail, but soon the movement was almost as a lightning flash. He grabbed the bait on the run, and started for his hiding place under the edge of the bank. However, his rapid movement was stopped by my long stick and line. The result was I pulled a trout up through that bridge that weighed a little over two pounds. This convinced me that fishing at home was better than two miles away in Blueye creek. This was the largest speckled trout that I ever saw except one. My brother and I were fishing in a mill pond about fifty rods from the bridge that is spoken of above, about one month after this, and he pulled a speckled trout to just above the surface of the water and not being able to bring it ashore let it sink back into the water again. Being older, and a little stronger, I grabbed his pole, and swung the fish to land. That one weighed over two pounds and a half. Garland had big speckled trout about 65 years ago.

A recent flood in the Brokenstraw creek reminded me of the old fellows of the rafting times which have passed away, when we had no railroads to carry the lumber. Such a freshet in the creek would have brought joy to the hearts of all the young men of the vicinity, for rafts would be running daily. Think of the changes! When I piloted my first raft on the Brokenstraw creek there was not a railroad in the United States. When the P. & E. road was built through Youngsville many people had never heard a locomotive whistle. One man played a great joke on himself. When he heard the whistle of the old Ohio locomotive, "Zenia," the construction engine, he seized his gun and started for town, about a mile distant, with the intention of killing what he thought was a panther.

The locomotive "Zenia" spoken of above, was brought from some Ohio railroad to haul the material for building the western division of the Philadelphia and Erie railroad. "Dick" Poor was the engineer and "Jim" Horigan was the conductor of the construction train. Scott Patten and William, his brother, were the contractors. Robert Beveridge, afterwards cashier of an Oil City bank, who died recently, was the store clerk. The people of this section were unanimous in thinking all those named were great men. They were bringing a railroad into our isolated country. When the old locomotive would leave Youngville for Corry after supplies, it would often be filled with women and men, anxious to have a ride on something propelled by steam. The crowd would be so dense that it was with difficulty that the fireman could shovel his coal. And "Dick" Poor, a big fat man, would share a seat at the lever with any of his free passengers. He was the very embodiment of good humor. In fact no one who wanted a ride on the old locomotive was turned away as long as there was room to sandwich in one more. Everybody in those days carried high heads and their faces almost said the words, "We are going to have a railroad."

## CHAPTER XXVIII.

### OLD TIME OIL TANKS.

This chapter will begin with a few remarks on tank building before it became a science. The first oil tanks that came under my observation were on the "Jim" Tarr farm. And, oh! what tanks they were! Perhaps a dozen or 15 were constructed at the Phillips well. They occupied all the narrow strip of flat land that lay between the well and Oil Creek. They were made of pine plank. A hole was dug into the ground about eight or ten feet deep, the diameter varying somewhere from 8 to 12 feet. The top of the tanks were just even with the ground, being covered over with pine planks to prevent pedestrians from walking into them at night. The few old operators who saw this kind of storage will bear me out in saying that there was a frightful amount of money in wastage. Oil was selling at from $8 to $14 a barrel, while the old Phillips well was gushing out hundreds of barrels a day, and the leakage from those home-made tanks ran into thousands and thousands of dollars. And it would make a young operator of the present day laugh, or cry, to see the owners getting oil into and out of those tanks. A three cornered trough was made of boards an inch thick, but any width that came handy, and the oil that did not escape through the cracks and holes in those crude little conveyors ran in great streams from the wells to those things called tanks. And when a pond "freshet" would come down the creek, away the greasy fluid would go to the Allegheny river in a "bulk boat," which means an open boat, previously filled by pumping the oil with a dandy looking pump from the tank to the boat through the wooden pipe. It was not many moons, however, before improvements began to appear in the tank line. The late Frank Tarbell, of Rouseville, soon began to manufacture a wooden tank that could be set up above ground. And soon after iron pipes were used in the running of the oil in and out of the tanks. Mr. Tarbell, aside from his tank business, ran the only lumber yard at Rouseville. In addition to all this, he put down a few oil wells and found no dry holes. I had the pleasure of supplying the lumber for his yard and tank business, and will say right here that in my long life I never dealt with a more honest and upright man. Nearly everybody has heard of Ida Tarbell. At the time I speak of, she was a bright and lively school girl of 16. My wife and Ida were good friends. The young girl made visits to our home lasting several weeks. She was a fine piano player and a very pleasant visitor. At that time she had never thought of becoming an authoress of national repute. The Tarbell family became residents, in after years, of Titusville, where Frank was a leader in the Methodist Episcopal church and in the up-building of the city in general. He continued in the oil business and other activities of life up to the time of his death not long ago.

I wish to make a few remarks concerning a very important part of the oil trade, showing that the present times are better than "Old Times in Oildom." I'll speak of the matter of leasing oil lands. There is not much said about land sharks nowadays. But in those old times was there not "wailing and gnashing of teeth?" Sharpers soon laid plans to catch the unwary farmers, and they worked their games for all they were worth. To prove this I will give one case which is but one of many. I called upon a man of 80 years in McKean county. I found him sitting on a chair on his porch, churning butter in the old fashioned way, moving a "dasher" up and down. He was the picture of despair. This is his story, given to me as he propelled the churn dasher. "I own a 100 acre farm that is without doubt one of the best oil farms in McKean county. But I am one of the most poverty stricken men in this county. I leased my farm to an oil company before I had given the subject any thought. I went into writings with this company blindly. The conditions of the lease were that company was to put down one well within one year. They fulfilled their part of the agreement. The well went down, but when near the oil they spoiled the well. They filled it about half full of sand and worked and fussed with it for a few days and pronounced it a failure. And that is the shape of things at present. Good wells are being struck all around my farm, but I am a poverty stricken man. The offer is so low that it is an insult to me. They know my situation and think that I will be obliged to accept their offer. Their offer is so low that it would not help my family much when I drop off and I never will accept it. I cannot force them to clean out this well or put another down. They have fulfilled their contract. And I am in an awful shape. I am 80 years old and I have the consumption and I have 30 acres of hay to cut and not one dollar to hire men to do the work. And I cannot do a thing except the very lightest of work. I would be a rich man today if not for these land sharks, but as it now stands I am one of the poorest men in this country. There ought to be a law to hang such men as these who took advantage of my ignorance. I don't know what I will do."

Thus ended my visit with the old gentleman and I left him looking the very exemplification of despair. A few months after that I saw the announcement in a paper of his death. Although really in the midst of wealth he died a poor man. But what a change has taken place in the last 25 years! We hear of few such complaints now. This leasing business has become a settled, honest business. Nearly all farmers are fully posted in this leasing business and at times they get the best of the oil man. Both know their business, and there is a kind of sameness in the contracts, which leaves both parties satisfied. All pioneer operators well know that the rough and tumble way of doing business at the beginning has now been systematized. This is the age of progress. Any man of my age can look back and see changes that could not be described in a book as big as a barn. I have often thought that I would like to look back upon this old world 100 years from now, and see how people would be doing things. If such strides in new inventions are made in the next 100 years as have been made in the last 100 years, what will this world look like? Perhaps the spirits of the dead can look back. The way things have been going for the last few years a man cannot consistently doubt anything. A few years ago if I had told people that two men could stand 3,000 miles apart and carry on a conversation with each other over a wire, or that men could converse with each other, standing hundreds of miles apart, with no wire, I would have been pronounced a fit subject for an insane asylum. Oh, how will it be 100 years hence?

I have just thought of a strange happening in my life, which is worthy of mentioning. The two extremes of heat and cold came to me at Conneaut Lake, Crawford county, Pa. About 26 years ago I was in the temperance work, organizing Good Templar lodges. I struck the lake about the middle of the afternoon on a fearful cold day. The first call I made was on the postmaster. I found in him a strong temperance man. He put his name and the names of members of his family on my list for application for membership, and invited me to take supper with him, which I did. It was the regular meeting night of the A. O. U. W. Being a member of that order I attended their meeting, engaged the use of their hall and organized a lodge the same night. The postmaster and family did not come to the meeting. After the organization was completed I went to the only hotel in town. I walked into the office, travelling bag in hand. A lot of men sat around, and no one made a noise. I inquired for the landlord. A big fat fellow clapped his hand on his breast, and said: "Here he is, this big fat fellow." I asked for accomodations. He said the rooms were occupied. Said he, "Some of the beds have but one man in them, but they don't like to double up." I asked him if there was any other place that a man could get shelter at that time of night, 11 p. m. He directed me to "a boarding house" down on the edge of the lake, the last house at the end of the sidewalk. I started out in the zero weather and pitch dark—no street lamps at that time. I got to the end of the walk, and found quite a large boarding house. I pounded on the front door, but got no response. pounded again, with renewed vigor. Same result. Then I tried my lumg power— for all it was worth, but it was just as valuable as the pounding. Finally I was obliged to give it us as a bad job. The next day I learned that the owner of the boarding house was a deaf woman, that could not hear me, and her helper was a foolish son. Between the two it was an impossibility for a belated stranger to gain admittance to that boarding house at 11 p. m. I then retraced my steps up town. I felt somewhat lonely, as everybody in town was in bed and asleep, except the lone stranger.

My next move was to rouse a doctor—one that I had initiated that night into the I. O. G. T. lodge—from his slumbers. In response to my knock at his door, he appeared. I then told him my situation; that I had been turned away from the licensed hotel because I had organized a society that night which would work against his liquor trade, and that I could not get into the boarding house. The doctor was a good natured and well meaning individual, but he said he had visitors and could not find room for me. He advised me to go to another of my Good Templar members. The doctor gave me verbal directions. Those directions were such that no one but an expert tramp organizer could follow them successfully. I failed as an expert. I was told to go down street a little way, then cross a street, then up a street, with several turns, and stop at the third house on the left. I undertook the job of finding this brother, as I had nothing else before me to do. It was not an easy task—looking for a strange house in a strange town and as dark as a stack of black cats, and zero weather at that. After I had turned as many corners as I thought would fill the bill and counted, in my mind, as many houses as the doctor had told me to—it really was so dark that I could not see a house—I walked up to a house that felt like the one that I was in search of, and rang the bell. I found it by sense of feeling and not by seeing. A man came to the door—I was at the wrong house, of course—and he scolded out the directions so plainly that there was no misunderstanding them.

The next hunt brought me to the hospitable home of my newly made brother Good Templar. I laid my case before him in as mild language as I could command. His answer was, "We are in just as bad shape as the doctor. We have visitors and could not make room for you." By this time I had crowded myself into his house and shut the door to keep out the zero air. I told my Dear Brother that as it was my first night in Evansburg—the town was plain Evansburg then;

it was before it became a noted summer resort—I would not care to stay out of doors, considering the temperature. By this time I had become almost saucy—perhaps desperate would be the better word. I cast my shivering eyes around the room and beheld a cold wood stove setting there with two sticks of green wood lying near it and a lounge sitting near it also. I said, "Is there any fire in that stove?" He said, "No." Then I said, "Could you put some fire in it?" He answered in the affirmative. Then I said, "If you will heat the stove and give me a comforter I will sleep on that lounge." The brother disappeared to his bedroom and consulted his life partner, and soon came with this answer: "My wife says she has no com forter to spare." Then I said, "Put some fire in that stove and I will use my overcoat for a covering." He obeyed my command and I laid down with all my clothes on except my overcoat, which took the place of what ought to have been about three comforters. I soon fell into a sleep, with uncomfortable dreams. I waked up about four hours before daylight—the coldest man in Crawford county, Pa. That stove was as cold as Alaska and I was nearly frozen. When I would wink, I could not only see stars, but I could actually see half moons. I examined that stove and found not a live coal in it. I saw two or three sticks of green wood on the floor. I concluded not to start a fire for several reasons. First, no matches could be found; second, I could not make green wood burn if I had had the matches, and I did not feel like arousing my brother twice in one night. So I doubled up and held my feet in my hands and kept up a little circulation until my brother and entertainer came with some dry kindling wood and built a good fire in that cold stove. After daylight appeared and after partaking of a good breakfast I said goodbye to these Good Templars and I have never seen them since. When I saw the doctor at his office before I left town, he eagerly asked me if I got a bed. I told him that I did and he seemed greatly pleased with the idea that I had found a downy bed. He never knew that my bones were aching and did ache for four days afterwards.

But now comes in the joke. I called at the postoffice the next morning after my freezing and the postmaster said: "Where did you stay last night? My wife reserved a bed for you and sat up until midnight, keeping up a warm fire for you.

We could not get out to the meeting, but expected you to stay with us." Just think of it! A woman sitting up until midnight, keeping a good warm fire and making a bed for me, when I was tramping all over town hunting for both and finding neither.

And now for the other extreme—the extreme heat. It will take but a few words to give the heat side of it. About 10 years after my work at Evansburg in organizing the Good Templars, I organized an insurance lodge. Another man conducted the hotel. I stopped at the place nearly a week. My room was on the west side of the house. The first night I slept in that room was the warmest in my life. I slept on a feather bed. It was in the middle of summer and one of the hottest nights I ever saw, or felt. The window had been open all day and the afternoon sun had poured through the window onto the feather bed, and to say that I had a hot night of it would be putting it mildly. There had been no rain for about six weeks. Now, reader, I think I have convinced you that I have met the two extremes of heat and cold in my experience in the same town. I would hesitate about visiting that place again, fearing that something awful might happen to me.

---

## CHAPTER XXIX.

### STARVING ANIMALS.

There was a lot of talk about Theordore Roosvelt's horseback ride of 90 miles in one day, at the time he was president. I suppose that not one of his "subjects" in the United States took as long a horseback ride that day as did the chief executive. It reminds me of my ride from Titusville to Garland, 75 years ago, a distance of less than 20 miles. I rode behind my grandfather, astride of a big white horse. When I reached Garland my legs were unable to do duty satisfactorily. When my grandfather, George McCray, of Titusville, lifted me from the horse and set me right end up on the ground, I staggered and fell, my legs being much benumbed. I well remember this, although I was but 6 years old. In fact, this is as far back as my memory runs. But I give up to President Roosevelt. I think he can hold the championship for years and years to come—at least so far as I am concerned.

The Rev. J. P. Burns, of the M. E. church, has been holding revival meetings here. He is a faithful Christian worker, and has started many souls on the Christian pathway. His oratorical powers are far above the average. As a proof of the appreciation of his parishoners, he has preached here over eight years. The year he was called to the ninth year, the call was signed by about three hundred petitioners. I mention these things in order to compare the present with the past. The first revival that I witnessed was carried on at what was called Whitestown, about midway between Pittsfield and Garland. People were affected differently those days. Strong men would jump, and dance around, and fall helpless to the floor, and lie as still as death for hours at a time. The leader of Methodism in Garland, John McCray, fell to the floor one day, about noon, and lay quietly nearly all the afternoon. He was a large, strong man, in both mind and body. To young unsophisticated eyes, this seems a strange sight. Men and women, old and young, were there on that barn floor. They had no church then, and James White's barn did its full duty in that line. Generally before falling there would be considerable loud shouting. There is a little of the same style of worship carried on by the Free Methodists at the present time. Indeed, a Free Methodist church stands directly across the street from the home of the writer of this, and sometimes they are quite noisy, but the noise of a Christian is music compared to the brawl of a drunkard, or profane man. There is one glourious feature about the Free Methodist church, and that is this: No man or woman can remain a member who uses intoxicating liquor or tobacco, in any form. If all the people on this old earth of ours, were Free Methodists, in this respect what happiness would reign supreme. Speaking of this invisible thing, which the church people call "The Power," I will say it is impossible for me to give any satisfactory explanation or reason for it. My good wife and I drove to Stilson's Hill, many years ago, to attend a United Brethren in Christ camp meeting, in the woods. The preacher was eloquent and interesting, but he did not get to the end of his sermon. When he had reached, perhaps, the middle of his sermon, he cast his eyes upward toward heaven and ex-

claimed: "He is coming! He is coming!" and fell over back-
wards on the floor of the platform. Another preacher took
his place and finished his sermon without a break. The preacher
remained there until the meeting closed for the evening, and
he had not moved a particle when wife and I left the camp
ground. Others, men and women were lying around in the
same comatose state. I have witnessed such exhibitions of "an
unseen power" many times in my life, but I am no nearer
solving the problem now that I was in the long ago.

There is quite a contrast between the winter this year and
one I recall about 61 years ago. The snow fell about four
feet deep and lay on the ground three months without thawing.
Not an icicle was seen on the buildings for three months. Hay
was "worth its weight in gold." On the fifth day of April
my father and I drove a team the length of Brokenstraw
creek hunting for hay or some kind of feed for our cattle, and
found two dozen sheaves of oats. The snow was three feet
deep the fifth day of the second month of spring. It thawed
just a trifle, enough to melt the snow in the road and to make
a little trickling stream of water. It was a hard winter for
the poor cattle, horses and sheep. There was too much snow
in the woods. It was so deep that the deer could not wade
through it and browse on the shrubbery, their usual winter diet,
and the cattle could not do any better than the wild animals.
Both the deer and the tame animals died by the hundreds.
My father lost a very valuable ox. It was starved to death,
and a half dozen cows did not make good shadows in the
spring. Such a thing could not take place now, as railroads
are great distributors. If any article becomes scare in one place
and plenty in another place, the railroads will even up things.
Just stop and think a moment. If we had been blessed with
railroads at that time not one of those poor cattle, horses,
sheep, etc., would have died. A farmer was simply obliged to
stand and see his poor suffering animals die, with no earthly
chance to feed them.

Many people are fighting railroads today who have never
lived without them. They do not realize the fact that all the
new inventions of the last 70 years are real godsends to the
very people who are fighting them. If those fighters had seen
81 years of progress, as has the writer of these lines, they
would not be ready for fight every time some little mishap

occurs. And in addition to the great and wonderful benefits of the railroads are the benefits of the telegraph, telephone and trolley lines. Now a business man can sit at his desk in his office and do business all over town. He can do more in 10 minutes at that 'phone that he could do a few years ago by footing it over town all day. He can do business with another man 10 or 15 miles out in the country in a minute, when before Edison's invention carriage hire and a whole day's time would have been required; or, if the business necesitates a personal interview, this business man can step into a trolley car, and within a few minutes he is face to face with his customer. In addition to this, if he wshes to talk face to face or tongue to tongue, he can interview a man a thousand miles away. On the other hand, if a farmer wants to do business with a townsman, he can step to his 'phone and in a minute the business is transacted. A few years ago this same farmer would be obliged, on all occasoins requiring his presence in town, to go to the barn, harness up old "Jim" or "Tom," hitch him to the buggy, if the farmer had one. If not he would have to go to a neighbor and borrow one, and drive over, at times, very rough roads to town and back, losing a half or a whole day.

And then another great thing for the farmer, outside of the inventions, is the custom which has grown up like a mushroom recently of the merchant delivering goods at the door of any customer regardless of the distance from the merchant's place of business. All the farmer has to do is to give a ring at his 'phone and say "Hello," and the goods are there when the horn blows calling the field men to the table. Is it any wonder that the farmers are paying off their mortgages on their farms? They are saving millions of dollars in time saved by these late inventions of big-brained men like Edison. In fact, the farmer is the favored person now. "Uncle Sam" is really partial to him. The United States mail carrier leaves his mail matter in boxes at his door, while the inhabitants of a town not large enough for free delivery must travel a mile or two and stand at the postoffice window until the "mail is changed" and handed out to him. The farmers will soon be, and some of them are now, riding in automobiles and looking down on common folks. And the millions of dollars that they are saving in time alone will be expended in beautifying this favored country, for as a class they are the most economical

8

of all workers. Edison never dreamed of the unspeakable benefits and the many blessings he has brought to mankind.

I have wandered from my subject of the deep snow. But I have never experienced such a winter again. Several very "soft" winters have come and gone since that time. The young people of this country will remember that 10 or 12 years ago, we were not favored with one day of good sleighing all winter. Farmers plowed nearly every day and could have plowed every day if they had wished to do so. Another winter, 45 or 50 years ago, was its equal. My father had prepared for an all-winter log hauling with two yoke of oxen. He had but one outfit, so he bought another yoke of oxen, bobsleds and chains, and all was ready for the hauling of those logs one and a half miles to Youngsville, to the nearest mill, to have them cut into boards, but not a day of sledding came, and consequently not a log was hauled. By the time of the next sleighing, one year afterwards, the logs were so badly de cayed and hurt by the worms that we had "cull" boards when they were sawed.

## CHAPTER XXX.

### OLD TIME QUADRILLE BAND.

In another chapter I spoke of dancing, but gave but little dancing news. It will be interesting to the people of today to hear a little about the dancing of the olden days. Time was when there was more dancers in this part of the country than musicians. The violinists who could play and call quadrilles at one and the same time were few and far between. Warren did not have a fiddler in the borough when your humble servant belonged to a quadrille band composed of players from Youngsville and Pittsfield, who had a corner on the dancing music in all Warren county. We played for private parties at Orris Hall's, Thomas Struthers' and other "upper ten" families of the county seat. One night we took but a part of our band— William Stright and son, Orra, and myself. When we ar-- rived at the stone mansion of the Hon. Thomas Struthers we found more guests than could dance in the parlors downstairs. We were obliged to split our band and Stright and son took the upstairs crowd and I the downstairs crowd. The Struthers house contained an organ upstairs and a piano downstairs. I lacked a piano player to make my music acceptable and I was more than pleased when the cultured, handsome and amiable daughter of Mr. Struthers offered her services and sat down and played a beautiful accompaniment from 10 p. m. until 4 a. m. without missing a set, although her young lady cousin offered to give her a rest by taking her place at the piano. She refused, saying that she was not in the least fatigued. A few years after I read of her death with much regret. The remembrance of her helping me out with my side of the music that night still lingers. Without her piano my lone violin would have given out doleful strains for that large crowd of Warren people.

Being the only quadrille band in the county and our music being in demand, gave us somewhat of a high opinion of ourselves, so we arranged a series of balls in this section of the country.

We commenced the round at Tidioute. The young people of Grandintown did not tumble over one another to reach our ball. Our aggregation of three musicians only made enough, at so much per couple, to pay our lodging, board and horse feed. We owned our own rig or we should have failed to reach our appointment at the next town, Titusville, where neither Drake nor oil was known at that time. When we arrived at Titusville we found a rather poor prospect of a turn-out. Jack McCray, then a mill man, came to the rescue, and saved us from an utter failure by getting out among the young dancers, with whom he seemed to be immensely popular, and in his impetuous way, got out enough of his young friends to save us from utter defeat. The next morning we found that we lacked one dollar of enough money to pay our hotel bill. As there was but one hotel in town, the landlord had a monopoly of the business, and his bill being a trifle larger than the Tidioute bill, left us one big dollar short. But we soon found that his confidence in us fiddlers was as big as his bill. He cheerfully took our word for it, that we would send him the dollar after we reached the moneyed town of Youngsville. And we kept our word. On our arrival home we enclosed a yellow gold dollar, and our band thereby kept itself in good financial standing. Our band held a council of war, and in about a minute came to the conclusion that disappointment would come to but a few if we would call off the appointments ahead of us, and take the shortest route to our homes in the Brokenstraw valley. When, after a pleasant sleighride through Enterprise, and where Grand Valley now stands—no town there at that time—the same with Torpedo, Garland, we called at Pittsfield, where on short notice the sprightly young people of that place got up a dance that exceeded both the others. Thus ended our self appointed dances—only three miles from home. We took this view of the whole thing, that what we lost in time, we made up in knowledge. We learned the fact that the young people knew when they wanted to dance better than we did.

After that we waited until we were sent for before going to play for a dance. And we were sometimes sent for as often as every night in the week. Once in awhile two dances would come off the same night. Then we would be obliged to divide our band. Several times I was obliged to "go it alone" both calling and sawing on the violin. I think I did more poor playing those days than any other man. I never was a match for Ole Bull, but as there were no Y. M. C. A.'s, basket ball, gymnasiums or women's clubs, the young people had to do something, and that something was shaking the "heavy" fantastic heel. Some call it the "light fantastic toe," but I like to have things changed.

But nothing lasts forever. As time passed along musicians became more plenty, some migrating to our country and some educating themselves. I finally bought a book called "The Violin Without a Master." It was a good and appropriate name for me. I never became master of the violin, consequently it was a violin without a master at our house. The first outsider that came to Youngsville to compete with our band and capture the affections of the best looking young ladies, was a very prepossessing young man named "Bob" Cross. He captured the whole crowd of dancing young people, both male and female. He had only to throw out a hint that he wished a benefit and the ball room would be crowded in a few hours. "Bob" ran the town, as far as the young people were concerned, and many old people thought he was "all wool and a yard wide." All doors were open to "Bob" Cross. He had only to crook his finger and what he wanted was forthcoming.

He was an extremely sweet player on the violin, but he "played by ear." He never learned to read music. But he was a sort of Blind Tom in picking up a tune as soon as he heard it. Politics came in handy then and we made him a member of our quadrille band, fearing that he would run us out entirely. He played several years in our band, then married into a wealthy family, finally dying a few years afterwards.

Others who have helped me out with my music and have since passed away were Josiah Duprey, who was an honest, easy going young man, and who died about four years ago, Enoch Duprey, brother to Josiah; William Stright, a composer of music, who led a quadrille band many years, and who in his riper years worked in a sawmill at Vowinkle, Forest county, Pa., for a period of ten years and loved his violin so well that he played nearly every evening for the free entertainment of the hardy lumbermen at his boarding house, and who died about five years ago—sending out sweet strains from his violin until 10 p. m., then went to sleep. In the morning he was found dead in bed. He had played his last tune. To my notion, Mr. Stright's only daughter, Nellie, is the best pianist in the city of Bradford, where she now resides. I know this is high praise, as Bradford is full of fine pianists. His only son, Orra, is one of the best violinists of the country. Chester Shaw, the bass violin player of our band, met a tragic death at Clarendon, Pa., by falling into a tank of oil and perishing by asphyxiation. Another, William Jewel, a justice of the peace for many years and a merchant of North Warren, died eight or ten years ago. Of the many who have helped me make music for the dancers of long ago, none but Calender Arthur, of Warren, Pa., and Perry Acocks, of Pittsfield, Pa., are alive today.

Before leaving the subject I must speak of one novelty. At one time our band consisted of William Stright, justice of the peace; Calender Arthur, constable of Brokenstraw township, Pa.; Chester Shaw, constable of Pittsfield township, Pa., and G. W. Brown, coroner, Youngsville borough, Warren county, Pa. This gave us a full band of peace officers—enough to keep peace at all times. In those days the balls were made up from mixed crowds. It was seldom that an invitation party was held. It required the whole population to make a "big crowd." The oil country crowds had not "arrived" at the time I am speaking of. And strange to say at all those private parties and public balls I never saw a fistic encounter in the rooms where the ladies and gentlemen were when I was one of the musicians. It is true in writing "Old Times in Oildom" I mentioned a knock down on a dancing floor at Petroleum Center, but I was not one of the regular musicians. I only assisted the regular musicians temporarily or until I was forever frightened away and stopped helping to make music for "wicked dancers."

## CHAPTER XXXI.

### CHURCHES IN THE OLD TIMES.

I will next mention the growth of the churches in the Brokenstraw valley. The first church that I in my babyhood attended, was no church at all. It was a school house—my first school house. We sat on pine slabs, with holes bored in them, and with wooden legs driven into the holes. These made seats, but very uncomfortable ones. There were no backs to them. The occupants were obliged to sit up straight, with no back support, or else they were forced to lean forward. The singing was carried on without the assistance of musical instruments. No church in Warren county had an organ to lead the untrained singers. Robert and Moses Andrews, two brothers, were the "standbys" in that school house in the singing line. Robert sang soprano, and "Mose" sang bass. To my young ears that bass voice of "Mose" Andrews was melody, indeed. It gave me a kind of liking for the bass part in music, either instrumental or vocal, which is still within me at the age of four score. It is very doubtful about my living long enough to lose my liking for this part of a quartette. Alto comes next in the four parts of a quarette, but I had not heard the sweet and captivating strains of the part named alto at that time. Soprano and bass was the whole dependence in all churches in Warren county. This congregational singing, at the old log school house at Garland, was participated in by John McCray, the real standby of the church—the Mandavilles, the Hamiltons, Browns—the father and mother of the writer— the Uptons and many others, had fine, natural untrained voices, and better melody than one would suppose—consider-

ing the absence of tenor and alto—floated out of the windows
and doors of that old school house. The preachers at this
"church" were just such as could be picked up occasionally.
The Bible expounders of those days were not men of very
much "book larnin'," but in the matter of real Christianity
they were full equals of the college bred doctors of divinity
at the present time.

Well, in the course of time, our family flitted down the creek
as far as Youngville. There we attended a frame church, with
a regular preacher. This church was a good type of the church
of that day. It had no steeple or belfry. It was a square sort
of structure, with a gallery all around, except the end where
the tall candlestick pulpit stood. The preacher was obliged to
climb a pair of stairs to get into it and when he reached it he
had barely room to stand in it. This pulpit had every indica-
tion of a scarcity of lumber and space for its diminutive proportions. The choir here had tenor and alto, in addition to
the other parts necessary for the making of a good church
choir. This was the only church in Youngsville and was a
Methodist church, with good and faithful members. The
standbys were the Meads, Davises, Whitneys, Siggins, Mc-
Kinneys, Hulls, Arthurs, Kinnears and others. The main singers
in the choir were the Arthurs and Davises. The choir sat up
in the gallery opposite the pulpit. After a few years an innovation came in the shape of a big bass viol played by a
stump puller named Evans. It was a short lived innovation.
After the first hymn was sung, with bass viol accompaniments,
an old member of the church whose word was law walked
down the aisle, climbed the stairs and came in front of the
choir and pointing his finger at the huge instrument exclaimed
in a voice not easily misunderstood: "Take that ungodly fiddle
out of this choir and keep it out." The command was obeyed,
with alacrity, and that was the first and last bass viol music
for that Youngsville choir. When the preacher read the next
hymn profound silence followed, not a chirp was heard from
any member of the choir. Finally a weak quavering voice
struck up a hymn and we had congregational singing in that
church for a long time. Then as time passed by a choir was
organized and strange to relate, an organ crept into this last
organization with but little opposition. A gradual change
came in music matters. The old member who vetoed the bass

viol was just as honest in his opinion that instrumental music was an evil, as the old members of today are that instrumental music is a blessing. If the old gentleman was alive today, and could step into General Charles Miller's Sunday School in the First Baptist church of Franklin, Pa., and hear the orchestra of a dozen pieces manipulated by professional musicians, and hear the soul stirring religious hymns that delight the hearts of a thousand worshippers, both young and old, every Sunday afternoon, the year around, he would no doubt enjoy the sweet and soft Heavenly strains as much as any other listener. No man in Youngsville was a more devout worshipper than he, and no man who knew this old man here on earth has the least doubt of his listening for these many years to the Heavenly orchestra that makes sacred music in the golden streets of the New Jerusalem.

Well, time moves on, and the church of Youngsville has been sold to the Lutheran Swedish congregation, who have torn it down and replaced it by a beautiful brick structure of late design, and the M. E. congregation has a brick building to worship in. In addition to the two churches mentioned above, Youngsville has a Free Methodist church and an Episcopal church, the two latter named built of wood, and before many moons the United Brethren in Christ will have a brick church building here.

And now a few remarks as to many churches in many places in this country. I'll begin with the Cumberland, Tarentum, Pa. I organized an insurance lodge there about 18 years since. It is the sociability and lack of sociability of churches that I will speak of. I had for my chaplain the pastor of the church named above. I attended the regular Sunday services at his church that first Sunday I spent in town. No man or woman spoke to me. Not one word to "the stranger in their midst." The next day I met the pastor and in a kind of non-complaining way told him that sociability was at a low ebb in his church. His answer was: "I am well aware of it and have been ever since I came here. Next Sunday I will preach a sermon on sociability." I was on hand the next Sunday and the good man preached a very eloquent sermon. After the benediction was pronounced I remained standing at the end of my pew until nearly the entire congregation had passed out, by me, waiting for a friendly handshake. I waited in vain.

One old, bald-headed, fat, good natured looking fellow came up the aisle. My hopes went up. Surely such a pleasant face and open countenance would not follow the example of those who had preceded him. But, like the Priest and the Levite who "passed by on the other side," his eyes were steadily fixed on the church door and soon he was wending his way to his Sunday dinner without a word for me. I gave all a fair chance to cheer the heart of a lonely stranger, but none seemed to act as if the forcible sermon of their pastor had "struck in." And the only hope I had was that the sermon might, like vaccination, work by degrees by giving it time.

The next place I attended church was in a high toned edifice in Pittsburg. Tarentum was reversed here. A very pleasant usher conducted me to a centrally located seat and soon the master of that pew came with his family, wife, daughter and son. After the benediction they introduced themselves in such an agreeable manner that I could not help drawing a comparison. The next church visited was the First M. E. church of Parkersburg, W. Va. I happened to sojourn in the West Virginia city three months. During that length of time I attended the First M. E. church 10 times. Here I found the members all "Priests and Levites." They all "passed by on the other side," except the pastor and his wife and one alderman and his wife. These four had joined my insurance lodge and had a fraternal hand to offer me. As to the effect of the lack of sociability, I will state the case of a railroad official's wife. She informed me that she had lived in Parkersburg two years, had attended that church regularly and had seldom been spoken to. She held a transfer letter from another M. E. church but she had concluded never to offer her letter. But now I come to the contrast. I was stopping at the Palace hotel and one Sunday evening got into conversation with a Presbyterian salesman from Cincinnati. He invited me to go with him to the Presbyterian church. He said he was a stranger in the city and would like to have company. I told him that I was a Methodist, but the M. E. church that I had been attending there was but a little above zero and I would try the Presbyterians that night; but as the Presbyterians had a great new stone church, resembling a fine theater, I had my doubts about finding a warmer atmosphere there than at the M. E. But there is nothing like making the effort to find out things. So I accompanied my new made friend and we were soon seated in a pew behind two ladies, who were dressed in their "silks and satins." We were not more than seated by a warm hearted and smiling southern usher than both ladies handed their hymn books to us and gallantly deprived themselves of those useful articles. When the services closed these Christian ladies took us by the hand, inquired about our place of residence and invited us to come again. It had been so long since I had been treated that way I hardly knew how to act.

The next Sunday evening I attended the M. E. church South and there I found a duplicate of the Presbyterian reception, only more so. A fine gentleman, son and two daughters, composed the quartette, and that church had fine singing. The leader, or father of the helpers, invited me to dinner the next day and I had good cheer all around, but a surprise awaited me when, in addition to the vocal music, they brought forth four instruments and rendered some very fine band music. Now don't think me egotistical, for I am writing this to show the great difference between social churches and non-social churches. No one but a wanderer can fully appreciate these things.

Now let me say a word about the ministers of the gospel. In all my organizing work in getting up and organizing 475 lodges, I never met a better class of men than the preachers of all denominations. They are the most provident men found in the country. Not more than one in 30 omits to carry insurance for the families. They look at it in this light: They are not expected to make and lay up a fortune to protect their families when they are gone. They cannot do it and follow the work of their Lord and Master, but they can pay a dollar or two a month from their salaries and keep their families safe at all times and they do it. No class of men in the country are so generally insured. A preacher without insurance is indeed a novelty. I have taken into insurance lodges over 300 preachers of different denominations. Indeed, I have never found a disciple preacher in all my work in five states who did not become a member of one of my lodges, securing his family against want at the time of his death. I have five ministers of the gospel in one lodge in Clarion, Pa., four M. E. clergymen and one Baptist. About a dozen of my clerical members died, leaving from $1,000 to $2,600 for the protection of their families. One Presbyterian minister, Rev. Isaac Smith, of Tonawanda, N. Y., died four months after joining, leaving his wife $2,600.

---

## CHAPTER XXXII.

### GOD BLESS THE SWEDES.

I am going back a little beyond "oildom" to begin this particular article. My mind wanders back 50 years to a time when we had springtime all winter. In those days the main business was either making shingles or boards, and the hauling of this lumber made lively times. From the break of day until long after dark a steady stream of teams lined the streets. Nearly every farm from Youngsville to Sugar Grove and beyond into York State had pine trees growing on the uncleared portions. And the uncleared was generally the largest part of the farm. All that a majority of the farmers had in those days was a log house in the woods, with a very few acres cleared. Each settler had a log shingle shanty close by his domicile, where, from 4 o'clock in the morning until 10 at night, the faithful builder-up of this wild country would be found either "riving" or shaving shingles. If he had a voice for singing he would use it for all it was worth. Trouble seldom came to him because of the fact that there was but little in the country to be troubled about—no railroad right of way across his farm to worry about; no trolley lines being surveyed through his orchard, garden or dooryard; no telegraph poles being set near "the old oaken bucket that hung in the well;" no telephone agent putting a machine in his house despite his remonstrances; no bicycles bumping up against him; no automobiles chasing him into the fence corner and causing his horse to run away; no millionaires being killed by their steam or gasoline wagons; no railroad accidents, for the good reason that there was no railroad; but few burglaries, because there was but little money or jewelry to steal; no flying machines, liable to light on the roof of log houses at any moment; no earthquakes worth speaking of; no oil or gas fires; and but few murders, for the reason that there were but few Harry Thaws and Hains brothers in the country. In fact, the hard working shingle maker had but little to worry about—barring sickness and death, which came to him, as to all mankind, in all ages of the world. Of course there were good and bad shingle makers. The good ones had nothing on their minds but the happiness of their families, and the bad ones had not as many chances to wander from the straight and narrow path as can be found nowadays. There was but little bank stealing, through dishonest officers, because there were few banks to "break." However, the bad shingle maker had one sin to answer for, and the sin was almost hereditary. In riving his shingles he would split the shingles so close to the knots in the timber that it was impossible to shave them so that they would be of any value whatever. It required five times as much labor to make this crooked shingle fit into the "bunch" nicely to deceive the buyer as it required to shave a good straight shingle. And the timber in many cases was stolen, costing the maker nothing. It was one of the puzzles "past finding out" why this extra labor should be put on these frauds, which only amounted to some tall swearing by profane carpenters down the Allegheny, Ohio and Mississippi rivers. It would try the heart of the best Christian purchaser of several thousand shingles to find his good money paid to the raftsman that had landed his raft by his river farm about one-fourth dead loss. When the purchaser opened the bunches of shingles his usual way of disposing of this fraudulent part would be to make a bonfire of them. The worst of this business was the fact that the purchaser always found himself short of the required amount of shingles and would be compelled to send off somewhere to buy again before he could put the roof on his building. I never heard of one of the defrauded purchasers putting the law in force against those rascals. The rafts immediately "pulled out" and floated down the river, perhaps cheating several more innocent buyers before the first purchaser had opened a bunch of shingles. The purchaser always pocketed his loss with as much grace as possible rather than undertake to find the man who defrauded him. Pinkerton was not around in those days. Now all the purchaser would have to do would be to give warning and he would be a cute shingle seller that could escape the penalty of such a transaction. At the present time no such crimes as the ones just described could take place, as no shingles are shaved by hand and the tall pines are few and far between. Shingles are now made by machinery, as nearly everything else in the way of manufactured goods. The old shingle shanties have all gone the way of the old log houses and indeed the occupants of both are nearly all gone. As a proof of this I will say that I, very recently, counted the deaths that have taken place on four miles of the street leading from Youngsville to Sugar Grove within 50 years. The number surprised me. Although not a village intervenes, only farms all along that road, the number is 137. "All are born to die." One family on this road, named Duprey, consisted of husband and wife and 14 children. All the children were married, save one, 50 years ago. Now all—father, mother, sons, daughters, sons-in-law, and daughters-in-law—are dead, but the youngest daughter.

When the timber was gone from this section of the country the people first thought they could not make a living without the tall green pines, but time has proved that the clearing and cultivating of the soil is much more to be depended upon than the pines. Considerable of the wealth of Warren county now consists in nice farms. And let me say that the light haired Swedes have done as much to bring these farms to perfection as the native Americans. Where a few years ago wooded hills, valleys and swamps abounded, beautiful farms, with orchards, painted houses and barns, fat cattle and horses, and everything pertaining to a well-equipped farm, are found. God bless the Swedes! They take to the American way of doing things as a duck takes to water. Just stop to think a moment what these people from the bleak country of the Scandinavians have done for us in this part of Uncle Sam's domain. They have built up whole streets in Youngsville and most of the neat farms surrounding the town are owned and occupied by families who spell the last syllable of their name with the three letters, "son." Then look at Kane, McKean county, Pa. The town would be in the woods but for these same industrious Johnsons, Swansons, Samuelsons, Thompsons and many other "sons." The traveler who has passed from Kane to Mt. Jewett has noticed the continual string of new farms all along both sides of the B. & O. railroad for the whole distance of 12 miles from Kane to Mt. Jewett. When I passed these two enterprising towns I was informed by an old settler that every farm, except one, and that was owned by a Frenchman, was owned and occupied by Swedes. It looks as if it were not for the Swedes, owls, bears, and wildcats might now be inhabiting these farmlands.

Almost the same can be said of the land along the B. & O. road west of Kane. Then look at Jamestown, N. Y. One wing, called Brooklyn, I think, is composed entirely of Scandinavians, and it is a very prosperous part of the city at the outlet of Chautauqua Lake. A few years ago I attended a county agricultural fair at Jamestown, N. Y. The first thing that attracted my attention was the Fenton, or Prendergast, guards marching down the sidehill street. When I spoke of the meloodious music and fine uniforms of the band and the precise step of the military company to an old resident he informed me that every member of both the band and the military company was a Swede. And when I visited the fair grounds and saw the military drill and listened to the strains from those "sons of a cold climate" I thought that surely Jamestown would have had a dull fair if not for her adopted "sons" from Sweden. And I do not have to go to Jamestown and Kane to see the beauties of this foreign population. I can travel a mile from the borough of Youngsville to the top of Hull's Hill and cast my eyes westward, southward, eastward, northward and I see a panorama of fine, well-kept farms stretch out before me. The question arises, "Who cleared up this rough wooded country and made it blossom as the rose?" The answer echoes back: "The Swedes."

But I have wandered away from my old shingle makers and left them sitting on a bench, pulling the draw shave. Before they were entirely through with this hard work shingle mills came by slow degrees and circular saws and steam have done the work in fast time. One set of four men will now make 25,000 shingles in a day, whereas 1,000 were a day's work for one man by hand. No other than sawed shingles can be found nowadays. The sound of the frow and maul is not heard in the land; neither are many of the wielders of the maul heard in the land. Their homes are the cemeteries in the many parts of the lumber region. Their farms are now generally occupied by their descendants, who perhaps but seldom think of the hardships their fathers and mothers endured. They do things so different and everything is so different that thoughts of the absent ones are seldom brought to mind. Sometimes an entirely useless old spinning wheel or some other old relic is seen tucked away in some old, dusty garret that is a reminder of times long since gone by. But the sight of an old "little wheel" for spinning flax or a "big wheel" for spinning woolen rolls into yarn, to be knit into stockings, has but little effect on a person who has never heard the buzzing or whizzing of them. The writer of this has heard this kind of music so often in the early boyhood that he can now—in his mind's ear—hear it distinctly as his mother sits, turning the "distaff" and feeding the "little wheel," and his eldest sister is making lively steps pulling out the woolen rolls and making long yarn preparatory to being sent to that intelligent being called the "weaver" of home made clothes on the big wheel. And added to this instrumental music would be the vocal music from both of those loved relatives.

And when it comes to the subject of derricks, how familiar they become to one who has lived in sight of them ever since the first derrick was built to be used in producing oil. I'll give a leaf from my own experience. About 15 years ago I took a trip into Ohio, organizing fraternal insurance lodges. I was gone from the old Keystone State four months and in that time organized 15 lodges. When I had worked about three months, without seeing a derrick or getting a smell of the oleaginous fluid, I landed at Prairie Depot, O. When I got off the train I saw tall derricks all around me and I also inhaled the, to me, delicious smell of "Seneca" oil. The odor was a little stronger than that in Pennsylvania, but not too strong for me. I will not try to tell the real joy of the moment. I had been deprived of the sight of a derrick for a long three months, the only three months since the striking of the first oil well in this country. I felt really at home among the "yellow hammers," all on account of the sight of those derricks and the smell of that Ohio oil. The last month of the four I stuck to the oil country and felt very much like being in Pennsylvania. In fact I was among Pennsylvanians. No oil town is complete without Pennsylvanians living in it. And it is a well known fact that all oil towns have new citizens from the old Keystone State, where the oil business was born, and the author feels proud of the fact that he and the oil business were born only nine miles apart. I tarried four days at Prairie Depot, organizing a lodge of 40 members, exactly half "yellow hammers" and half "bluejays," the latter name given by the Ohio citizens and the former given by the Pennsylvanians, who had taken up their abode among the Ohio oil wells.

I found a novelty in this town. A native born citizen in the shape of a young man of 20 years took it into this head that he was a barber. He hired a room, bought a chair and a razor or two and put out a striped pole and commenced shaving men, no, not shaving, but pulling out their beard by the roots. His method was to seat the customer in the chair, put a dirty towel around his neck, mix up some lather, dip his brush into it, spread it on the face of his customer, grab his razor and try to cut off the growth. He made an utter failure of getting all the beard from the face that he made no attempt to soften. He didn't give one second to the rubbing of the lather. I stood this kind of torture twice while I was a guest of that town of rich soil, covered with big oil wells and droves of black hogs. I have given this space to the barber free of charge, knowing full well that it will not interest the general reader. Commercial men, who are shaved by many different barbers, will wonder at this, as no doubt nearly all have endured such chairs. I have been shaved by more than a thousand different barbers and I never found this young man's "double."

I must not close without giving a winding up word to the reader. Those old pioneers have all gone on to a land where the golden gardens are already cleared and awaiting their arrival. Their descendants are enjoying the improvements of the age. The shingle shaving was finished before their fathers left this earthly abode. Now a trolley runs from Youngsville to Sugar Grove, also three 'phone lines and a mail delivery route, so you see these descendants have no need of losing a day occasionally going to town on horseback, in a buggy or afoot for little errands. The old settlers never dreamed of these conveniences. These time savers make wealthy tillers of the soil. The farmer now raises blooded horses and cattle and sells them for double the money that his father could get, and chickens, eggs and crops of all kinds bring a price unbelievable to the "old man," who split and shaved the shingles. The prices on farmers' goods now make the farmer smile and the townsman frown. The next thing that happens will be the opulent farmer riding in his automobile, and some of them do that very thing now, and others are financially able to do so. So the world moves on at a great pace.

---

## CHAPTER XXXIII.

### YOUNGSVILLE FOUNDERS AND BUSINESS MEN.

What will the end be?

I thought I had "Old Times in Oildom" finished when I wrote the last chapter. But since that time I have thought of many things that ought to be said of Youngsville that would show the great changes that have taken place in this one little spot since I made my appearance on this earth.

About 65 years ago Amasa Ransom owned and occupied a farm one mile from Youngsville. He also owned a sawmill at Garland. Most all owners of sawmills were farmers also at that time. They raised the hay and oats on their farms that kept their teams in good order while hauling the logs to the mills. The farm and mill ran in connection, a kind of "a wheel within a wheel." When a farmer would get a little money put away in a stocking—no banks then—he would build a sawmill. It did not cost as much to build a mill in those days as it does now. The farmer and his boys would cut down big trees and make a dam, hew out some square timber and make a frame building, put in a little machinery, consisting of a water wheel, wooden frame or sash for one saw, set in an upright position, the only saw of any kind in the mill, make a wooden carriage, and that was about all there was to it. The owner and his farm help would do all the work except a few days work by a millwright, who made the water wheel and bossed the hanging of the saw in the sash and looked after the "scientific" part of the business. A good millwright stood as high in the estimation of the community in general as Edison or Marconi does now. He was paid the magnificent sum of from $2 to $3 a day. It required but a few hundred dollars to put a sawmill in running shape. But it took a great real of hard work to get the money back with the best of pine lumber bringing

9

$4 per thousand feet, or about one-eighth part of the present price in Pittsburg. Perhaps it brought half that amount at the mill.

Our family lived near Garland. Mr. Ransom, having bought the mill and lands belonging at Tiona, Warren county, Pa., afterwards known as the "Joe" Hall property, and still later owned by Clapp, Stone & Co., with 7,000 acres of oil lands, came to Garland and persuaded my father to rent his farm near Youngsville, as he wanted to move to his newly acquired property. My father did not need much coaxing to induce him to lease his log house in the woods and come to the "big city" of Youngsville, with one store and two black-smith shops, one tavern and one church and two little wooden school houses, one on each side of the creek, and perhaps some other "big places of business" that have escaped my memory. The first work that I did after being settled on our newly rented farm was to yoke up the oxen "Buck and Bright," and join a procession of four yoke of oxen and their drivers and travel one mile and a half up Matthews run to the farm now owned and occupied by O. P. Brown, and hitch to one of the largest hickory trees ever seen in this section. In a few hours that mammoth tree was lying on the bank of the Brokenstraw creek, in the village of Youngsville. In a day or two the best Democratic carpenters in Youngsville had that big tree peeled and shaped into one of the largest "James K. Polk" liberty poles in Western Pennsylvania. And in a few days more a great gathering of Democrats took place and with rope and tackle, "a few jugs of that which gave them courage," and spread eagle oratory and fuss enough to launch a war vessel, and Colonel William S. Roney for boss, the tallest and straightest Democratic hickory pole, with the largest flag waving from its tiptop, in Warren county, honored the Democrats of Youngsville. My father was always an ardent Democrat. He raised three sons up true to his doctrine, but only one remains true to this father's teaching. That one still lives on the old homestead where the big "Polk and Dallas" hickory pole was cut. Two of his sons have for many years voted the Prohibition ticket.

At the time I made my debut into Youngsville society by driving our oxen on the occasion mentioned above, 12 young men, the cream of the town, had a society organized named

"The Youngsville Glee club." They had a wagon box with this name on the outside in large letters. About once a month they would hitch two spans of horses to a wagon and put that box on it, each taking his best girl with him, making 25, counting the driver, and go to some outlying village, take supper—it would be dinner now—and have a good time in general. One of their number, in the course of time, went west "to grow up with the country," and left a vacancy. At their next meeting the writer of this was duly elected a member to fill the vacancy, the ox-driver, a mile out in the country, the only out-of-town boy in the club. I felt somewhat lonely, but happy. To think that of the many out-of-town boys I was the chosen one was enough to give me the "big head." But I put on the brakes and my head kept its normal size. And not to be egotistical, I tried not to dishonor the club and stuck to it until the old wagon box rotted away and is now only a memory.

I am going to speak of a few of the old settlers that made Youngsville what it was at that time. The first that comes to mind are John Mead and William Siggins. Judge Siggins lived at Youngsville and owned a sawmill and a gristmill, had a wife and 13 children. The judge was a very tall man—over six feet—and his wife was a very short woman. Nine of the judge's children were boys. There were no mowing machines and the hay was all cut with scythes. The judge would march at the head of his line of sons and when they would reach the meadow the 10 would start in, the judge leading, and how that timothy did come down at their bidding. When one or more are mowing in the same field they have to "keep stroke." Watching this one family of 10 taking the even swing together was a sight not seen every day, even in the day of no mowing machines. And then, in a field of ordinary length when they came out at the end of the field, an acre of new mown hay was drying in the sun. The old judge was a character. When he took hold of anything he generally "got there." At one time he served as constable 12 years. Every year he was elected without much opposition until the twelfth year, when the people thought they would make a change and let some one else have a chance. But they elected the judge to the office of high constable, an office which at that time carried but little business with it. A high constable could only do a

little borough business. The judge surprised everybody by
getting a special law passed by the legislature giving the high
constable of Youngsville borough a legal right to any kind of
business that the regular constable could do. And that has
been the law to this day. The judge made an excellent constable under the old law and the business was nearly all put
into his hands under the new law, and the income was as great
as it was under the old law. The regular constable regarded
it as a good joke and took up another business. At 88 years
of an active, well spent life the judge said good bye to all
earthy things and passed away.

And now comes in the coincidence. John Mead's family was
a double of the William Siggins family. John Mead had a
sawmill and gristmill, a mile up Brokenstraw, and a family of
13 children. He was as tall as Mr. Siggins, and his wife was
as short as Mrs. Siggins. Seldom, if ever, could such a coincidence be found. The nearest of this case that has come under
my observation is a Mr. Cross and a Mr. Morrison, living at
Parthenia, six miles below Irvineton, on the Allegheny river.
They were next door neighbors; only a school house between
them, and each had 13 children.

Another of the pioneers in the Brokenstraw valley was H. P.
Kinnear. He was born and reared in Youngsville, and as he
grew into manhood be became a leader in the business of the
town. Everything pertaining to the good of the town he
engineered to the best of his ability. To tell all the benefit that
Henry Kinnear was to this town would take more time than I
have to spare. But I mention a few of the things that he did to
help make Youngsville a nice, well-regulated place to live in.
It was by his movements that the little village became a
borough more than 50 years ago. There was no other
borough in Warren county except Warren. Now there are
eight boroughs. He succeeded in organizing Youngsville lodge,
No. 500, I. O. O. F., about 60 years ago, and was elected as
representative to the Grand Lodge every year while he lived
after the organization, 40 years. He, as burgess and councilman, brought about many improvements that will stand as
monuments to his love for Youngsville for all time to come.
One of the principal landmarks is the Odd Fellows cemetery.
The cemetery overlooks the brough from a beautiful eminence
about a mile away. This "City of the Dead" was the pride of

his life until life ended for him about 20 years ago. He gave of his time freely in bringing about borough improvements of all kinds, one of which was to make a nearly level grade on all streets and sidewalks. If a rise of ground appeared anywhere on the main streets it was plowed and scraped and carted away until the surface was smooth and even. The same with the sidewalks. If a bump appeared it was soon leveled, and if a shade tree was an inch or two inside the six-foot limit it had to be shoved out to the proper place or taken away entirely. In getting this accomplished Mr. Kinnear made many enemies, but he went his way unmoved by the grumbling of the tree owners and now when he and a majority of the grumblers have gone to their eternal homes, about 10 miles of shale brick sidewalks are laid on a level foundation, the grading being done years ago under the supervision of this same H. P. Kinnear. I was not one of the grumblers, but I was obliged to lower the ground at one end of my sidewalk and cut nearly half the roots off of some nice hard maple shade trees. And I am one of the inhabitants of the town who have been permitted by the Great Ruler of the Universe to live to see the time that I can walk about 10 miles on the different streets on level brick walks and not stub a toe. But I am not done with Mr. Kinnear yet. He, at different times in his rather eventful life, filled town offices, being sheriff, member of the state legislature and treasurer, chairman of committee on Grand hotel and superintendent of the grounds of Point Chautauqua. In fact, he held all of these offices at one and the same time. And at the time of his death he was president of the Youngsville Savings Bank. Hon. H. P. Kinnear has left his footprints in Youngsville for all time to come. The borough has the appearance of a park in certain places because of his work.

Charles Whitney was another old-time citizen who did a great deal to make a beautiful place of Youngsville. He owned nearly half the land inside the borough line, nearly all west of the Brokenstraw creek. He owned a sawmill about two miles up the creek and was both a farmer and lumberman. His big farm in Youngsville was covered with pine stumps. He bought a stump machine and summer after summer could be seen from break of day until dark working with his men, not bossing alone, but doing as much work as any of his hired men. Mr. Whitney raised four children. All are, however' dead now. His oldest son, Captain George Whitney, did his full share toward putting down the Rebellion. He got up one company, took it to the front and turned it into Colonel Roy Stone's Bucktail regiment, then came back and raised another company and took it to the front. He stayed with this company until the war closed.

Another citizen of this place is R. P. Davis, a sweet singer, born and reared in this town. He has been singing tenor in the Methodist Episcopal church for the last 50 years. He has missed but few Sundays in his time and considering special occasions would more than average twice. But calling it twice each Sunday, it would count 5,200 trips and about the same number of miles traveled. Counting three hymns to each service, this shows that he has sung 15,600 hymns. He has, in addition to that, spent about two years' time in the 50 years, in singing at funerals. He has done all this free of charge. In the above mentioned time he has worked a farm, has been sexton of the cemetery 16 years, has been either burgess or councilman 14 years, and has been superintendent of the county farm here three years. All of this inside 50 years. Truly, Reuben has been on the move within the last half century.

Alden Marsh was one of Youngsville's well-wishers and workers for the town's advancement. He was a successful lumberman and retired with a competency in middle life. He filled the office of county commissioner for three successive terms with great ability. He was a leading Odd Fellow and the I. O. O. F. band turned out and played solemn dirges at his funeral. When he was in business and had plenty of money, and I was a young chap, just commencing business without money, all I had to do was to ask Mr. Marsh for a thousand dollars to use in buying and running lumber to Pittsburg and selling it, and it would be forthcoming. He never refused me, and this borrowing was repeated many times. When he died he left his property and cash in bank to his wife. He had no children and when his wife died the property and cash all went to Mrs. Marsh's relatives in Minnesota. No provision was made for keeping his lot in the cemetery lawn mowed and in proper order, but in these long years since Mrs. Marsh's death no weeds or briers have grown on the Marsh lot. For I cannot bear to see a tangle of weeds and briers growing on the grave of such a good old financial friend of the long ago.

John McKinney was another of the moulders of Youngsville. He was one of the first born after the old Scotchman, Matthew Young, drove stakes and marked out the site for the town of Youngsville. He was the oldest of a family of seven boys and a girl. He, like every provident young man of nearly a century ago, went into the lumber business, and accumulated a large quantity of land on the waters of the Brokenstraw creek and its branches. Part of it cost him but a few cents per acre, which he bid off at tax sales, as unseated "lands." But the bulk of his land was bought privately. He paid the full value for it. But the full value was not a large amount at that time, when men were working hard, cutting, piling up and burning nice pine timber to make room for very scant crops. Land that was groaning under the weight of the very finest timber that ever stood out of doors was sold at $1.50 per acre. I have bought, at that rate, of the Huidekopers, rather than just take it. It was "all the go" to cut where one could find it, but I always felt a little safer cutting my own timber than Huidekopers'. However, I don't feel like bragging because of my honesty. The reader can just call it cowardice. and let it go at that.

But to return to John McKinney. His pine-covered lands kept rising, and then how they did rise when Drake struck oil at Titusville! Mr. McKinney owned 100 acres near Hosmer run, a mile above Garland. When they drilled with a spring pole he got a smell of oil and sold it for $20,000. This hundred acres was bid in at a tax sale for a few cents an acre. Great is oil. At that time Mr. McKinney could walk from Youngsville to Irvineton—three miles—on his own land, by zigzagging to the sidehill at a couple of places . He sold several hundred acres of his land holdings at oil prices. When Mr. McKinney was transacting this business mentioned above his two nephews, John L. and "Curt" McKinney, two miles from Youngsville were helping their father James McKinney, run a little sawmill, propelled by an old fashioned wooden water wheel. But when their uncle John died several weeks later, worth nearly a quarter of a million dollars, these two boys were beginning to lay the foundation for their fortunes of millions of dollars.

John McKinney was a man who loved to help those who tried to help themselves. A case in proof of this: When I was emerging from boyhood to manhood I borrowed $150 of him to pay the Huidekopers' for 100 acres of pine timberland. Two years later I called with money and interest to pay back the borrowed money. When I spoke of interest his answer was this: "I don't charge interest to young men who are trying to do somehting for themselves." He would not and did not take a dollar of interest, although I expected to pay it and came prepared for it. John McKinney was a business man all his lifetime of about 80 years. He never bothered himself about office, with the exception of one term of three years as sheriff of Warren county, which the voters forced upon him. When he died he was the richest man on the Brokenstraw creek, from its mouth to the headwaters in the state of New York. His oldest son, Arthur McKinney, now lives in this place and has done much to test the territory between Youngsville and Irvineton for oil and gas. He is more encouraged at the present time than ever before; has faith that we have a paying oil field between Youngsville and Irvineton. The big flood of 1892 swept everything before, it and business had not been resumed until recently. As one well had put 150 barrels into a 250 barrel tank before the flood, and oil, tank and all were swept down the Brokenstraw and the well has not been touched since. Mr. McKinney has faith enough to clean out that well and try again.

Philip Mead, Esq., was one of the substantial residents for 50 years. He held the office of justice of the peace for 25 years without a break. He was one of the leading merchants of this place for 40 years. And when it came to church matters, he was an authority., No service was complete without his presence. He was always to be found at the Thursday evening prayer meeting at the M. E. church, as well as all Sunday services. He leaves a son, W. J. Mead, who keeps up his father's reputation for business. He runs the leading hardware store of the town, and a daughter, Callie Mead, now holds the position of assistant cashier in the First National Bank of Youngsville.

## CHAPTER XXXIV.

## NEW TIMES IN OILDOM.

In a recent chapter I spoke of the pioneers who have make Youngsville what it is. Now I am going to write something which will sound more like "New Times in Oildom." Here goes: Sixteen years ago Youngsville was like a majority of the small towns of the country, nearly at a standstill. Although the location was far ahead of any town of its size in Warren county, being situated in a beautiful valley, averaging a mile wide, ten miles long, underlaid with gravel, where an iron pipe can be driven down 30 or 40 feet in a few hours, and the very best of pure, cold, soft water obtained, its growth was slow, It lacked manufactories. There was considerable money, owned by people who were very conservative. They preferred to keep their money in the banks, at small interest, to risking it in any kind of speculative business. Money makes a poor showing in that way, in fact no shownig at all. That was about the condition of affairs at Youngsville when W. P. Nutting, a young oil operator who had formerly lived in Youngsville, but who for several years had been a very much alive Clarendon oil operator—came to his former home town and started a bank. Then "Charley" Kay came from Stilson Hill, with little money but with lots of business energy, and went into the steam sawmill business. From that business he entered the steam gristmill business, with John Sheldon, another Stilson Hill man as a partner. The big flood of 1892 carried the mill off, leaving nothing but a big hole in the ground. The engine was found nearly a quarter of a mile down the creek, almost hidden by gravel and stones. That ended the mill business for "Charlie," but he had an appetite for business that could not be quenched by the loss of one mill, and a few weeks after the flood found him with Peter Turner and Amil Sagerdahl, starting up a furniture factory in a building reconstructed from a private house. One addition after another was put to this small beginning, until a large and rather commodious furniture factory reared its proud head in the heretofore quiet Youngsville. Then, when "everything was lovely," one quiet evening the fire bell rang, and Youngsville's pride was soon a heap of smouldering ruins. And Youngsville lay all summer "in sackcloth and ashes." But C. H. Kay, superintendent, and his always to be depended upon secretary and treasurer, M. D. Whitney, were not covered with ashes. They were planning the building of a new factory of triple the capacity, and built in a much more convenient place than the old one. And the result is a $250,000 factory, which has paid for itself, and is now bringing to its stockholders enormous dividends. But a word of explanation is necessary in this connection. Only $15,000 of stock was sold at the beginning. It now pays dividends on a $250,000 plant. No stock is for sale in this institution. And this is not all. Both Kay and Whitney are interested in nearly all the improvements of the town. This large factory employing 150 men is not all. Both the gentlemen named above have done good work for the town, both in erecting of new buildings and in all things pertaining to the advancement of Youngsville. Besides the individual efforts of these two gentlemen, their example has been far-reaching. Two years ago another furniture factory was built, with a capacity for 200 workmen. The main instigators of this factory were Amil Sagerdahl and E. Swanson—Sagerdahl being superintendent. Then the Gem Mirror Works of Jamestown, N. Y., came and put up a plant as the result of the influence exerted by these two furniture factories. This shows that in the business line one thing follows another. And in building for private families A. F. Swanson takes the lead. This man is an enigma. About 20 years ago he opened a little grocery store with about $400. Today he owns a half dozen stores, dwelling houses sheltering 20 families, owns a hotel, the Youngsville house, owns considerable stock in both furniture factories, in the Gem Mirror Works, in the First National Bank, of which he is a director, also the Forest Manufacturing company. He owns an opera house, owns stock in the Standard Shale Brick plant, and other properties "too numerous to mention." Mr. Swanson has not made any sensational strikes in the way of speculation. He has conducted a store all these years, and has quietly accumulated somewhere in the neighborhood of $100,000. E. C. Swanson, brother of A. F. Swanson, has also done his full share of helping Youngsville.

C. A. Hazard is another man who believes in making homes for new-comers. For several years he erected two first-class tenement houses each year. A. F. Peterson is another gentleman who has built a nice row of brick houses along West Main street. Mr. Peterson is the president of the Gem Mirror plant and is one of the foremost capitalists of our town. He owns stock in nearly all the industrial plants in the place. E. A. McDowell, superintendent and secretary of the Forest Gas Company, is another of our foremost business upbuilders of the town, assisted by his three sons, one of whom, Forest, has gone west, "to grow up with the country." Roy is one of Uncle Sam's "mail route agents," and Fred is cashier of the First National Bank of Youngsville. Charles Newgreen is another man who has been active in the work of helping to double the population of the town in the last five years.

Hon. J. B. White, a former resident of Youngsville, but now a resident of Kansas City in the winter, and Chautauqua Lake in the summer, has done his share in the educational line. Three years ago he built a High School building costing $25,000 in memory of his son Frank. In the same year the Currie Memorial Industrial school building was erected. J. T. Currie, a wealthy resident, died about 19 years ago, leaving money on interest for the purpose of putting up a building where the boys can learn to do carpenter work, iron work—work at other trades—thereby educating the hands as well as the head; a place where the girls can also learn the art of cooking and sewing. At the same time the old four-story wooden school huilding was veneered with No. 1 standard shale brick and overhauled generally. Now we have a row of three brick school buildings, fronting on College street, with a background of three acres for a playground for the children. I have traveled a great deal in New York state, Pennsylvania, Ohio, West Virginia and Canada, and I have never seen a town of 2,000 inhabitants have as many nice school buildings as this town has. And we have the living J. B. White and the dead J. T. Currie to thank for two of the finest of the buildings. Both of these magnificient gifts were turned over to the Youngsville school board as free gifts.

C. S. Mead, the leading dry goods merchant of this place, has also been one of our town builders. He owns the old H. P. Kinnear farm, which is situated near the center of the borough and has there a little village of his own.

Among the newcomers is Robert Slater, a man who has made a great deal of money along the Allegheny river at the lumber business. He is a good citizen to have lying around loose. He takes stock in all manufactories that are being built.

This is an answer to the question often asked, "What makes Youngsville grow so fast?" It is the enterprising moneyed men. And let me add that the town is often helped by the enterprising and "moneyed ladies." Mrs. Laura Jackson and Mrs. Frank Kay built two of the finest of the many brick houses erected last year. Mrs. McCormick, Miss Callie Mead and other ladies own nice brick houses. Oh, yes, the ladies are doing their full share of the work of making Youngsville what it is today; the only town of its size that I know of which has laid about ten miles of shale brick sidewalk within the last five years, and doubled its population in the same length of time, except of course towns that have struck oil or gas, or opened coal mines.

Another who must not be left out among the helpers in Youngsville, is H. C. Preston, who has been the superintendent of the Rouse hospital farm here for the last 12 years.

John A. Day, a man who was born here, about 50 years ago, is counted among one of the most enterprising citizens of the borough. He, single handed and alone, promoted the Warren County Traction Co. He brought C. H. Smith, G. W. Wood, Mr. Gibson, Mr. Bailey and other moneyed men of Sheffield, and William Culbertson, of Girard, the wealthiest man in Erie county, Pa., into the company which made it a success from the start. The roadbed is cut and filled the whole nine miles, making it a road for both passengers and freight. The road will soon be extended from Sugar Grove to Chautauqua, a distance of about 16 miles, and from Youngsville to Warren, a distance of nine miles. Then it will be one of the best paying properties of the kind in the country. No roads, either steam or electric, parallel it from Youngsville to Chautauqua. It has a splendid farming country all to itself. Mr. Day has not let this monopolize his mind entirely. Just to fill in his time while he has been building the trolley road on his own hook he has built telephone lines nearly all over Warren county. And his only son, Archie, "is a chip of the old block." Archie has stuck up his poles and strung his wires and does the "hello" business for the wealthy and enterprising town of Sheffield, 22 miles east of Youngsville.

## CHAPTER XXXV.

## "DUNC" KARNS AND "TOM" KING.

Noticing the announcement of the death of S. D. Karns brings very forcibly to my mind once again "Old Times in Oildom" in Parker City. I owned a lumber yard in that noted city at its inception. "Dunc," as he was called by everybody, lived in his oil country house, next door to my lumber office. He was a lively oil operator and no mistake. All he had to do was to drill a hole in the ground and get a big gusher of five or ten hundred barrels a day. Oil was four dollars a barrel, and his income was simply immense. Everything he took hold of melted into great piles of money. He bought, or leased, the McClimens farm, one mile and a half south of Petrolia, and aside from the gusher oil wells, he made a nice little pile in lots, on which to build "Karns City." The writer of this bought ground for an opera house, a restaurant and hotel and a city office, where was located the lumber business and Western Union telegraph office, and land on which the lumber yard was situated. All these pieces of land were situated in the western part of the town, and when the town burned, a cross street was all that saved my property. My chief loss was simply some ornamental cut glass in the "telegraphic" part of the building, worth but a couple of hundred dollars. This would have been saved if the wild, noisy crowd of men had obeyed my instructions not to carry it out, but to let it take its chances, as there was a cross street between my building and the fire, and as the fire companies from Parker City, Petrolia and Millerstown each had a stream of water on the fire, I felt in but little danger. But they paid not the least attention to me. They were crazy, and they rushed past me as I stood in the front door, and a half dozen grabbed the frame work and carried the whole business out and into the middle of the street, where they dumped it into the mud, and the fire companies soon made mince meat of it. After that fire, Karns City was partly rebuilt, but it never fully recovered from the damage. But it is today far from being a toad-stool town. It is a pretty little farming village, reinforced by many old time wells, and it will be a success as long as good producing farms abound in that region.

But back to "Dunc" Karns. He was "it" in everything pertaining to the business of Parker City and vicinity. Any kind of business that did not have Karns attached to one or the other end of the names of it was considered "small potatoes." It was "Parker and Karns City railroad," "Karns bank," "Karns bridge," "Karns City," "Karns pipe line," in fact he was the main spring. "Dunc" was not one of those business men who go around with a troubled look on his face. No, indeed! He scattered sunshine every day. He mixed pleasure with business, and had a good time generally. He was a young man, full of life, and energy when his great piles of money fell upon him. The weight of his money did not crush him. He never put on money airs, and make himself disagreeable to the average man. He would play a game of billiards with a respectable oil worker with as much enjoyment as he would have had playing with the owner of a thousand-barrel well. I recollect one little mark of pride on his part, however. He bought a billiard cue, finished with silver trimmings. The billiard man kept Mr. Karns' cue in a separate receptacle from the other sticks. Although this looked somewhat "uppish," "Dunc" bought it for what it was, a finely wrought plaything.

The first sign of opulence on "Dunc's" part was the building of a fine brick mansion a few miles below Freeport, Pa. He graded a lawn all around it, large enough for a common sized farm, with a nice setting of evergreens all over it. This place was on the opposite side of the Allegheny river from his boyhood home—Karns eddy. But the old saying it, "It's a long lane that has no turning." The lane was turned with "Dunc," but turned the wrong way. He was not the first to dip in a little too deep, nor will he be the last. The oil country is paved with men who have made and lost money. The writer speaks from experience, he having earned a small fortune in two years and lost it in one. You see by this that you can go down hill twice as fast as you can go up. At a certain time when the oil business was at its height, there were 30 lumber yards in the lower oil regions. These lumber yards were all doing a good business, when, lo and behold! oil dropped from $3.00 a barrel to 50 cents a barrel. Then the lumber men got it "in the neck." Oil operators by the score, who had been paying their lumber bills every 30 days, went into bankruptcy. One little bit of an example is this: One operator, who had been one of my best customers failed for $1,500,000. Then where was my $900 lumber bill? This kind of thing was not uncommon. Out of this number, 30 yards, only two came off unscathed—28 having found the oil country a slippery place to do business in. Money slipped into the dealers pocket easily, but it slipped out again much more easily and quickly than it came. You may ask 28 lumber yard owners if they do not agree with me. One of the surviving two is now dead, leaving but one witness in favor of the beauties of the lumber business in the "lower oil regions."

The Parker City of today in a business point of view, is not a shadow of its former self. I feel inclined to give one incident of many that could be given to show the strenuous way the Allegheny Valley railroad had of doing business. The railroad being on the opposite side of the river from Parker City, with only a wire cable to guide a ferry boat across the stream, made it anything but easy to do business in the new and hustling town. Everything was "hurly-burly." The short side track at the "Phillips House" could not hold half the cars sent to the new oil town, and the cars would be "switched" off at Foxburg, three miles above, or at Bear creek, one mile below, and they would lie there until a small opening on the switch at the Phillips House could make room for one or two cars. Then the cars destined for Parker City would be "switched in." One day the freight train men put two car loads of lumber for my yard, lumber needed at once for oil well purposes, on Bear creek end of the side track. No room was made for cars for nearly a week, and no team could get near the cars to unload the lumber. As "gondolas" were in great demand about that time the railroad could not well spare its cars a week at a time lying idle on a side track. Consequently "Tom" King, assistant superintendent of the road, came up from Pittsburg and ordered his track workers to pitch my lumber down the steep bank onto the gravelly beach. There it was, partly in the water and partly out of the water, before I was even aware of the "King's" decree. Well, my customers were in a great hurry for the lumber and I put my own team and a couple of other teams at work hauling that lumber nearly a half mile up that river beach over gravel, and rocks and up a steep bank. A team could haul about one quarter of a load at a trip, and it was fully $100 damage to me considering the breakage and extra teaming, lost time and everything. I had not time to sue the railroad company. "Tom" King had not time to lose with a law suit, and the most important of all the reasons for not suing the railroad was that I had a free pass over the road from year to year, and if I had resented "Tom's" mean action it would have, in all probability, had a bad effect on the pass. And as the pass covered the Allegheny Valley road and its branches, and I was over the road very often, I figured that it would not take a great while to "deadhead" $100 worth of transportation in my kind of business. So "Tom" King was not put in the sheriff's hands to answer for his unheard of way of doing unheard of things. I hear that "Tom" King, with a big "K," is still railroading in the western country somewhere. If he takes such liberties with some of those cowboys as he did with me he would have to "excuse himself" at the point of one of their playthings, a revolver. But what is the use of being named King if you can't be a King.

It was uphill and downhill business those days to run a lumber yard in the new Eldorado even when the hard-worked yard master could get a car on that little short side track at the Phillips House where wagons could reach it. It was no picnic to get the lumber to the yard on the other side of the river. When the teamster was lucky enough to get his team in through the crowd of teams it required two men to load the wagon, one on the railroad car and another on the wagon. Then the brakes had to be put on good and hard to get down the steep river bank and onto Fullerton & McLaughlin's chain ferry boat. Then upon reaching the Parker side of the river a steep bank had to be ascended before reaching the yard. It cost something to get lumber from that little crowded side track to the yard, the wages of two men and team and the tremendous ferry toll of Fullerton & McLaughlin on small loads. And now I will give the other side for there were two sides to the business: I bought a raft of 100,000 feet of boards from the Weston mills, three miles above Olean, N. Y., on Monday morning, paying $10 per thousand feet for it in the water. Saturday evening it was all gone at $19 per thousand feet. This was without cost to me. The oil operators would drive their teams into the water beside the raft and load their wagons from the raft. I cleared $900 on that raft in one week without touching a board. Another $900 easy transaction took place a short time after the last mentioned. A bridge was built across the river and the contractor gave me the contract of furnishing the square hard maple timber to put under the bottom of the stone piers. I gave the contract to a Springcreek mill owner at his own price and cleared about $900 without tounching a piece of this timber. This looks like making money easily. But old saying is: "Come easy, go easy." As stated heretofore in these chapters there is no trouble about the reader seeing where the "go easy" came in. All the old operators will remember the method, if there was any method in it, of doing business. It was up and down and up and down again and again and all branches of buisness were in a state of chaos until the Standard Oil Company, through marvelous management, gradually brought things in the oil country into understandable shape.

---

## CHAPTER XXXVI.

### WARREN'S BIG MEN.

At this time there comes to my mind many of the old business men of Warren, Pa. There were among the members of the bar Judge S. P. Johnson, Judge Rasselas Brown, Judge Glenni W. Scofield, Thomas Struthers, Judge L. D. Wetmore, William Parmlee, J. D. James, and Judge W. D. Brown. Of those named all are dead but the last named, who has good health and the prospect of enjoying the well earned fruits of his former efforts for many years to come. Judge Johnson was noted for his stern visage and plain talk. During his long and successful legal term he never spoke but he said something in a manner to be plainly understood. Many were offended at his plain speaking, but those who knew him best knew well that underlying his stern outward appearance was a warm and tender heart. The writer had business relations with him and was never more kindly treated. The last interview was just before the opening of the World's Fair at Chicago. I found him in the consulting room of Thomas Struther's law office, writing that philanthropist's last will and testament. It was a somewhat sad sight to meet those two substantial old lawyers trembling on the very edge of eternity, making a disposition of their very large inheritance. The judge dropped the will writing and accompanied me to the court house. On the way he, the judge, informed me that he had been at Chicago to see the "White City." He said he was well paid for his trip. Said he: "I am 84 years of age but I am in good health and active for a man of my years. I can walk nearly as nimble as ever." He then proceeded to give me an example of his nimbleness. "And," he said, "I hope to live long enough to make the second visit to the World's Fair, after those buildings are filled with the best products of the world." But, alas, for the uncertainty of all things mortal. The judge was seized with sickness and died before those buildings were filled. These old lawyers were an honor to Warren. At the time of which I write Warren and Erie counties were one congressional district. Warren furnished the member of congress for both counties for many years, Erie being left out of the race. The large county and city of Erie seemed to be content to help elect Warren county men to represent them on the floor of congress. G. W. Scofield was elected and re-elected several terms. Then Colonel L. F. Watson followed him a couple of terms, and when Erie did put forward a man and elected him, Mr. Scofield was chosen congressman-at-large. The congressman elected in Erie was C. B. Curtis, a former lawyer of Warren. Then came a genuine Erie county man, Mr. Brainard. All those named above were Republicans, but then a Democrat—Erie's pride— walked over the 4,000 Republican majority a couple of times, and represented his, the "wildcat district"—with much credit to himself and to his constituents. Colonel Scott was as smart as he was rich. He was an honor to the Democratic party, but the old saying is "the good die young," and years ago Erie's lamented citizen, W. L. Scott, passed away.

But let us return to Warren. All the old set of lawyers were full of legal lore and an honor to the legal profession. One of the recent deaths of the Warren judges was that of Hon. L. D. Wetmore. His 10 years on the bench as president judge was a pleasant term for both himself and people. He did not seem to grow old under the pressure of that responsible office, but rather appeared happy, but he, too, had to obey the call of the Great Judge of the World.

Another of the president judges was "Charlie" Noyes, as he was familiarly called by his innumerable friends. Although a Democrat, in a strong Republican county, he was elected to the high office of president judge by a good majority. Judge Noyes was a man of many parts. He was connected with all good societies and everything tending to make Warren one of the finest and best towns of its size in the country. When he died the newspapers were filled with eulogies. He was indeed missed. He was a young man at the time of his death, but was old in the knowledge of the laws of this country.

I will now make mention of the younger and at present active lawyers at the Warren county bar: These are D. I. Ball, D. U. Aired, Hon. O. C. Allen and his son, Samuel— Bordwell, W. W. Wilber, W. M. Lindsey, who has just completed a 10-year term as president judge with honor to himself and to his constituents, and Charles W. Stone and son, Ralph. C. W. Stone has filled about all the offices worth having in the state of Pennsylvania. From principal of the Warren schools he has passed through the state assembly, state senate, lieutenant governorship and three or four terms of congress. Mr. Stone stood second best of the hundreds of congressman at Washington. When "Tom" B. Reid, the then speaker of the house, was absent for a week at a time he chose the Hon. Charles W. Stone to take his place.

But let me now tell of the old, old lumbermen. There were Orris Hall, "Joe" Hall, Chapin Hall, and Judge Hall, Boon Mead, Guy Irvine, A. H. Ludlow, S. H. and S. V. Davis, James Eddy, "Zack" Eddy, Judge L. D. Wetmore, Hon. L. F. Watson, Andrew Hertzel and a host of others, who made fortunes in the lumber business, when nearly the whole county and the adjoining county of Forest were literally green with as fine pine trees as were ever found anywhere. Many of the old settlers of Warren made their fortunes by "bidding off" unseated wild land. I'll take Colonel Watson as an example. He came to Warren from Titusville when a mere boy, with 25 cents in his pocket, but full of energy, business and integrity. He commenced work in a store on a very small salary, but he, unlike many young men, saved his money. When the day came for the selling of unseated lands—unseated land means that many owners of wild land though it not worth while to pay their taxes in the wilderness of Forest and Warren counties, and let the assessors place them on the unseated list—young Watson was possessed of a keen vision and he could look into the future and use good common sense. He expected and knew that this country would grow and this isolated timber would come into the market sometime in the future. Consequently he bought large lots of this wild land. It cost but a few cents an acre and a small amount of his savings would buy large tracts of land.

I'll give a conversation that I had with Mr. Watson a few years ago in the directors' room of the Warren Savings bank. I was seated in an easy chair when Mr. Watson entered the room. After a cordial shake of my hand, and a warm hand was always extended to his friends by that genial gentleman, he said, "I have just got back from quite an extended trip over in Forest county. Yesterday I saw for the first time a thousand acre lot that I bought at tax sale 50 years ago. I paid a few cents an acre for it. It is completely covered with pine all over, except about 20 acres in one corner, and that 20 acres is covered with the best of hemlock timber. I had heard that it was a good pine lot, but there are about 8,000,-000 feet more pine than I expected." I made this remark: "The surplus, or the timber that you did not know that you owned, is worth more than your whole bank here." He said "yes."

Since the interview above mentioned all timber has raised more than one-half in price. Mr. Watson became several times a millionaire. This certain piece was one of many pieces of his early purchases of wild lands at unseated sales on the court house steps. Many other old settlers, the late Hon. L. D. Wetmore among the number, became immensely wealthy by the same fair methods. And no wonder that Warren is one of the wealthiest cities of its size to be found anywhere.

The late Hon. Henry Brace helped Mr. Watson with some of his land sales and afterwards went to California and became wealthy himself in timber and other transactions. He was buried in the Odd Fellows cemetery at Youngsville only a short time ago. Mr. Brace was at Mr. Watson's side when he (Watson) dropped dead in Washington, D. C., and like a coincidence death came to Mr. Brace at his California home instantaneously. All of the above named old time lumbermen have sent their last rafts down the Allegheny, except the last named, Andrew Hertzel, and it is to be hoped that he will live to be 100 years old to superintend the beautiful Odd Fellows' cemetery at Warren as he has managed it for the last 40 years without one dollar of cost to the society. Can Mr. Hertzel's equal in this respect be found in this or any other country? Nearly every day finds him driving "over the river" to the beautiful city of the dead, where he keeps his eyes on all the workmen and gives them friendly instructions. There is only one Andrew Hertzel. Two other gentlemen, S. V. and S. H. Davis, twin brothers, were helpers of Mr. Hertzel in his laudable work while they were busy citizens of Warren. Their twinship has ended here on this earth and has commenced again in the unknown country beyond. A word about these two that were nearly always seen together here while alive on this earth will not be amiss: They were both Democrats living in a county with 1,500 Republican majority. S. V. received the Democratic nomination for sheriff of Warren county and was elected over his Republican opponent by a majority of 85. When S. V.'s time expired his twin brother, S. H. Davis, repeated the performance of his twin brother, S. V. Davis, the only difference being that the former had a trifle more of a majority than the latter named. Those three workers for the cemetery were also three good workers in the I. O. O. F. lodge at Warren which controls the cemetery. The two last named are missed in the councils of both the lodge and cemetery.

Away back, 60 years ago, Guy Irvine was the king lumberman of the Allegheny river. He owned many sawmills, all propelled by water, and it required many mills those days of single sash, upright saws, to manufacture his dozens of "Allegheny fleets." On the pring freshet Mr. Irvine would float to Pittsburg fleet after fleet, and tie them up to both shores of the river for miles above the city. He would pay off his army of "hands," leaving one to each raft to keep it afloat as the water would recede. After each man had received his nine to twelve dollars, about the amount paid in those early days for a down the river trip, Mr. Irvine would take them to the Red Lion hotel, on the Pittsburg side of the river, or to Old Tom Gardner's hotel on the Allegheny side of the river, and treat them to a "cityfied meal." And let me say right here that no landlord ever got rich from those men's meals. After a week on the raft, subsisting on bread, meat and potatoes, prepared by some man who was taking his first lessons in cooking, those hungry up-the-river men got away with all the apple butter, apple sause, stewed peaches, stewed cherries, etc., that came before them. No newfangled side dishes were used in those early day taverns. The victuals were heaped up on single plates, and each fellow pitched in and helped himself. If the "tavern keeper" got full pay for the raw material of one of those meals—the cooking thrown in—he came off lucky. When those Pennsylvanians and New York state Yankees had more than satisfied "the inner man," a large majority of them indulged in something stronger than river water, and then would commence the foot sore march toward their homes up the Allegheny.

Those raftsmen were a lively set, both floating southward on an easy going raft or trudging northward over hard stony roads. The denizens of the scattered farms along the way generally let those raftsmen run things in their own way. And let it be said to the credit of those pioneer raftsmen, whom I have accompanied many times, that their wild deeds were few and far between.

But let me return once again to Guy Irvine. He, with all his riches, had not the enjoyment of his northern home only a small part of the summer months. He could not, as now, slip up home in a day or in a night and visit his family and back again in the same length of time, but he had to stay away a long time to sell and deliver his vast amount of lumber. And when he did get away, sometimes nearing the fall of the year, he would come home on horseback, loaded down with money. And he was bold enough to ride along through farm and woodland without a companion. One of the great wonders is that no highwayman even "interviewed" him.

A story was rife at one time that one robber stationed himself in a dense piece of woods, with a gun, and awaited the passing of Mr. Irvine. But in vain, as Mr. Irvine had happened to take another route and thereby spoiled the robber's fun.

Let us look at the great strides in the manner of doing business now, compared with 60 or 70 years ago. Instead of running the risk of being robbed, if Mr. Irvine was selling lumber now at Pittsburg, he would only have to drop his pile of money into a Pittsburg bank, take a certificate of deposit and drop it into a Warren bank when he got home, ask for a blank check book, and draw his money at his pleasure. And instead of that tiresome ride on horseback, he could step into a Pullman car and sleep until he reached his home.

I would like to speak of more of the old time business men of Warren, but to do the beautiful island town full justice I would have to write a whole book. I can, with my mind's eye, look back and see Judges Galbraith, Vincent, Johnson, Brown, Noyes, Lindsey and Wetmore. The reader, who was acquainted with those legal lights, will see that five out of the seven have presided at their last suit, Judge Vincent having only recently passed away.

---

## CHAPTER XXXVII.

## WEST VIRGINIA EXPERIENCES.

I think a few words about West Virginia will be interesting. The writer of this spent the largest part of two years in the "Mountain State," organizing insurance lodges. It was easy work to get a list of names of men and women and organize a lodge, but when it came to paying dues and assessments, in some of the 20 towns where I organized they were "not in it." I organized five lodges in Wheeling, the largest city in West Virginia. The members were always on hand at the meetings of the order, but when it came to paying their assessments and keeping their protection safe, they were not as good as the Pennsylvania people. In the way of entertainments they were the best in the world. I made an appointment with 10 lodges for a visit from the supreme president of the order. I notified each lodge of the time of his appearance. The meetings were for all members of the order and non-members. Well, those 10 meetings were 10 big picnics. They had entertainments galore. We had brass bands, mandolin clubs, quartets, duets, solos, recitations, oratory and everything that would add to the entertainment of a crowd. At Wheeling the entertainment was far in advance of anything ever witnessed before, or since, by such a "jiner" as I, and I belong to nine different secret societies. I'll not try to describe this entertainment, but I'll give a few pointers that will give the readers a chance to guess at the magnificence of the performance. The Grand opera house was the place of the meeting. The orchestra belonging to the building made splendid music. The best performers of the city gave their efforts on all parts of the varied program. The members of the order were all dressed up to their special parts in the program at great cost to themselves. In fact, this could hardly be called an amateur performance. The performers—many of them—were professionals. This is one of the "unguessable" things. To think of men and women attending so faithfully to the frivolous parts at great cost and neglecting the impotrant parts at little cost.

Let me make a little correction. I said I had organized five lodges at Wheeling. One was at Benwood and another at McMechen, but all were on the trolley lines. Of the 20 lodges organized in West Virginia, they were nearly all in oil towns. Many, in fact a majority of my members, were Pennsylvania oil men and women. The inhabitants of West Virginia are largely made up of Pennsylvania and Ohio people. The Pennsylvania people are a little more appreciated than the Ohio people. Senator Stephen B. Elkins informed me, in the town named after him, that the Pennsylvania people took much more kindly to West Virginia than the Ohio people. The former are accustomed to a mountainous country and the latter to a level country. The Senator says it makes more difference than one would suppose at first thought.

There is but one difference between the two states of Pennsylvania and West Virginia. The sidehills are very much more precipitous in West Virginia than in Pennsylvania. When I first saw Wheelng it was a black little village, not much thought of by the raftsmen who rode lazily past it from the Pennsylvania and York State lumber woods. Black coal smoke rose in several places as a nest egg to Wheeling's future greatness in the iron business of the country. Parkersburg was the next largest town on the Virginia side of the Ohio river—it was old Virginia at that time, as no division had been made. Parkersburg was a little huddle of old fashioned houses. Just make the comparison now, and then. Now it is a city of nearly 20,000 inhabitants. All the recent buildings are up-to-date— built in the latest fashion. Oil has been largely instrumental in making Parkersburg what it is today. Many of the inhabitants of the city came there full-fledged oil operators, as they generally came from the Pennsylvania oil fields up the river. I spent four months within the confines of the old-time city and found a very social and intelligent lot of cizitens. I, for the first time since railroads were built, did not ride one rod in a railroad coach in four months. I organized a lodge of over 200 members before I left the town, and, unlike Wheeling, all the insured members paid their assessments promptly each month. It was the best lodge of the 475 that I have organized within the last 32 years.

I stopped at the Palace hotel that winter, and one peculiarity of the situation was that nearly all the young couples who came across the river from the state of Ohio to be joined in wedlock put up at the Palace hotel. The proprietor of this hotel had a preacher within easy call always when one of these matrimonially inclined couples were ready to put on the yoke, and he had a standing witness in the person of your humble servant. I became regular in my attendance at weddings. The name of that landlord and my own decorated the marriage certificates of dozens of new beginners as sailors on the matrimonial sea.

I found myself in a rather noted crowd at dinner one day. There were seven Hatfields and one Brown at the table. The McCoys stopped at another hotel. The relationship did not seem exactly cordial between the two famielies, although they were both making a visit to Parkersburg at the same time. A word of explanation is due here. A great land suit was on in the United States court, then being held at Parkersburg, and the Hatfields and McCoys were there as witnesses. But they demonstrated their good sense by not mixing up the names of the two families on the same hotel register. Well, I had the honor of dining at a table full of Hatfields, with "Devil Anse" as one of the number. As they had been stopping at the "Palace" and boarding quietly with people that were not murderers, for nearly a week, we all got used to them and it was no great feat to be one of eight who was not a Hatfield, at the same table at the same time. In fact, I became somewhat intimate with the family. I was assured that if I behaved myself I would be in no danger of bodily harm. I'll give a little conversation that one of the crowd and I indulged in one evening while we sat quietly in the hotel office. I said, "People up your way say that you fellows are not a very bad lot in general." He replied, "Oh, we are not the worst men in the world, but a little fiery." I told him that I "would write them up" for the Parkersburg Journal and that I would hand him a copy of the paper. He said, "all right, I would like to have it." The next day I went to the railroad depot and just as the train moved off toward the mountain home of the Hatfields I handed him a copy of the Journal. I will explain why I held the paper until the departure of the train. I thought that if he should take offense at any part of my remarks I would rather he would take offense riding on a trian speeding way from Parkersburg than before he left the city. Now, to show plainly how we can be deceived in appearances, one of those Hatfields had every appearance of being a perfect gentleman, both in dress and actions. I said to myself there is no danger of that man ever murdering anyone. But in less than two years from that time I read an account in the papers of a man being murdered by this same quiet looking Hatfield. But time mellows all things. I have since read of the two noted families intermarrying and thereby modifying the feud between the world renowned Hatfields and McCoys.

I never in my 32 years of organizing lodges met but two editors of newspapers who refused to publish the list of officers of my newly organized lodges. The first was a Pennsylvania editor, a U. P. preacher, by the way. Secret societies were not to his liking. The other was a McCoy, of West Virginia. He was a lawyer, editor, owner of a big oil farm and a trustee of the Presbyterian church. It was not because of his religious scruples that he refused the publication of the list of officers, but he felt that it was "paid matter." He did not seem to know that editors in general are very much pleased to have items of local news of that character. Often the managers of daily papers in large cities have sent their news gatherers to the ante room of the lodge rooms with orders to stay until the list of officers could be obtained. I have had them wait two hours before the installation was finished.

The first locomotive that I saw running along a track was in the state of Ohio. I was on a lumber raft, lazily floating down the Ohio river, when we met an engine, with no coaches attached, coming up the river, on the Ohio side. It was a sight for our up-the-Allegheny river eyes, and I also actually had my first ride on steam propelled cars on the same side of that same river. After landing our Ohio fleet at Cincinnati, and staying as watchman on the raft until my employer, the late Eben G. Mead, than whom no better man ran lumber to the lower markets, sold and delivered his raft, I got into a coach and took my first railroad ride to Cleveland, O., then on a lake boat to Dunkirk, N. Y., then in a stage coach to Jamestown, N. Y., and "footed it" across the line into the Keystone State, 18 miles, to my home in Youngsville, Pa. Was not that going around the bush some, if not more?

I have mentioned the down-the-river people learning how to land a raft with a long rope. Let me just mention the beauties of this long rope business on the rafting trip just described. After we landed this big Ohio raft, I took up my abode in the raft shanty until the raft was sold. One nice warm day during the first half of the month of May, I laid my sleepy head on the straw pillow in the raft shanty and was soon in the land of dreams. The river was very high, over its banks in many places. My dreams came to an end very suddenly when four Clarion timber rafts, owned by Mr. Ford, of Ridgway, Pa., broke their cables and came down against my raft with a crash that broke my cables and sent me down towards Cincinnati. I was "monarch of all I surveyed," sailing down into the heart of the city on a very large "Ohio fleet," with no one to boss me and thousands of feet of square timber floating after me. Now comes in this long rope business. When the raft had made about two miles toward Porkopolis, I saw two men jump into a skiff and row towards me. I first thought that they intended to take me to shore. But I soon found that they had a better object in view. They rowed vigorously until they reached the side of my runaway raft. They then asked me for the privilege of landing the raft. The reader may guess that the privilege was instantly granted. They then, with my help, lifted a coil of rope, 900 feet long, one and one-half inches in diameter, and carried it onto the raft. Next one of the men took hold of one end of the rope and got into the skiff and the other rowed him to shore, and while the man with the rope took a half-hitch around a big plum tree, the other man rowed back to the raft and took a hitch on the raft snubbing post, and played out the 900 feet of rope, bringing the big raft to shore, safe and sound. I felt like the passengers who offered prayers and thanked Marconi when the big vessel went down recently, when the wireless telegraphy saved 1.650 lives. These two men will always have my best wishes. Their act, the next day, when Mr. Mead called to pay them for the job, proved them to be fair minded indeed. Their charge was only $10. Mr. Mead expected to pay about $100, as their work saved him over $1,000. If not for getting that raft landed above Cincinnati, where it was sold, it would have gone below the city, and would have been sold for a much less price than it was already sold for at Cincinnati. Mr. Ford's timber went on below the city and he afterwards informed me that he lost $6,000 by the breaking of his ropes. His rafts were towed ashore by tugboats after they had passed the city, where they were sold.

This rafting was a peculiar business. One instance is worth mentioning on this trip. On the Ohio river we ran night and day. Not so on the Allegheny river. There were too many islands and bars and crooks. It required daylight to navigate it safely. Sometimes when the water was falling or when a pilot failed to make a landing in a safe eddy he was obliged to run all night and it was remarkable the small number of mishaps that did take place. When we take into consideration the large number of rafts that passed Oil City every rise of the water it fills one with wonder that so few rafts were wrecked. Why, the old inhabitants of Oil City can recollect the time that they could stand on the bank of the river all day and never be out of sight of rafts either opposite or up or down the stream.

The description in the Derrick recently of the lights of Oil City at night reminded me of the Pan-American show at Buffalo a few years ago. And it also reminded me of Oil City many years ago. Then, instead of the glorious blaze of light of the present, about all that could be seen in the way of illumination was a tin lantern, with holes cut in the sides, and a "tallow dip" standing in the bottom. There was but little difference between those old fashioned lanterns and a common sized lightning bug. Why, did you ever think that we are 2,000 years behind the times? The Bible tells us that in A. D. 70, Antioch had street lamps, water running in the streets and into the houses. Once or twice Oil City has had water running in the streets and into the houses, too, and Antioch was not "in it" in regard to fire, but Oil City was "in it" to a sorrowful degree. Many of the older citizens and some younger ones will agree with me in this. It is to be hoped that the fire fiend will never again make such disastrous visits as it has done when that beautiful city was first springing into its wonderful growth.

The Derrick recently spoke of John Haliday being a pioneer in the ferry business in Oil City. My next door neighbor is John Haliday's son, Thomas, and he is a "chip of the old block," interested at present in the oil business between Oil City and Pleasantville.

Speaking of Pleasantville, reminds me of a little lumber transaction when things were running wild. Very late in the fall of that exciting year, when Plumer was the terminus of the only railroad in sight of Oil City, I landed a raft of hemlock derrick lumber at Oleopolis, or at the mouth of Pithole creek. I sold the raft to a New York City man who was operating quite extensively in the rather prolific Plumer oil territory. This man gave me $15 per thousand feet for this lumber. He drew a part of it for his own use and sold part of it to other parties for $60 per thousand feet, and nearly half of it floated off down the river in the great flood of 1865. I was the only man who did not lose on that raft, and taking out the cost of one day's run, I made one-third on my investment. I mention this to show the uncertainties of the lumber business, as well as the oil business. And while talking of lumber, let me make the remark that something like dreariness comes over me when my mind wanders back to rafting times, when water floated the lumber to market instead of steam pulling it on wheels. The beautiful green pines have been cut down and are gone, and nearly all the sturdy axe-men who cut the trees have been overtaken by Old Time and cut down as ruthlessly as were the thrifty green trees. The places that knew them both will know them no more forever. But in time the places of trees will be filled with a new growth of flourishing trees and the work of these pioneers—good men and true—will live long after them.

## *CHAPTER XXXVIII.*

## RAMBLING RECOLLECTIONS OF THE LAST FIFTY YEARS IN THE OIL AND LUMBER COUNTRY.

(Published in the Oil and Gas Man's Magazine in 1909.)

I have been requested by my friend, C. R. Wattson, of Butler, Pa., Secy-Treas. of the Oil Men's Association of Western Pennslyvania, to write an article for this issue of the "Oil and Gas Man's Magazine." I take up the task willingly but hardly know where to begin. A flood of incidents lie calmly on the surface of the sea of 50 years' memory. To cull the best out of the lot is something of a task—but I have no misgivings about the interest the readers will take in it, if well culled. To show the extent of the field of knowledge I will say: I saw the old Drake Well, or first well, putting out its second day's production. Strangers and residents of the then litttle village of Titusville were standing around so thick that to get near the great American wonder required both strength and skill.

Every onlooker was surprised to see pure grease, covered with white heavy froth, pouring so abundantly from sixty-nine feet below the surface of mother earth. People from all around the country farms and towns were equally astonished at nature's new departure. Visitors were present from all the great cities of the nation. New York, Chicago, Philadelphia and Boston were well represented. They all were of the same opinion relative as to how so much oil was to be utilized. Up to that time the little that had been gathered along Oil Creek by soaking it into blankets had been sold in the crude state as a panacea for all the ills that poor human nature is heir to. The query, therefore, with everybody was, what will be done with this heavy production of oil ? No one thought of using it as an illuminant. The question was left to be answered by John D. Rockefeller and his coterie of intelligent and energetic helpers. Just stop and think a moment, dear reader. The man that was at the head of the greatest of the world's discoveries, namely, petroleum and its by-products, is one of the best abused men in this country. Little did Mr. Rockefeller think when he was racking his young brain for the everlasting benefit of the oil business that he was bringing down on his devoted head more abuse than any other man ever carried in these United States. I mean misplaced abuse. It was ever thus for greatness and success to receive its reward by the historical pen of future writers after the Tarbells and the like have passed into oblivion, and there is no doubt Mr. Rockefeller will get justice in the pages of history yet to be written.

But let me leave this Drake well in its present loneliness (it has nothing to mark the spot at present, but thanks to the good and enterprising ladies of the oil country, this will soon be remedied) and take a look at the Williams well on the John Watson farm, a mile north of the Drake well—here was the pioneer spouter. It was my good fortune to see this well two days after it was drilled in. The oil went skyward to a great height and the first flowing well was doing business with great energy. This well was planned and put down by Mr. D. M. Williams, the then leading dry goods merchant of Warren, Pa.

Although Mr. Williams was the moving spirit in putting down the first flowing oil well of the thousands that followed, for some reason he vanished from the oil business and died with "nary" a well. This Williams well, although the wonder of the world, as regards gas, did not cause the commotion that the Drake well did—for the reason that the Drake well uncovered the fact that large deposits of heretofore unthought-of wealth underlaid this country. The Williams well only demonstrated the fact that said wealth could be boosted out of mother earth by a hitherto unseen power, called natural gas. By direction of Divine Providence, Titusville had the first pumping oil well and also the first flowing oil well. The inhabitants of the "Queen City" are justly proud of this. California, Illinois, Oklahoma, Kansas, Texas, Mexico and Indian Territory must take a back seat at the discovery business, as many slow moving years passed after Titusville pointed the way before these now prolific states knew that they were in it.

Shortly after the Williams well began to spout oil I did my first and only work on an oil well. It was helping John Duncan, of East Titusville, "kick" at a well on Pine creek. We used a spring pole, and did not make a very long hole in a day's "kicking." I left John at the end of six weeks, satisfied to abandon the drilling business with a spring pole. Medical authorities say the exercise of the lower limbs is healthful. I did not quit because I disagreed with said medical authorities but I thought I would rather take their word for it than to prove it by prolonging my "kicking" job. Duncan filled my place with another "kicker" and soon got a fair producer. But even then it would have been hard to convince the average settler on Pine creek, at that time, that the oil belt ran up the creek as far as Grand Valley and beyond. It was left for the years to prove that Pine creek was oil territory from the Drake well to the Summit on the D., A. V. & P. railroad. As a matter of fact, the drill is the only way to test the location of petroleum.

Among the many old-time lumbermen of this country was John McKinney, uncle to John L. and J. C. McKinney, two of Titusville's wealthy and leading citizens. His father, also named John, was one of the first settlers of the Brokenstraw valley. John McKinney, Sr., had a family of seven sons and one daughter. The old gentleman had a good farm for each, but his son John outdid all his brothers in adding to his fortune. He was a fixture each early spring in the Pittsburg lumber market. Mills were strung along the Brokenstraw creek, every place that high banks were found, and many places where the banks were not high enough, artificial banks were thrown up to make a head race and tail race, as they were called. The mills beginning at the mouth of the creek were owned by Dr. William A. Irvine, William Freese, Judge William Siggins, John Mead, John Garner, James McKinney, father of the Titusville men mentioned above; A. H. Ludow & Co., Eben Mead, Wm. White, John McKinney, (the first mentioned), Robert Andrews, William Cotter, Daniel Horn, Dr. W. A. Irvine, Daniel Donaldson, William Demming, E. Hyde, Ogden Demming, John Walton, and here the creek crosses the state line and I don't know the Yankees' names that owned the mills on the creek over on the "York State" side. Those water mills would run nearly the year around and in the early spring when the melted snow raised the creek to a rafting stage, the Brokenstraw creek would get a move on it. All day long the board rafts were pulling out from the many mills and crowding each other around the crooked bends of the creek. Many times they would crush together and pile up, completely blocking the navigation until the swift moving water would force a passage through. The men that pulled the oars and piloted the rafts were skilled in that work. A

large majority of them were born and reared about those sawmills and were real water ducks. They were right in their
element, when manipulating those raft oars. The writer
prided himself on his skill as a creek pilot and always got his
raft through to the down river markets without mishap. For
years upon years he enjoyed himself hugely floating rafts out
of Brokenstraw creek, and after the creek pieces were coupled
together into the Allegheny fleets bossing the men at the oars
from Irvineton to Cincinnati and still further down the Ohio.
This rafting business was only a part of the floating done on
the Allegheny river. The iron business came in for a share of
the trade of this country at that time. Iron furnaces were
numerous and the man that was not interested in pig iron in
some manner was considered a back number. Making pig
iron along the Allegheny river and running it to Pitttsburg in
flat boats was generally considered among the money making
pursuits of life. A man that had not a pig metal furnace of
a few tons capacity was looked upon as a man of not much
consequence from a business standpoint. Those old pioneers,
while pecking away at this laborious business, had never an
idea that they were working above a sea of oil that would lay
in the shade their iron ore, and not only outstrip their business,
but bury it in everlasting forgetfulness. When a man gets
after oil and gas it is good bye to pig iron. And let me here
remark "where in this world will be found a more favored
set of men than the Western Pennsylvania farmers?" In
some single counties is found iron, coal, oil, gas, limestone,
salt, rich soil, good timber, in fact nearly everything that mankind needs in this vain world of ours. A farmer doesn't need
to go away from home to provide for his family, everything
is right on his farm. Where—oh, where can its equal be
found?—echo answers, where? No need of a young man taking Horace Greeley's oft quoted advice "to go west and grow
up with the country." Many a young man has grown up with
this oil country since good old Mr. Greeley gave his advice
and has nothing to regret at staying at home, and the end is
not yet. Human nature, however, is never satisfied. Many
young men have gone west since the advent of the Drake well,
and some of them have come back to this country that flows
with milk and honey and some have grown up with the western
country in poverty; of course, some have struck it rich, as they

11

would probably have done in any other country. I said a farmer had everything on his farm. I'll take it back—I have not discovered or heard of gold, silver or diamonds being found on Western Pennsylvania farms, but would not be surprised to see or hear of their discovery before I die. Perhaps some, if not all, of these metals will, ere many years, bob up in the face of these aforesaid farmers while peacefully harvest-ing their buckwheat crops. The reader may think me too optimistic, but listen, more strange things have happened to the honest farmer in the striking of oil and gas than the discovery of the last three wealth producers mentioned above.

As a stimulus to young men just starting out in life "on their own hook" I wish to hold up an example in the person of Hon. J. B. White, a former resident of Youngsville, but now of Kansas City, Mo., and Bemus Point, N. Y., the latter being his summer home.

Mr. White was born and reared in Watts Flats, Chautau-qua county, N. Y. When but eighteen years of age he came to Stillson Hill, five miles from Youngsville, and taught school in that district one term. He then bought a pine timber farm and took up his residence in Youngsville, which turned out in years afterward to have been a good move for the town. He commenced lumbering from his pine tract and the business had a peculiar charm for him. After he had cut the timber from his Stillson Hill farm he transferred his lumber business to Tidioute. With the advent of Parkers Landing as the center of oil operations, Mr. White began business at that point. He prospered so well that the eagle eyes of the million-aire Grandins alighted on him and prevailed upon him to go to Missouri and buy yellow pine timber, by the tens of thous-ands of acres. The Grandins and the late lamented Hunters, and Capt. H. H. Cumings paid White a liberal salary and gave him a sixth interest in the business for his services. White was as full of energy as an egg is full of meat and he proved to be the very man to carry the deal to a successful issue. After making piles of money for the company and finding himself owner of fourteen lumber yards in as many states and owner of vast amounts of long leaf yellow pine in Louisiana and other southern states, and a fine Chautauqua Lake property with unlimited means, Mr. White did not lie down "on flowery beds of ease" while doing this work, but while attending to the superabundance of work in building and putting in order a very large lumber town (Grandin, Mo.), he traveled over all the southern states adding to the holdings of the company in the way of the best long leaf yellow pine found anywhere in the south. The lucky part of this whole business is that this immensely valuable timber was bought before the wonderful upward jump in the price of lumber. Another most favorable point is that at the rate the lumber of this country is being cut there will be no decrease in price no matter what the tariff tinkers do in the matter of rates.

The benefit resulting from the young school master from Stillson Hill selecting Youngsville as his home at the close of the first school will now appear. After Mr. White became a citizen of Kansas City his oldest son, John Franklin White, M. D., received his diploma and became a prominent physician. He accidentally shot himself, dying within three weeks. Before his death his father promised that he would build a memorial high school building to his memory in Youngsville. This promise was made good last year, the school board receiving from Mr. White's hands a $25,000 building. The building has all the latest conveniences that go to make up a first-class building of this character. It stands between another memorial building, erected by the estate of the late J. T. Currie, and the old four-story high school building. The Currie building, is an industrial school. It is supplied with all kinds of tools, suitable for learning the different trades to boys and girls.

Mr. White is a strong believer in educating the fingers as well as the mind, and years ago induced Mr. Currie to leave money at his death to perpetuate his memory in this manner. Mr. White is, therefore, credited with two of Youngsville's fine educational buildings. Mr. White says, "as I have a father, mother, two sons and wife buried in the beautiful I. O. O. F. cemetery in Youngsville, it is only natural when I quit active business I will move to Youngsville and spend my declining years there." Mr. White has a warm side towards Warren county, as it sent him to Harrisburg to help make the laws for the great state of Pennsylvania when he was a mere boy. He is not the man to forget past favors even if many years have intervened.

Our postmaster, Clyde Wright, says his father put down an oil well at Tidioute 41 years ago that is at the present day producing a half barrel of oil a day. We have a well in Youngsville that was drilled by A. McKinney and John Black 22 years ago and is now flowing a half barrel a day. So the operators of the present time may not feel discouraged if they don't strike gushers every time. Small wells will produce longer than larger ones. At the rate some wells start off Lake Erie could not supply them forever and forever. Besides a little slow well will run on for years and years, until petroleum gets scarce and rises in price. My good friends and operators, don't get in a hurry—take it cool. The oil business will not down.

---

## CHAPTER XXXIX.

### INTERESTING LETTERS TO THE AUTHOR.

When I wrote the preceding chapter of "Old Times in Oildom" I thought I had finished. But since the publication of the first of the articles in the "Derrick" I have received many letters from the readers of that paper, a few of which I would like to have printed. One is from a brother of the late Charles Dinsmoor, Esq., of Warren, and who is now an expert botanist, of St. Marys, W. Va. The letter explains itself. It does more than explain itself. It gives a little insight into the size of my feet that might otherwise have remained a secret, so far as those who never saw me are concerned:

St. Marys, W. Va., June 29, 1909.

Hon. G. W. Brown, Youngsville, Pa.

Dear Sir:—Your "Old Times in Oildom," now running in the Oil City Semi-Weekly Derrick, is most intensely interesting to me. It is barely possible that you can remember me. I was "head" sawyer at Tiona and cut lots of tank plank for you along about 1871, '72 and '73, and remember you quite distinctly. You frequently gave me directions of the kind you wanted. You were then quite grey, somewhat stooping and had feet nearly as large or larger than President Lincoln's. One instance I can recall. You were standing near the "edger" in a slightly dangerous place. I motioned to a young fellow of Irish extraction, directing him to have you stand in another place, as you might get injured. He replied, "Be jabbers, he is long enough for this world," meaning that you were very "tall timber," as we domoinated six-footers I regret not having had the pleasure of "hoeing it down" after your "scraping" the "fiddle" and keeping time with your No. 10s.

Many pleasures have come my way in the last half hundred years; none that surpassed the old-time dances of the mill and woods men and women of "Old Lang Syne." As you recalled the names of leading lumbermen of Warren county, a sweet, sad remembrance stole over me that I can scarcely shake off yet. I was personally acquainted with nearly every one of them. Guess I did my share in tearing up the noble wilderness that once covered so much of Warren county; perhaps sawed as many logs as any young man of that period; every piece that went into Pleasant bridge at Warren in '72; also the timber in Dunkirk, Warren & Pittsburg railroad; hundreds of walking beams; also stuff that went as far as Boston. Came near being a resident of Youngsville, with L. B. Wood, but commenced to roam; have since spent 20 years in the west; have taken the Derrick for 25 years at least; have had, and still have splendid health; am on "Easy street;" have fine children. Was born on the very summit of Quaker hill, 1,900 feet above the Allegheny river; was the youngest of 15 children—one only settled in Warren, Charles Dinsmoor, all having crossed over except three. Am now living one and a quarter miles from the Ohio river, 550 feet above the same. On my next visit to Warren county will make it a point to see Youngsville and the "15 miles of sidewalk." Should you come down in Ohio be sure to stop at St. Marys. You will have no trouble in finding Dinsmoors in plenty.

Sincerely younrs,

G. W. Dinsmoor.

Another letter from the secretary and treasurer of the Oil Men's Association of Western Pennsylvania is as follows:

Butler, Pa., April 16, 1909.

Mr. G. W. Brown,
 Youngsville, Pa.

Dear Sir:—I have been reading your reminiscences in the "Derrick" with interest. These old stories bring up memories of the past and are worthy of being preserved.

The Oil Men's Association meets this year at Conneaut Lake, August 5th, and would be glad to entertain you there for a couple of days.

I don't know whether you recall me or not, but I remember meeting you here several years ago, and like yourself, I have been on the Derrick staff for a decade or more,
 I remain, with best wishes,
                    Yours respectfully,
                         C. R. Wattson.
 The Oil Men's Association of Western Pennsylvania.


Another letter is as follows:

Butler, Pa., May 8, 1909.

Hon. G. W. Brown,    -
 Youngsville, Pa.

Dear Sir:—It is these reminiscences that the oil people like to go over again.

Will you kindly send me a photo of yourself? Thanking you for your kindness in this matter and with best wishes, I am,
                    Sincerely yours,
                         C. R. Wattson.
 National Transit Company, United Pipe Lines Division.

## GENERAL CHARLES MILLER.

This portrait represents a gentleman from Franklin, Pa., who is a power unto himself and all that he comes in contact with. It is beyond the power of my pen to describe him—a book the size of this would not be large enough to do him justice. There is but one Gen. Charles Miller. He is a gentleman of so many parts that it is impossible to describe all, and it seems unfair to leave off any, when all are equally interesting. It is a real puzzle to the writer and everbody else how any man can handle the vast amount of fiancial business, social matters, church matters, military matters and other matters relating to a busy life, and act in each capacity as if he has nothing else on his mind. For instance, how does the General find time with his multiplicity of business of many kinds on hand, to commit to memory every hymn in his Sunday school singing book? The writer of this has had the extreme pleasure of atteding his unequalled Sunday School many times, and never saw him look at his book while leading his thousand singers. If a stranger attends Sunday School at the First Baptist church, Franklin, Pa., at 3 :00 p. m., any Sunday, when the General is not out of town (and the strangers names are legion that embrace the opportunity of seeing and hearing the General in his role of Sunday School superintendent) he would be led to think that the General had been occupied all the past week in preparing the program and had no business matters on his mind. His immense oil business, railroad business, manufacturing establishments and military business must be merely playthings to him, as it seem to be enough to fill any man's head to do the church work that Mr. Miller does with the expenditure of about $600,000 on one church in the beautiful little city of

Franklin, Pa., alone, not to mention his open hand to all calls from numerous other churches. When General Miller presents himself for admission at St. Peter's gate, the keeper of the gate will not be obliged to count pennies to ascertain whether he has won a seat in Heavenly mansions by a close financial shave. "God loves a cheerful giver," and if any man or woman can take comfort in this Bible promise in this part of God's universe, it is General Charles Miller of Franklin, Pa.

---

## HON. O. C. ALLEN.

This portrait shows the face of one of the leading lights in the legal line in Warren county.

Mr. Allen was born on a backwoods farm in Pinegrove township Warren county, Pa. He was a good farmer boy, but early imbibed a desire for a knowledge of the law. He belonged to a law loving family, Samuel, Harrison, George, brothers, all were admitted to the Warren bar (the first two named have long since passed over the divide where God's law is supreme, and where no legal discussions arise). George went toward the setting sun many years ago, and has honored the judicial bench of some western town, by his being chosen to decide question of law for his newly made neighbors. Of the quartette of Allen lawyers, only ex-state senator Hon. O. C. Allen, pleads at the Warren county bar, and let me say right here that his natural eloquence is not excelled in this neck- o'-woods." Senator Allen has a large and growing clientage, and as Warren does not lack for "limbs of the law" the senator does well to stay at the head of the flock. As I have said before in this book, Warren has furnished more good judicial timber than any town of its size in Western Pennsylvania, and has held its own up to the present time. Senator Allen has held many important officers, borough, county and state, and one of the most important which he has held for many years is a trustee of the North Warren Insane Asylum, where his good judgment has been a boon to the management and inmates.

## JOHN L. McKINNEY.

The cut here is the shadow of one of the best business managers in the oil country, beginning to operate in oil in the earliest stages, when the spring pole done duty in the drilling line. He was one of the "A B C" scholars. He commenced by putting a few hunred dollars in a well and following said few hundred dollars with faithful and muscular "kicking"—

kicking at a spring pole was the only power used in reaching the greasy fluid when John, in his teens, commenced the oil business, and being a boy "man grown," both his muscle and disposition went in harmony towards a good solid day's work. He met with losses at first that would discourage any but the earnest, in an unknown business. When he commenced to lay the foundation for his fabulous fortune, he met with many discouring circumstances. The fortune did not push itself upon him, it required an indomitable will on his part to climb to the financial heights to which he has attained. He comes from solid stock. In 1792 John McKinney, (John L.'s grandfather) came from Belfast, Ireland, and settled at Philadelphia, Pa., then came to Irvineton with a party of surveyors, pre-empted the broad, wild river flats there. Then learned that Gen. John W. Irvine held a claim ahead of him. He then relinquished his claim on the banks of the Allegheny river, and came to Youngsville and got a claim on nearly all the land in sight. Mr. McKinney then returned to Reading, Pa., and married Miss Rebecka Arthur, and brought her into the wilderness. Shortly after the couple were settled in their log cabin, a Scotchman came and boarded with them, named Matthew Young. He soon made himself so useful in the embryo town, that Mr. McKinney consented to the town being named Youngsville instead of McKinneyville. Eight sons and one daughter was born to Mr. McKinney and his wife. The eight sons and one daughter are all dead. Two of the sons never married. Four sons and the daughter have each but one living representative, at present. Two sons, Arthur and James, have fair sized families (the latter named, James, being the father of the well known oil men, John L. and J. C. McKinney, of Titusville). The two named in brackets, have very recently (a couple of months ago) placed an eight ton monument on the cemetery lot containing the remains of their grandparents, named above, in Odd Fellow's cemetery, Youngsville. The monument is of Barre granite and of beautiful design. The good man, Mr. McKinney, sent money to Ireland and brought his two brothers to this country and presented each one with a farm and sawmill. He also presented a farm to each of his eight sons, and to his only daughter. The reader of this can see from this statement that the McKinneys have done their share of business in the commercial world and made a wilderness "blossom as the rose."

## HON. CHAS. W. STONE.

Hon. Charles W. Stone, M. C., four terms, was in reality the second best member of the United States congress. When "Tom" Reed was speaker of the house and was obliged to vacate the chair Mr. Stone was his choice as his substitute, and had the high honor of filling Mr. Reed's place a week at a time. This is something for the wildcat district to be proud of. Mr. Stone has the qualfications of a first-class business man, in addition to his high statesmanship. During the last six months he has made two trips to Mexico, and has purchased immense tracts of timber lands which is an investment not loaded down with uncertainties.

Lawyer, ex-congressman; born in 1843; among his ancestors there were revolutionary blue-coats, intermarried with the families of Prescott and Greene. He was educated at Lawrence Academy and Williams College, earning his way by teaching and other work, graduating with honor. He accepted a position as principal of the Union school at Warren, was elected county superintendent of schools in 1865, and later in the same year was chosen principal of the academy at Erie. He took up the study of law, was admitted to practice in the courts of Warren county in 1866, and entered into partnership with Judge Rasselas Brown; served three years in the borough council, nine years on the board of school directors, and the last three years as its president. In 1869 he was elected to the legislature from the counties of Warren and Venango, and was re-elected without opposition. In 1876 he was state senator, and served as chairman of the General Judiciary Committee, and in 1878 he was elected lieutenant governor. Mr. Stone was one of the three commissioners in 1883 who located the United States public building at Erie, and later was a representative of Pennsylvania at the Inter-state Extradition Conference, called by the governors of the several states; subsequently he was a delegate from Pennsylvania to the Prison Congress, over which ex-president Hays presided. In 1877 he was appointed by Governor Beaver to be Secretary of the Commonwealth, and served until his election to congress from the twenty-seventh district in 1890; and he was four times re-elected by large majorities. During two of the terms of his service in congress he was the efficient chairman of the committee on coinage, weights and measures. In 1890 he was a candidate before the Republican convention for the nomination for governor and received one hundred and sixty-five votes, one hundred and eighty-three being necessary to nominate. Address: Warren, Pennslyvania.

---

### HON. W. M. LINDSEY.

This photo shows the face of another of the self-made men of Warren county. He was born and raised on a farm, like the majority of the legal lights of Warren, but left agricultural pursuits and studied law and joined issue with that strong minded lawyer, Hon. S. P. Johnson, and for many years worked in harness with Mr. Johnson and when the latter named died, was chosen to fill the chiar recently vacated after a ten years service by his long-time partner. The Hon. W. M. Lindsey has just finished his ten year service as president judge of this district and leaves without a blemish on the judical ermine. Although entirely competent to fill any office in the gift of the people, Mr. Lindsey has refused to mix in politics very deep, preferring to give his rich talents undividedly to the laws of his country. The ex-judge is comparatively a young man yet, and no doubt he will be one of our law-makers before he quits this mundane sphere. He is fitted for a politician in many respects, the one best respect is geniality. It is his nature to be social, the best hold of a politician.

## C. N. PAYNE.

The man whose photograph is seen here is one of the many self-made men of the oil region. He pitched into the oil business when a boy and took hold of it just as though he had served an apprenticeship at the business. At the time of his leaving his father's farm, the oil business was an untried proposition. There were no precedents to follow and nobody had learned the business for the reason that it had never been a business. It had to be worked up to a point where it could be called a business. Nobody could impart knowledge to anybody else. All men stood on an equality, each could guess as close as the other, but all were not good guessers. C. N. Payne was one of the "cut and try" good guessers, he had a way of his own and his way was crowned with success from the beginning. Much pluck, good sense and good management put him to the front and he is now one of the valuable advisors of the greatest business aggregation in the world today. Mr. Payne owns three automobiles and his son-in-law owns one, four housed in the same garage. His dwelling house in Titusville, shows signs of opulence on the part of its owner that are unmistakable. His high standing in the oleaginous world has not unhinged "Cal's" mind in the direction of geniality. He don't let his immense business spoil him socially. He can make an old acquaintance feel as much at home in conversation as before he climed the oily ladder.

## HON. FRANK M. KNAPP.

Frank M. Knapp, of Warren, Pa., was born in the township of Farmington, Warren county, Pa., June 29, 1851. His early life was spent on his father's farm, where during the summer, he did such work as is required of those engaged in this occupation, and during the winter months he attended the district school. At the age of 18 and for several years thereafter he followed the occupation of a "school teacher" during the winter and attended the Jamestown Collegiate Institute and the Edinboro State Normal during the fall months. In 1873 he entered the law office of Johnson & Lindsey as a student and in 1875 was admitted to the Warren county bar. He followed the law profession until 1880, when his Republican friends elected him county treasurer. At the expiration of his term in 1883 he entered actively general manufacturing, production of oil and gas and general business. From 1898 to 1904 he held the office of prothonotary and clerk of courts of Warren county. He was twice elected chairman of the Republican party of his county.

At the present time Mr. Knapp is the president of the Jacobson Machine Manufacturing Co., the treasurer and vice president of the Warren Table Works, the secretary of the Allegheny Foundry Co., and secretary and treasurer of several large carbon companies operating in West Virginia.

He is a member of the First M. E. church of Warren, Pa.

In politics he has always been a true and loyal supporter of the principles of the Republican party. His first presidential vote was cast for General Grant and his last for William H. Taft.

Mr. Knapp in addition to his law business takes a hand in the business of building up the city of Warren. He is pres-

ident of the Glade Oil Refinery, treasurer of the Jacobson
manufactory, half owner of the latest big brick block built in
Warren, on a corner near the New Struthers hotel, and lives
in and owns a dwelling house that shows opulence on the part
of the owner. Taken all in all he is a good man for the up-
building of his home town.

## CAPT. H. H. CUMINGS.

Captain H. H. Cum-
ings was born in Mon-
mouth, Illinois, but spent
his youth and early man-
hood in Madison, Ohio.
He graduated in 1862
from Oberlin college and
immediately entered the
Union army—served un-
til the end of the war—
was captain of the 105th
Ohio Volunteer Infantry.
In September 1865 he
came to the Pennsylvania
oil regions, and was located in June 1866 at Tidioute, Pa., engaged in buying and shipping crude oil and operating an oil
refinery, as a member of Day & Co. Late in the year 1873
he formed a partnership with Jahu Hunter, of Tidioute, in
operating for oil the fourth sand or "cross belt" in Butler
and Armstrong counties, Pennsylvania, successfully for many
years, and is still owning oil wells in these counties, also in
the Bradford district and recently in Oklahoma, since 1880
to the present time. He is considerably interested in lumbering in Missouri and for the past few years in Louisiana. At
one time he was interested in lands in the Red River Valley
in North Dakota. The captain represented the Warren and
Venango districts in the senate of Pennsylvania for eight
years, 1899 to 1906.

Such men as Captain Cumings are an honor to Warren county and the state of Pennsylvania, as a helper in making laws for the Keystone State he has no superiors and but few equals. Oh, for more Cumings as law makers for the great state of Pennsylvania and the nation.

---

### HON. J. C. McKINNEY.

This portrait is a good reminder of a former mayor of Titusville, and one of the upbuilders of the Queen City. He was born near Youngsville, before oil was discovered in this country. He was a faithful helper to his father, James McKinney, who owned and run a sawmill a couple of miles up the Brokenstraw creek, above the town of Youngsville. The rich soil of the Brokenstraw valley was drawn upon in the summer time to bolster up the lumber business in the winter time. The mill was always run when the water was at a good stage, or not frozen to thick ice.

The ancestral history of Hon. J. C. McKinney, will be found in the souvenir number of the evening Titusville Courier, for 1906, and also in the biography of an older brother, Hon. John L. McKinney, in the "History of Petroleum," written by J. T. Henry, in 1873.

Hon. J. C. McKinney, like his brother, John L., pitched into the oil business on his own account when but a boy, and prosecuted the work with wisdom and vigor for five years, being unusually successful in several fields. He then went into partnership with his brother, John L., and has remained a partner up to the present, about 39 years. It is doubtful if a like history can be found in the archives of oil country history.

## HON. R. E. DICKINSON.

He whose picture adorns this page of "Old Times in Oildom" is the present mayor of Titusville, the city and birthplace of Seneca oil. He also enjoys the distinction of acting as confidential secretary to the millionaire, Hon. John L. McKinney, for the last 15 years. As a sign of good standing in his adopted home he was elected as a Democrat mayor in a city which is largely Republican. The Hon. Mr. Dickinson is the youngest mayor that ever occupied the executive chair in Titusville. He was elected in February, 1908. He is qualified for any position that the far famed city of Titusville may put upon him. He is the son of Augustus Warren and Clara Olney Dickinson. Born in Butler county, Pa., July 30th, 1877. Was graduated from Titusville high school in 1895, and then secured a position with the South Penn Oil Company and has been associated with Hon. John L. McKinney and Hon. J. C. McKinney, vice president and general manager, respectively, of said company, ever since.

Mr. Dickinson was married April 17, 1901, to Miss Mary Theobold, daughter of Mr. and Mrs. Peter Theobold, who was a pioneer in the oil refining business, being president of the Independent Refining Company, of Oil City, Pa. Hon. R. E. Dickinson is in the prime of life and no doubt but his past success will cling to him for many, many years to come. His host of friends all hope so and he will not be likely to disappoint them.

## A. J. HAZELTINE.

This portrait represents one of the best bankers in the state of Pennsylvania. Below will be found a brief history of his rise to a self-made man.

Born on the Hazeltine homestead in Chautauqua county, New York, in 1847. Educated in the common schools. Began business life in a country store and was partner in business at the age of 18.

Was deputy clerk of the board of supervisors of Chautauqua county in 1869, but came to Warren, November 10, 1869, as bookkeeper for the Piso Company. Was chosen bookkeeper of the First National Bank, in March, 1870, and teller of the same bank in September, 1870. He was elected cashier of the Warren Savings bank February 1, 1872, president of the same on the death of the former president, Col. Watson, in November, 1889. Is still president of the bank. Has been on the United States Assay commission, treasurer of Pennsylvania Bankers Association and on legislative committee of the association which drafts the new law as to reserve of state banks.

His son, Dr. Harold Dexter Hazeltine, is now professor in English law at Cambridge University, England.

## HON. J. B. WHITE.

The picture that this represents is familiar in more than half the States that make up this most glorious country, Hon. J. B. White is the best known and the most popular lumber dealer in the United States. He was born in Chautauqua county, N. Y., December 8th, 1847, son of John and Rebekah Barber White. He received a public school and academy education in the Empire State; taught school in Warren county, Pa., two winters, and one winter in Chautauqua county, N. Y., and when yet in his teens, crossed over the line into Pennsylvania and began the lumber business, which has increased with gaint strides, until he today is one of the best known men in the business, owning a majority of the capital stock in seventeen lumber yards in different states. He has interests in over five hundred thousand acres of timber lands mostly in the Louisiana yellow pine region.

He married Miss Arabell Bowen, of Chautauqua county, N. Y., in 1874 (now deceased), and his second marriage was with Miss Emma Siggins, of Youngsville, Pa., December 6th, 1882. He taught school winters 1866-9. He was engaged in lumber manufacturing at Youngsville, Pa., and East Brady Pa., as a member of the firm of White and Kinnear until 1874. He was a founder of the Warren County News (weekly) in 1874, and later sole proprietor. He was a member of the committee of seven elected by the Pennsylvania legislature in 1879 to prosecute bribery cases. He was president of the board of education, Youngsville, 1877-9, 1880-3.

Mr. White moved to Missouri in 1879. He is president of the Missouri Lumber & Mining Company, Louisiana Central Lumber Company, Forest Lumber Company, Reynolds Land Company, Salem, Winona & Southern Railroad Company,

Ouachita & Northwestern Railroad Company, vice president
of the Grandin-Coast Lumber Company (Kansas City and
Seattle), director and secretary of the Louisiana Long Leaf
Lumber Company; secretary, treasurer and general manager
of the Missouri Lumber & Land Exchange Company; director
of the New England National Bank (Kansas City) ; president
of Bank of Poplar Bluff 1886-1907; member Pennsylvania
House of Representatives 1878-1879; postmaster Gradin, Missouri, 1887-1892; appointed by President Roosevelt November, 1905 as his personal representative to investigate affairs
on Cass Lake, Minn., Indian reservation, as to whether the
reservation should be opened up in part for settlement; appointed by President Roosevelt in 1907 as member of Forestry
Commisison; appointed by Governor of Missouri in 1909 as
member of the State Forestry board; delegate to the first
National Conservation Congress, Seattle, Wash., 1909; delegate to Southern Conservation Congress, New Orleans, 1909;
member of executive committtee of National Conservation
Association; chairman of executive committee of National
Conservation Congress since its organization.   He organized
the first lumber manufacturers' association in the Southern
States in 1882, called the Yellow Pine Manufacturers' Association, and was its first president, serving for three years;
director Y. P. M. A.; member of board of governors National Lumber Manufacturers' Association; deputy governor
general Missouri Society Colonial Wars; fourth vice president
of the Missouri Society of the Sons of the Revolution; life
member of the American Academy of Political and Social
Science; member of National Geographic Society; life member of Holestein-Friesian Association of America; life member of the New England Historical and Genealogical Society;
life member and vice president of Historical Society of Heath.
Mass.; member of Virginia Historical Society, vice president
for Missouri of Ohio Historical Society; member of Kansas
City, Mo., Historical Society; member of Missouri Historical
Society; member of Harleian Society of London, England.
Trustee of Kidder Institute, Mo., (Congregational school);
member of Commercial Club of Kansas City; member of Mid-
day Club of Kansas City; 32nd degree Mason.

Has published four volumes of the genealogy of John
White, of Wenham, Mass.; also the Barber and Gleason gen-

ealogies; author of ten pamphlets on "Conservation of Natural Resources." Chairman of the conservation committee of the National Lumber Manufacturers' Association and chairman of the conservation committee of the Yellow Pine Manufacturers' Association. He is a member of the Missouri State Board of Education of the Congregational Church; vice president of the Fisher Flouring Mills Company; vice president of the Fisher-White-Henry Company; vice president of the White-Dulany Grain Company, the last three of Seattle. The reader will, no doubt, think that Mr. White has reason to be troubled with a disease commonly named "big head." But he is far from that. He is the same socially inclined individual that he was when he taught school at Sugar Grove and Stillsons Hill, Pa. He has a good reason for being pleased with his record. A few days ago we read in the newspapers of the country of his being one of a quartet of speakers at Kansas City, Mo., composed of President Taft, the governor of Missouri, and a member of the Conservation Committee.

## CYRUS A CORNEN.

The writer of this sketch was born in the city of New York, November 3, 1844. At the age of ten years my parents moved to Ridgefield, Connecticut, where I attended select school until seventeen years of age, at which time I taught a district school, the school house being located on one of the many Connecticut mountains, the district being known as the "vast mountain." One term of school teaching was sufficient for me. Upon Good Friday, 1862, my father and uncle, W. H. Beers and myself left Ridgefield for at that time the far west, Oil City, Pa. We left New York the same day via the broad gauge railroad, the Atlantic & Great

Western, arriving in Corry, Pa., the next day. When we changed cars for Garland, the nearest railroad point to Oil City. We staid over Sunday in Garland with Landlord Stout and on Monday morning, with Charlie Johnson, as commonly known, the regular stage driver between Garland and Oil City, a distance of some twenty-eight miles, we made a start on our overland route. After turning over twice that day, spilling out trunks, seat cushions and all, we got as far as Enterprise, where we stopped for the night.

The next morning, Tuesday, we started for Oil City, after crossing what was and is known as Cherry run some ten times, we arrived at Rouseville, where we concluded to leave the stage and make it our headquarters to investigate for future headquarters. After a few days investigation we rented for $5.00 a month from one Mr. Wilhelm, a small portion of a building he had built for a store at McClintockville. We went to work at once putting in bunks for beds, having brought bed ticks and bedding from home, made a table, stools for chairs, etc., where we lived two and a half years, and let me say I never enjoyed two and a half years of better health in my life. I embarked in the butcher business at this time. Soon finding out that I did not have the facilities to carry on the butcher business I did not follow it but a short time. My father, I. Beers and myself under the firm name of Cornen & Beers, went directly into the buying and shipping of oil to the Pittsburg market; the dry season came on and Cornen & Beers had a flat bottom boat at what was known as the Breedtown well on the upper end of the Story farm. Oil was selling at this time from ten to fifteen cents a barrel. Either the land owner or well owner I have forgotten which, dug out of the clay a large hole in the ground near the creek, (Oil creek) planked it, puddled it, etc., but the scheme was a failure and the oil oozed through the clay and found its way into the creek; this came to my notice by seeing the oil going to waste on the surface of the creek. I spoke to my father about it; he gave me the use of the boat I have referred to, I rigged a boom out into the creek; took a common pail and with a stone sunk it to the surface of the water; as the oil came into the boom it found its way into the pail. With a long tin pump I would stand in the bow of the boat and pump the oil out of the pail into the boat. I was not long in the filling the boat and I sold considerable. That was hauled to Union, Pa., a station on the P. & E. railroad, averaging about 50 cents per barrel, the market having advanced in the meantime. I took into partnership, one John Gilbert, of Connecticut, who was a carpenter. He worked at his trade to pay living expenses while I pumped the oil. The oil in the boat became exceedingly heavy from evaporation from the sun's rays, so we bought a boat, bought it about half full of fresh oil from the well. We pumped the fresh oil into the heavy boat to and fro, mixing it thoroughly, the lye productions in those days being worthless. The first natural freshet that came we started for Pittsburg with our two boats of oil, as the water in the Allegheny was quite low, our pilot, Arnor, did not wish to take chances of going over some of the lower bars in the river so we stopped at what was known as the Success Oil Works above Kittanning, I think, where we sold our oil for 16¼ cents a gallon, netting us something over $1,200.00. I never was so wealthy before, I never will be again. We continued for a time buying along the creek and selling in the Oil City and Pittsburg markets. I then devoted my time for a while in going in among wells and buying what oil was in the bottom of tanks. I would dig three holes in the ground, tap the tank and the sun's rays from the first to the third hole would separate the water and other impurities and when it was barreled and hauled to the Oil City market it sold at the same price as oil fresh from the wells, after which I devoted my time in trying to become a producer. In the meantime my father and Mr. Beers had bought from one Mr. Parsons, of Westfield, N. Y., fifty acres on Cherry run for a nominal sum and had the same surveyed and plated into leases 99 feet square, the royalty being one-half. The writer was one of four eastern parties who took the first lease from Cornen & Beers, and known as the Cherry Valley Oil Company and drilled the first well upon the property, and as the four owners were from Massachusetts and Connecticut we named it the Yankee well. When the stake was driven for the well she proved to be a fifty barrel flower. Oil was sold from this well the first season she produced for $13.00 per barrel. It was quite common in those days to sell one-half of ones interest before the well was completed for a sum of money sufficient to complete the whole interest.

which was the case with my interest in this well. I drilled many wells upon this property with various results. In one case I was awarded with a one-fourth interest in one of the largest wells ever struck upon the property. At one time Cornen & Beers had an auction of some of the leases; at this I paid $1,700 bonus for one lease 99 feet square and half the oil. Little did I think when going down this run to Rouseville that I would ever assist in taking out of this property the hundreds of thousands of dollars that was taken out. This same property is owned by Henry I. Beers today and I am of the opinion it is still producing. The derrick to this Yankee well was hewn from chestnut timber and morticed together, being 56 feet high. The entire rig in those days cost $600, 250 barrel tank, $250; drilling $3.00 a foot. An eight-horse power second hand portable boiler and engine was purchased at Franklin for $1,800 and hauling the same from Franklin to Cherry run $200; Butwell 2-inch tubing, $1.25 per foot; Cranberry coal $1.25 per bushel, (did we get a bushel?). Any one who might suggest to drill upon the mountains in those days was a fit subject for an insane asylum. In 1867 I bought from one Dr. John Nevins 160 acres on Haliday run. I drilled many well and made many leases; while the caliber of the wells was small they were very lasting; the property is producing today. It proved to me to be a lucrative property. My south line was the dividing line between Oil City and Cornplanter township. My first visit to the Bradford field did not impress me with favor. I could not believe that oil produced from a chocolate rock could be lasting, but as time rolled on I soon followed the rush and with my brother, who had arrived to a business age, we formed a partnership under the style name of C. A. & D. Cornen. We drilled many wells in various parts of the field, having as our motto to buy the property and drill on free ground. It came to our ears there had been a new well struck at Clarendon, Warren county, Pa. We at once investigated the matter and found the same to be a fact, with from 20 to 25 barrels daily output, with a number of wells that were flowing at Stoneham, about one-half mile from the new well, and had been for a number of years, but they were small. We looked upon the situation with favor and at once bought in fee the Davis farm at Clarendon, 200 acres. The fee of 556 is 165 acres, of 531 is 165 acres. The oil and gas, right in fee of 586 is 165 acres, the oil and gas right in fee of the west half of 563, 80 acres, all in Mead township. Also the south half of the oil and gas right in fee of lot 608, Cherry Grove township, aggregating some 887 acres. Every piece of property proved productive of gas or oil or both except the west half of 56, 80 acres. In drilling a well upon 586, which was known as a wildcat, pure and simple, not knowing the altitude, we intended to drill deep enough, at a depth which we afterward found out was 140 feet, below the level of the Clarendon oil sand, we struck a very large gas well. We set to work at once to pipe the same to Clarendon for domestic purposes and through the oil field for drilling purposes. The caliber of the well gave us a large clientage of consumers from this well. A 450 line was run by Peter Grace, of Jamestown, N. Y., to 646, which opened up the famous Cherry Grove oil field. Operating a short time in northwestern and southeastern Ohio and also in West Virginia, neither of which swelled my bank account, this writing finds me and mine, after traveling over 43 years of life's journey together, in possession of the old homestead in Ridgefield, Connecticut, in a house large enough for a moderate sized hotel with 11 feet 6 inches ceilings on the first floor, with 11 windows, each of which can be made a door if you wish it, with cultivated sugar maples of some forty-five years' growth on either side of a wide highway for over three-quarters of a mile, and when foliage is out they form an arch of grandeur and beauty and comfort to man and beast, as the hot rays of the summer's sun seldom finds its way through the foliage; of a cultivated sugar maple orchard of some 250 trees of the same growth. With a trout stream running through this 300 acre property where my two sons from the banks of this same property last season caught six trout that weighed seven pounds and seven ounces. It is not uncommon to fill an 8 pound basket from this stream. Two of the trout weighed 1 pound 9 ounces, the other 1 pound 8 ounces. I have fished many of the mountain streams of Pennsylvania and I don't know where to equal it in that state.

With a new railroad, for which they are now procuring the right of way, bringing Ridgefield within one hours run of

New York City, will almost make us feel we are living in the confines of the metropolis. This connection brings the Berkshire hills much nearer New York City which will be a great convenience to the city tourist.

---

## E. B. GRANDIN.

Alhough E. B. Gradin's photo does not appear in this "Album of Self-made Men," he is entitled to a short biography, being one of the subscribers who has bought a large number of copies of this book to distribute among his friends. Mr. Grandin stands out conspicuously as one of the best types of an oil man. He commenced the business when it was an unknown quantity. It required genuine grit and sticktoitiveness to produce oil before tools were made to produce it successfully. It was much easier for Mr. E. B. Grandin to follow the business than many other boys who started in and fell by the wayside, as his was an exceptional beginning. I have my doubts of finding another boy, (he was a mere boy when he took his first chance of the greasy fluid,) that had such universal good luck as he had from the beginning to the present time. He handled more different interests than any operator of his age and made a strike every time he took an interest in an oil lease, either in fee simple or lease. To know that E. B. Grandin owned an interest in an oil well when drilling was to know that it would be a great money maker and the same may be said of other investments outside of the oil business. He has now a heavy interest in 325,000 acres of wheat and pine timber lands in many southern states that keep swelling his already immense fortune.

## GEORGE WELLINGTON DINSMOOR.

George Wellington Dinsmoor was born in Elk township, Warren county, Pa., June 20, 1847, being the youngest son of G. F. and Catherine Dinsmoor. He received a very meager education, attended school not to exceed one year in all. He had to work hard at an early age being the youngest of a very large family, he helped his father and brother on the farm, also doing odd jobs for neighbors. At the age of fourteen years he secured employment of a farmer in Cattaraugus county, N. Y., at twelve dolalrs a month during the summer and during the winter worked in the woods and sawmill for a lumberman by the name of Edward Reynolds, in Elk township, and at intervals during the following summer and winter. The next summer back to Cattaraugus county for the same farmer, milked ten cows and made a hand in hayfield also. Getting the war fever he enlisted and was rejected on account of age, tried again with same result, the third time he was accepted and assigned to the 111th New York Infantry. A splendid organization standing fourteenth in fatalities of all the two thousand or more regiments of the Union army (according to Colonel Fox, late of Oil City). Mr. Dinsmoor being present and in many of the hardest fought battles of the latter part of the war was right on the "firing line" when General Lee surrendered at Appomatox.

On returning home he worked at lumbering and in sawmills in various places and for different men. Sawmills at that time were principly uprights, Mulleys, Gangs. Once or twice he undertook to farm but the farm had no charms and was soon abandoned.

In the late 60's Joseph Hall's splendid sawmill at Tiona (then called Tionesta) was burned to ashes but was soon re-

built by that enterprising lumberman and an up-to-date circular mill established. On going over to see it work he at
once became fascinated. So delightful to see a circular take
swing on hemlock knots. He at once secured employment
from Mr. Hall and commenced at "tail" sawyer (off bearing
would be proper), and was soon promoted to setter, next to
handling the levers. Studying closely he became head sawyer,
filing saws and having about full charge of the entire establishment and had a good understanding of every part. When
E. G. Wood & Co. sold to Clapp, Stowe & Co. he left and has
not done an hours' work in a sawmill since. In 1874 he
went into the lower oil country, Venango, Clarion, Butler
counties were the "front" at that period. He worked in country coal mines, soon went to pumping, dressing tools, drilling,
done some of all kinds of work in connection with the oil
business and kept at it until 1884. Then with his son, L. D.
Dinsmoor, a "husky" lad of seventeen years, started out to
see a little of the world. Went to the Pacific coast, followed
it from Mexico to Vancouver, B. C., but returned to the
southern part of Missouri, where they spent one year, then to
Moberly, Missouri, where they worked in and around coal
mines and in 1888 was a candidate for representative from
Randolph county. He did not get elected but got a fine vote,
(the county was almost three to one Democrats). He spoke
in several places where a Republican had not been before.
In 1889 he went to Macon county, Missouri, it looked good
and he concluded to settle down and "hew" out a home.
He was census enumerator in 1890, worked at mining, was
hoisting engineer, weigh boss, etc., until 1905. Meantime
he had built up a beautiful home with unequalled surround-
ings, conventional designs, exquisite flowers, etc., the finest
in that section of the county and was justly proud of the
same. In 1895 his son, L. D., had returned to West Virginia
and had been very successful in the oil business, securing
quite a large settled production, urged him to come and take
charge of some of it which he did. He has been pumping
for Dinsmoor & Co. up to the presnt time. He is pleasantly
located on a high hill above the city of St. Marys having a
fine view of over five miles of the Ohio river.

On August 2, 1909, his son, L. D., was thrown from a
horse and fatally injured, only surviving about three hours,

the saddest shock of his entire life. His solace being his son's children, four in number, one born four days after the fatal accident.

He is a fair "off-hand" speaker, always in demand at camp fires, encampments, decorations, anniversaries, etc.

He is patriotic to the core, displaying the flag on all occasions, presenting flags to those that will display them. Never meets an old comrade, Union or Confederate, in need of assistance without rendering every assistance in his power.

At one time in life he was fairly well posted in geology, at present entirely superceded by botany. His chief delight is in roaming woods and hills, with congenial companions, studying wild flowers, forestry, rocks, etc.

Always makes a rule to work for the best interest of his employers.

He makes it a strict rule never to speak cross or angry.

The little advance in education was prompted as necessities appeared.

Is optimistic in regard to the future. Thinks most people, especially financiers, take life too seriusly. Hence tries to be cheerful under all circumstances.

He is fairly well posted in history, war history a specialty.

In religion and politics he is extremely liberal. Does not belong to any church but believes there is good in all of them, also that there is good in nearly all societies, secret and open. For a number of years belonged to the Knights of Labor. For two years, 1886 and '87 was worthy foreman of district No. 11, embracing all territory between the Mississippe and Rocky mountains. Was presiding officer on several occasions.

Has belonged to the Grand Army of the Republic about twenty-five years. Commander of Posts several times. Was delegate at large from West Virginia last year (1909) to National Encampment at Salt Lake City.

Entered the campaign in 1896. Made addresses in several states in the west in the interest of the Republican ticket. Was member of National League of Republican Clubs from first congressional district of Missouri.

Has this advice to all young people, "Do not be mean, and the longer you live the more firmly you will be convinced it is the best advice you ever received."

## E. O. EMERSON.

Mr. E. O. Emerson was all through the Civil War, and when it was over came directly to the oil regions and located in Titusville. His first venture being in Pithole in 1865 when he bought a half acre near the famous Grant well, paying for the same $5,000 bonus and half the oil. Starting to drill two wells on this little piece of ground, the estimated cost of which was $10,000. After this was done there was nothing to do but await developments; one day upon climbing one of the adjacent hills, where he could look down upon the innumerable derricks thickly covering the valley, he observed a line of teams nearly half a mile in length awaiting their turn to fill their barrels at the Grant well, then flowing 1,000 barrels a day, and it occurred to him that if all these drilling wells got oil it would swamp everybody in the business, there being no pipe lines to carry away the oil then. There was also the danger of getting dry holes, so he decided it was too great a risk to take and at once decided to sell. Very soon he found a purchaser by which he doubled his money inside of a month and went back to Titusville. His two wells when completed were both dry, and nearly everybody there went broke or sustained large losses. Later Mr. Emerson bought the lease of the famous Riddle farm off Dunc Karns, located at Karns City, containing 200 acres, and secured a large production.

In 1880 Mr. Emerson went into the natural gas business at Olean and Pittsburg, in company with J. N. Pew and laid the first pipe line for commercial purposes into that city from Murraysville, about eighteen miles from Pittsburg. When they struck their first well, the gas could neither be seen or smelled, it was just as if a blast of wind was coming out of the hole. All of his experience with gas up to this time was that it had distinct odor and could also be seen as a vapor, so when the question of laying the pipe line to Pittsburg came up, Mr. Emerson was like the man from Missouri, he must be shown; people would laugh if he laid a line to carry wind to the city, so he insisted that a pipe be carried out to a safe distance, and then prove by lighting the gas. This was done and all doubts dispelled upon applying the torch.

Mr. Emerson has had forty-five years of experience in the oil and gas business, and is still more or less actively engaged in various enterprises, in all of which he is noted as a conservative operator.

## GEORGE COLIN PRIESTLY.

George Colin Priestly, now a prominent oil producer of the Mid-continent field, was born at Fort Kent, near Houlton, Maine, June 10, 1862. His father and mother were of Scotch parentage, thus by birth he was e n d o w e d with good health and great vitality, which have assisted him in the great struggle to attain his present position. His early years were passed in Pleasantville, Venango county, Pennsylvania, where his father moved his family in August, 1866. His boyhood days were full of hard work, Leaving school before he was twelve years old, he assisted his father by driving team, hauling coal from Titusville to the oil wells near his home. At that early age the oil business seemed to have a fascination for him that grew with age. He wanted to be an oil man. Getting a little money ahead he attended Duff's Commercial school at Pittsburg one term, and

then accepted a position in the general store of S. Q. Brown
& Co. Clerking did not seem to appeal to him and a pumping
job being offered to him by W. B. Benedict and D. McKelvey
he quit the store and went to work for them. He soon adapted himself to the work and was made superintendent of their
properties at Wardwell run farm, near Glade, Warren county,
Pa. He was then under twenty years of age. At the opening
of the Grand Valley oil field he was transferred to Goodwill
Hill and developed their property there. On December 25,
1885, he was married to Miss Julia Ruland, of Enterprise, and
moved to the little home on the Hunter farm, which he had
prepared for his Christmas present. He remained with the
company until they sold their property. About this time Mr.
Gillam, who owned the small store on the hill, died, and Mr.
Priestley bought the property from the heirs. This was his
first venture and in a measure showed his ability to do things.
From a very small trade he built up a business that surprised
the oldest. He soon had a shingle mill, then a sawmill, and
took great pride in selling the best shingles and lumber that
went to the trade. During these years his family increased to
six, four children being born: Willis, Hazel, Bessie and
George. School matters began to interest him and he was
elected school director and was president of the school board
for several years. His activity in politics (Republican by the
way), fighting as hard to elect a township official of his faith
as he did a president, soon attracted the attention of the leaders
of his party at the county seat and he soon became a strong
favorite for county treasurer to which office he was elected
in 1900. At the expiration of his term of office he immediately went to Oklahoma and plunged into the fight for leases and
wealth. On his arrival at Bartlesville he was told that he was
too late, that everything good was taken up and in less than
two weeks he bought from local parties the Lumberman Oil
Co., which today is one of the best companies in the state.
Since then he has acquired the Wolverine, Fort Pitt, and
Pickwick companies, all gilt edged and good paying properties. His outside interests are large, some good real estate in
Bartlesville, a nice interest in the Indepdendence & Coffeyville
Traction company, one of the best investments in the state of
Kansas, an interest here and there in various manufacturing
concerns in the city, seem to indicate that he may attain the

position which he smilingly mentions when politics have been broached to him, viz: I am out of the game until I make a fortune.

Southern courtesy has attached colonel to him and from his second month there he has been addressed in no other way. His eastern friends do not seem to catch onto the title, but if you are in Bartlesville, ask for Colonel Priestley and every citizen can tell you where to find him. His success has not changed him in the least, he is still George to all his old friends and the "latch string has never been pulled in to them."

From the first he has been a member of the Commercial Club of the city. No public improvement or anything for the good of Bartlesville has ever passed his door without a contribution.

His Scotch blood shows in his religion, Presbyterian, but none of the others can find any fault, as he treats them very nicely when called upon to assist them. His donations to charity are known only to those who receive but they are second to none in one of the most charitable cities of its size in the United States.

Bartlesville is proud of her citizenship. Coming from all parts of the world, all working to build up the best city in the state, she gives credit to all upon her roll of honor among whom you will find the name not far from the top, Colonel Geo. C. Priestley.

## McKINNEY'S CORNET BAND.

This band is one of the oldest in Warren county. It is 37 years since its organization. W. S. McKinney, when but a boy of 15, joined and was elected leader, which position he has held up to the present time. For the first four years the band hired Mr. George Gross, a German gentleman, who had played 20 years in a military band in Germany. He taught the McKinney band two nights each week, and at the end of four years the members of the band were fully competent to play beautiful dirges at the funeral of their faithful teacher. They played at many noted places during that time, among which was the laying of the corner stone of the insane asylum at North Warren, the dedication of the I. O. O. F. cemetery at Youngsville, at the I. O. O. F. grand lodge of New York at Jamestown, N. Y., where they took second premium at a contest of many bands, at the laying of the corner stone of the magnificent high school building erected in the memory of his son, Dr. Franklin White, by his father Hon. J. B. White, a former resident of Youngsville, but now of Kansas City, Mo., in the winter and Bemus point, N. Y., in the summer, and other noted places, too numerous to memtion. All these years this band has made music for their home town free of charge, dozens and dozens of times. They have made music nearly all over the country and are more widely known than any band in Pennsylvania outside the large cities. One novelty is, that every member belongs to the Odd Fellows, and they make free music for the initiatory ceremonies. They are called the I. O. O. F. band. In fact, they proclaim the fact by carrying the big letters I. O. O. F. on the end of the bass drum. The names of the members are, reading from left to right, seated: W. H. Gray, W. F. Schnell, W. S. McKinney, leader; H. Babcock, W. B. Phillips.

Back row, standing: Sam Rima, Archie Davis, A. Schnell, Elmer Sederburg. Members absent, R. A. Head, George Schuab, Ross Mead.

## NELSON P. WHEELER.

N. P. Wheeler was born at Portville, N. Y., and grew upon a farm with its work and lumbering, attended district school. At the age of thirteen began attending O l e a n Academy, six miles away, caring for the horses and cows, pigs and chickens, getting the wood and driving down and back each school day. When seventeen years of age he made his first trip on the river, pulling an oar the whole distance from Portville to Cincinnati and going out with the line at each landing. At twenty-three he went on the Tionesta to take charge of the lumbering establishment of H. Stow & Co. At twenty-six he was elected county commissioner. In 1878 was elected assemblyman from Forest county and refused another term on account of increasing business. In 1906 he was elected congressman in the twenty-eighth district of Pennsylvania and re-elected in 1908. He has been an active lumberman all his life.

## JOSEPH ANDERSON SCHOFIELD.

The portrait herewith is a good likeness of Joseph Anderson Schofield, a prominent attorney and oil producer of Warren county, Pa. Mr. Schofield was born in Philadelphia, December 31, 1860, his parents being Albert R. Schofield (a prominent attorney of the Quaker City, and a member of the state legislature for two terms) and Mary E. Anderson, a descendant of Patrick Anderson, who fought in the Revolutionary War as one of the aides to General Washington.

Joseph A. Schofield received his education in the schools of Chester county and Philadelphia, where he resided until 1885, when he came to Warren, Warren County, Pa., where he has resided continuously since.

He is an attorney of ability and is the principal owner of the largest oil production, consisting of one continuous property, in Warren county, being known as the J. A. Schofield & Co. oil lease. This property was originally purchased from O. W. and D. W. Beatty, but Mr. Schofield has added to it adjoining lands from leases until now it consists of over 1,500 acres of land on which is situated 220 oil wells. It is conceded by all that it is the best fitted up oil production in Warren county, all the wells being pumped by the latest machinery, the foundations of the powers being laid in cement, wire rope being used for pull rods, maintains its own thread cutting machnery and machine shop, and everything up-to-date in every particular.

Mr. Schofield is an ardent Republican, has been chairman of the Republican County Committee and is a member of the Warren borough school board, and has been prominent in Warren for many years as a public spirited, progressive citizen.

In 1889 he married Clare C. Braddock, of Philadelphia, who is also a descendant of revolutionary stock. They have four children, Braddock, Albert R., Anderson and Rebecca.

---

## YOUNGSVILLE FIRE DEPARTMENT.

The photo on the next page shows the very efficient fire fighters of Youngsville, Pa. They are a set of firemen that a borough of only 2,000 inhabitants may well take pride in.

Several years ago the city fathers built a town hall of brick and bought a fine $3,000 engine. An addition is being built at present to make more room for the big engine. Since buying this, it has, in saving property, paid for itself over and over, many times. Several fires have started that would have swept streets if not for this engine and thirty-two lively fighters. Twelve were absent when this photo was taken, but the twenty present show determined faces. All take pride in the good they do for the town.

The names of these members beginning at the left of the lines are: Sitting—Foreman Wickham; Chief Bradway; Assistant Foreman Black. First row standing—Dalrymple, R. McKinney, J. M. McKinney, Benson, Phillips, Weaver, Hanson, Yarling, Kirkham. Second row—Lightner, Haupin, Wickwire, Brooks, Bartlett, F. Black, Davis. Engine Master Ralph Dalrymple; Driver Ed.. Johnson.

## JOHN CALHOUN DINSMOOR.

At one time in his life John Calhoun Dinsmoor, of Marietta, Ohio, aspired to the profession of the law and as disciple of the illustrious Blackstone, he would, no doubt, have won enduring fame, as his keen and analytic mind admirably adapted him to a career in the forensic world. But at a critical moment the alluring fascinations of the oil field served as a magnet to draw him away from well-laid plans, and as a result the profession of the law, no doubt, lost one of its most shining satellites. That he made no mistake is strongly accentuated in the fact that he has won enviable prominence in his chosen field, not only accumulating wealth but making a reputation among the leading oil operators of the country as a man of remarkable business ability.

John Calhoun Dinsmoor was born March 21, 1838, in Warren county, Pa., and his ansectors were noted for their many intellectual attainments. His father, a lumberman and farmer, was a son of Governor Dinsmoor, of New Hampshire. The Dinsmoors were of Scottish origin, while James Calhoun Dinsmoor's mother, who was Katherine Harper before her marriage, and noted for her Christian spirit, came of fine old English stock.

The subject of our sketch first attended the common schools of Warren county, and later in Jamestown and Randolph, N. Y. The early years of his schooling constituted only a few months in the winter and the balance of the time he worked on his father's farm, endeavoring to secure enough money to obtain an education, and one of his ambitions was to possess knowledge. He taught school for several winter terms and then read law with his brother, Charles Dinsmoor, in Warren, Pa., with the expectation of adopting the profession as his life work. But when the oil excitement broke out at Oil Creek, Pa., he cast aside legal lore and got a position boating oil on Oil creek. Later he went to Cranberry township, where he engaged in the coal business, making his first money. After two years he sold out and was next heard from in the west, where he followed agricultural pursuits for six years, returning to Clarion county, and again started in the coal trade, from which he realized considerable money.

Although he had been wandering in other fields, he still looked forward to a career in the oil business, and with the money acquired from his coal business he obtained a small lease of several acres including two wells, which he operated and realized a very fair production. The oil market finally got on a down grade and Mr. Dinsmoor sold out to pay his debts, but his credit remained good.

He then went to Oil City, Pa., and located in the Tarkill oil field, not far from the city, purchasing a small interest in a large lease and went to work pumping. He bought in on this lease, but oil again taking a drop, lost everything he had. His credit remained good, however, and he retained the property, which he operated later with eminent success. Since then he has been an extensive buyer of oil lands in Pennsylvania, having an immense production. Since 1901 he purchased large properties in West Virginia, where he now has 450 producing wells.

Our subject is a heavy stockholder in the concerns of Dinsmoor & Co., Dinsmoor Oil Co. and J. C. Dinsmoor & Son, besides having large individual holdings in oil and gas interests in various parts of the country. He is a member of the Oil City Gun Club, Oil City, Pa., St. Marys Gun Club, of St. Marys, W. Va., and the Odd Fellows.

Mr. Dinsmoor was married in 1865 to Miss Jane Holt, of Warren county, Pa., and they have two children, James Denton and Lyell Emerson. Club life holds forth no charm for Mr. Dinsmoor, whose chief delights are the associations that surround his home, and when not engrossed in his multifarious business affairs, can always be found in the society of his family.

Mr. Dinsmoor made his way up to his present enviable position by work, his alma mater was the college of hard knocks, and he had the rare faculty of never getting discouraged when failure stared him in the face. He has been blessed with the best of health all his life, and he was thus enabled to prosecute his labors without interruption. Our subject has an extensive acquaintance among the oil fraternity, and is one of the most popular men in the business. He is an omniverous reader, having a magnificent library of scientific works, and is an expert on the geological conditions of the early oil fields, a subject of which he has wonderful knowledge.

He attends the Unitarian church and his religious views are broad and liberal. He attributes his success to being ambitious and keeping his credit. He has rubbed elbows with all conditions of life, and as he puts it himself, been thousands of dollars worse off than nothing. His experience has made him a good man to tie to when in trouble, as his perseverance and wise counsel have frequently brought success to an enterprise that appeared to be doomed to failure. He assures the young man that refuses to become discouraged and works hard that he will ultimately sweep all obstacles from his path and attain the fame and success to which he aspires.

## LANSING DITMARS WETMORE.

Lansing Ditmars Wetmore was born in Warren county, Pa., on the 18th day of October, 1818. He was decended from Thomas Whitmore, whose name has become abbreviated to Wetmore.

Thomas Whitmore, a member of a well known English family, came to Boston in 1635 and later lived at Hartford and Middleton, Conn.

Lansing Ditmars Wetmore was a son of Lansing Wetmore and the grandson of Parsons Wetmore, who married Aurelia White, daughter of

Judge Hugh White, the founder of Whitestown, N. Y., as western and central New York in 1784 was then called.

His mother, Caroline Wetmore, born at Newton, L. I., was decended from mixed Dutch and French Hugenot ancestry; from the Dutch families of Ditmars and Remsen, and the ancient Hugenot family DeRapelye.

He received his early education at the district schools of Warren county, graduated with honor from Union college in the class of 1841 and then began the study of law in Warren. He was admitted to practice at the bar of Warren county in 1845 and from that time on he conducted a large and successful practice in Warren and the adjoining counties, first alone, later associating with him younger men, the firm name of Wetmore, Noyes & Hinckley being the most widely and best known.

In 1870 he was elected president judge of the sixth district composed of the counties of Erie, Warren and Elk. Soon after he retired from the practice of law to take up the duties of the bench, Hon. W. E. Rice became a member of the firm. It is a fact of interest that Judge Noyes, Judge Rice and Judge Hinckley, have succeeded Judge Wetmore on the bench of this judicial district—four judges from one firm, including every member thereof. He was one of the founders of the First National bank of Warren, and president of it for many years. He was elected president of the American Lumbermen's Association at its meeting at Williamsport, Pa., in the early seventies. Like his father, he was always remarkable for the affability of his manner and his social disposition in all the relations of life. His judicial decisions were almost always correct, notwithstanding the fact that he was engaged in private business enterprises that would alone fully tax the energies of most men. He studied all the questions that came before him for decision with the thoroughness of a student in love with his task, and refused to neglect the minutest detail of his position.

As a citizen he was both public spirited and liberal to a marked degree. His influence and purse could be relied on in every movement for the benefit of the community. He was a generous contributor to the fund to purchase the site for the Struthers library building and was one of the original trustees appointed by Mr. Struthers. He took an active part in securing the location near Warren, of the State hospital for the insane; was an original trustee of that institution and for many years president of the board. The Warren Emergency hospital was made possible by the subscriptions of Judge Wetmore, and several other like public spirited men.

After the expiration of his term as judge, he purchased a plantation where the Lynnhaven river enters Chesapeake bay, in Princess Anne county, Virginia, and devoted the latter years of his life to the development of that property. He died at his home in Warren on the 30th day of December, 1905.

Judge Wetmore was twice married. His first wife was Betsy Weatherby, of Warren, who died in 1856, leaving one child, now the wife of J. P. Jefferson, of Warren. In 1858 he married Maria C. Shattuck, of Groton, Mass. There were three children of this marriage: Edward D., Frederick S. and Albert L.

---

## LEWIS EMERY, JR.

Lewis Emery, Jr., of Bradford, was born about two miles from the pretty little village of Cherry Creek, Chautauqua county, N. Y., August 10, 1839. In 1842 his father had been engaged constructing a railway near Olean, N. Y., for the old Erie, now the New York, Lake Erie & Western railroad, and lost a great deal of money through the failure of that corporation. After severing his connection with the railroad he secured a contract on one of the levels of the Genesee canal, and when that company defaulted he was again a sufferer, financially; and, becoming disgusted with the state of affairs in the east, determined upon going to the west. In January,

1842, he started, with his family, to drive overland to Janesville, Wis. He was a thorough general mechanic, and an adept in all the varied details of woolen cloth making. When he reached Jonesville, Mich., on his westward journey, the loss of some of his live stock compelled him to make a halt, and the people of the surrounding country, learning of his ability, persuaded him to settle among them, and they agreed to and did build a mill for him, allowing him to pay for it from the profits on his sales. He remained in Jonesville for seven years, during the latter part of which period he built another mill at Hillsdale, the county seat, to which place he moved with his family in 1849.

Hon. Lewis Emery, Jr., the subject of this sketch, after spending his early youth learning the trade with his father, and acquiring what rudimentary education the country schools afforded, was sent to Hillsdale college, Hillsdale, Mich., where he finished his mental training. At the age of nineteen he engaged to teach the district school of Wheatland township, and continued to do so for two years; after which he resumed work at his father's flour mill, which he continued until he left the state. During his attendance at Hillsdale college he met with, and formed an attachment for, Miss Elizabeth A. Caldwell, and on December 29th, 1863 he married her at the home of her parents, in Vistula, Elkhart county, Ind. Four children were the result of their marriage: Delevan Emery, born September 26, 1867; Grace Elizabeth Emery, born January 27, 1874; Earle Caldwell Emery, born December 12, 1875, and Lewis Emery, born August 27, 1878. In May, 1864, he went to Southern Illinois and engaged in general merchandising, and also built a mill. The war was brought to a close soon after he went there, and, business coming to a stand-still, he concluded to seek other fields, and in August, 1865, started for the oil regions of Pennsylvania. He made his first stop at Pithole, Venango county, remaining a short time, and in that memorable year located his first well at Pioneer, that county, and shared the ups and downs of the producers of that period. For the next five years he followed the excitement, so characteristic of the oil country, with all its varied successes and disappointments, until in 1870, he went to Titusville, Crawford county, Pa., and was fairly on the way to wealth. He rapidly rose to the top rank among the well-known producers of that field, and by his determination and enterprise, coupled with a strong sense of honor in all business dealings, he soon commanded the respect and confidence of the whole community. Like hundreds of others of the then prosperous producers, the financial panic, precipitated by the failure of Jay Cooke & Co., of New York, caught him with the floating obligations that could not be quickly enough protected to save him from the desolating ruin that followed, and in the parlance of the country he "went to the wall," almost hopelessly ruined. With a recorded debt against him that would have driven a less intrepid man to lunacy, or, possibly, to the grave, he, with his characteristic enterprise and confidence in himself, was soon looking about for a way to recover his lost fortunes. He had often viewed the hills and vales of McKean county, Pa., with the strong suspicion that they held beneath them a vast lake of petroleum, only waiting to yield up its wealth to the pioneer who should tap it. Now, in a spirit of desperation, almost, he determined to test his ideas with a drill. He had leased and purchased about 14,000 acres of territory, without a cent of money. The people had confidence in him, trusted to his ability to pay, and never questioned his honor. He commenced operations in this field July 28th, 1875, his first well being at Toad Hollow, on what was known as the Tibbets farm, about two miles south of the city of Bradford. This well opened up at the rate of forty barrels per day, and not only proved of vast financial importance to him, enabling him to wipe out every cent of debt, and accumulate a handsome fortune, but it virtually opened up the greatest oil territory the world has ever seen. His wealth piled up, and each year saw acres of territory falling into his possession, until over 50 wells were pouring their wealth into his store-house. In thus entering such a vast undertaking without money, the firm of Eaton, Cole, Burnham Company, of New York, proved great friends to him. They gave him unlimited credit, though he was a bankrupt. They realized that a man who had gone down two or three times, and as often came out of the ordeal with honor unstained, would not long remain down, and so it proved. In 1878 he was elected by the people of McKean county to represent them in the general assembly, where, in the session of 1879, he took such a warm and untiring interest in the wants of the oil country, that the people returned him to the legislature, in 1880, with credentials of a senatorship. During his sitting in the lower house of the legislature, he manifested an independence of spirit in political labor similar to that which had always characterized his action elsewhere. While he did not object to the party caucus, he would follow no leader whom he suspected of packing the caucus, either by purchase or the party lash. He ever edvocated the most frank and honest dealing where the rights of the people came into the question; and never could reconcile the mandates of packed caucuses with either frankness, honesty or honor. It was for this reason he refused to go into the senatorial caucus of 1879. At that time the Republican party was being wielded by and for the interest of a few individuals, and the "gag" rule and caucus packing were two of their favorite instruments to carry on their plans. The continuation of these practices led to the memorable senatorial dead-lock in the legislature in 1881, when fifty-six Republicans remained out of the party caucus, many refusing to be tied to Galusha A. Grow for the United States senatorship, and this action ultimately resulted in the election of Hon. John I. Mitchell, and was followed a year later by the three-cornered fight for the gubernational chair, by Hon. John Stewart, Robert E. Pattison and James A. Beaver. He was re-elected to the State senate from the twenty-fifth district in 1884, by a largely increased majority. In the same year he was chosen delegate-at-large to represent the State of Pennsylvania in the National Republican convention, that convened at Chicago, June 19, and was in attendance during the memorable contest which ended in the nomination of James G. Blaine and John A. Logan. He was a warm advocate of Mr. Blaine's nomination, and an ardent supporter of him in the election that followed. In 1886 he was a candidate for congress from the sixteenth district, and again in 1888 from the twenty-fourth district, but both times was compelled to yield his claim, because of the rotation system so determinedly clung to in that part of the state. During his ten years of public service he was unflagging in his opposition to the tendency of corporate monopolies and trusts to prostitute their rights to private purposes, and the crushing out of fair competition. In this direction he was the recognized leader of the anti-monopolists, and, though tempted to withdraw his opposition to the monopolists, by prospects of ample financial returns in the way of business facilities, he consistently stuck to his principles, and refused to be cajoled in any manner. In

1879 he went to Europe, and made a thorough investigation of the oil fields of the Baku region in Russia, to learn, if possible, what its competition with American oil would ever attain. In 1881 he made a second visit to Europe, this time traveling through France, Germany, Italy, Turkey, Greece, and up the Nile 1,000 miles, as far as the second cataract. He has also traveled extensively in this country, and in the Canadian provinces, and has equipped himself with a vast store of general information as to the needs and capability of the country. While traveling he was always a keen observer and a painstaking student of the men and things he met. He is a man of broad views, a ready reasoner and most determined in execution. His philanthropic work, while it has been very extensive, has been directed in a modest and unostentatious manner, and many are the institutions and private personages who have felt the influence of his quiet beneficence. In his personal habits, as in his public actions, he is plain and unpretentious. His home life is one of domestic peace and happiness, and furnishes him a harbor from the labors of business and public service, to which he always hies with pleasure unfeigned. His public spirit, coupled with a firm conviction that the rights of the common people must be sustained against the encroachment of individual or corporate gain, has made him an object of admiration among the people, and one to whom they have always shown a readiness to entrust their welfare. He is now engaged in the production and refining of petroleum on a very extensive scale in Bradford, McKean county, Pa.; has large wheat land interests in Northern Dakota and is owner of a large oil well and general supply store in Bradford, McKean county, Pa.

## LEVI SMITH.

Levi Smith, of Warren, Pa., was born April 12, 1844, in Lowhill township, Lehigh county, Pa., son of Gideon and Eliza (Reber) Smith. His father was a farmer and his ancestors were from Germany and Holland.

Levi Smith, our subject, attended the common school, in Lowhill township, only spending four months of the winter at school, and his summers were spent working hard on the farm until he was nineteen years of age, when he left home and school, and engaged with Kressley brothers at Lyon Valley, Pa., to learn the agricultural machinist trade, where he remained two years for $75.00 and his board; he then went to Allentown, Pa., where he worked at his trade until he left for the oil region of Pennsylvania on June 22, 1865, with a worldly possession of $72.00. His first work in the oil regions was at East Sandy, Pa., where he helped to build a hotel; from there he went to Pithole, where he helped to build an oil rig and drill the first oil well he ever worked on. After having worked at this well about one year, a proposition was made to him by Miram Judson, of Conneaut, O., to take possession of an oil well nearby on a percentage of one-half of the production, which he accepted, and increased the production of the well from four to eighteen barrels per day, oil being worth about five to eight dollars per barrel.

He afterwards formed a partnership with Peter Schreiber, and operated for oil at Pithole, Pleasantville, Henry's Bend and Tidioute, Pa., and when this partnership was dissolved after four years of agreeable business relations, he formed a new partnership with Brady & Logan, of Tidioute, Pa., in the oil business, on Triumph Hill, of which he had charge; his partners being also engaged in the hardware and oil well

14

supply business, with a branch store at Triumph at the same time, who during the time of the "thirty day shut down" requested him to take charge of their branch store at the latter place, which position he accepted, and when later on Brady & Logan went into bankruptcy, our subject formed a new partnership with A. J. McIntyre and purchased the hardware and oil well supply stock and machinery, in which B. & L. had formerly been dealing largely, from Grandin brothers, of Tidiuote, who purchased the stock at sheriff sale, being the principal creditors of Brady & Logan; he remained at the head of this partnership for about seven years, with a moderate degree of success, when he determined to get out of partnership, though with kindliest feelings and regards for his partner, to whom he disposed of all his property interests in and about Tidiuote; after disposing of his interest at Tidiuote, he purchased an oil well supply stock at sheriff sale, formerly belong to J. W. Humphrey & Co., at Clarendon, Pa., and later on also a large stock of oil well fishing tools of William Robertson & Son, and in 1884 he became associated with John Japes and Robert Thompson in a very crude and cheaply constructed oil refinery of twenty-barrel capacity for which a ditch of water served as a condenser, and of which the entire inventory amounted to a little less than $850,000, of which he purchased the undivided one-third interest, but took no active part in the management of the works. The first year's business showed quite a little loss, and then Japes' interest was purchased by the remaining two partners, and the second year also proved profitless, apparently for lack of still capacity and other necessary improvements. At the end of the second year Mr. Smith bought Thompson's interest also and devoted most of his time to the refining business from that time on; he rebuilt and improved his plant from time to time, as he was making financial headway, until his still capacity reached over 1,000 barrels per day, and excellent success has attended his untiring efforts in the refining as well as in most of his other varied lines of business. He is and has been largely interested in western lumber and timber business, Portland cement, in and Kansas and Texas, mining and milling interests in Colorado, soap and grease business in Warren, Pa., and has also been president of the Citizens' National bank of Warren, Pa., for a number of years until he resigned that position.

Mr. Smith was married January 1, 1873, to Miss Amanda J. George, of Lyon Valley, Pa., by which marriage four children have been born to them, two sons and two daughters, the oldest son having died at the age of six years. His residence is located on Market street, in Warren, Pa., where he is surrounded with every home comfort. He is naturally of a cheerful, musical, poetical and mechanical turn of mind and all of the family are musically inclined. He is a fine marksman and hunter, and is possibly the only man who ever encountered a huge grizzly and a cinnamon bear at one and the same time and came off victorious after ramming his rifle barrel down the grizzly's throat, which incident happened in the Rocky Mountains in Colorado, in 1882, while on a hunting expedition with several others, who witnessed at a distance, the horrifying, fearless experience on his part, with hearts in their months, and which he regards as having been the busiest moments of his life.

Mr. Smith has taken much interest in school matters in Warren, and other places, but more especially in instituting the various industrial and physicial culture departments, being a great believer in combining the cunning of the brain and hands for the benefit of both the individual and national welfare, and he says if it were in his power to bring it about, he would make physical culture and manual training compulsory in every school in the United States, to the extent that it could be made practical. He has equipped the Warren high school with a first class manual training outfit for boys, domestic science and sewing departments for girls, and an excellent gymnasium, and donated to the same also, what is said to be the finest collection of crystallized minerals in this country, and which is a magnificent mineral flower garden. In addition he has also contributed largely to other schools and institutions. He is and has been sustaining a number of foreign missionaries in China, Korea, and India for a number of years also, and had at one time proposed to erect a first-class municipal building and donate it to the town of Warren for the use of the necessary town offices, the W. C. T. U., the Salvation Army, and other homeless organizations, but which. on account of objections raised by some who will never make such a proposition themselves, he decided not to force it upon the community. He neither uses tobacco or liquor in any form, having smoked but half a cigar when a boy, and never learned to play any games except dominoes, and his advice to young men would be never to adorn themselves with a necklace of such millstones.

Mr. Smith has enjoyed good health most of his life, and has kept a diary since 1865, which he writes up regularly every night before going to bed.

Fraternally Mr. Smith is a Mason, being a thirty-second degree Consistory Mason, Knight Templar and Shriner, and socially he is most affable, genial and respected by all who know him in a business and social way. He can be termed a strictly self-made man, who has paved his own way to his present enviable position, by industry, perseverance and strict integrity.

> We're spreading on life's records
> The acts of our careers;
> Our deeds of good and evil
> Throughout our mortal years
> Whereby we may aid others
> To win life's doubtful race
> Or prove ourselves a hindrance.
> A failure and disgrace.

## GUY C. IRVINE.

Guy C. Irvine was born December 15, 1792, near W a r r i e r s run, Northumberland county. Pa. His brother, James Irvine, wrote him to come to the Little Brokenstraw creek, and work at his trade—blacksmithing. He walked to Pittsburg in 1817 and was kicked by a horse, while working at his trade, and was laid up with a broken arm. He then went to Broken-

straw township, and found a chance to buy some lumber, sawed, rafted, and ready to run down the Allegheny river. He did not have the money to pay for it, so he walked back to Warriors run, and borrowed the money—$400—from his step-father, walked back againi bought the lumber, run it to Pittsburg, sold it, and within forty days, was on his way back to his home, in Northumberland county, to pay back the borrowed money.

He later bought a mill from James Irvine. He was married to Miss Mary (Polly) Cotton, February 5th, 1822, by 'Squire Donaldson, of Youngsville, and began housekeeping in a log house which they named "Castle Comfort," on what is now known as the Brooks farm, near Dugall, Pa. In Castle Comfort they had born to them three sons and one daughter. Then in 1826 he founded Irvineburg, near Russellsburg, in Pinegrove township, and was engaged in the lumber business until his death in August 24, 1868. He had a partner when founding, Irvineburg, Refus Weatherby, his brother-in-law who died April 21st, 1833.

This firm, Irvine & Weatherby, commenced the building of a large gristmill and storehouse. Mr. Weatherby died and never saw it finished. Mr. Irvine carried out their plans alone, after the death of his brother-in-law. From that time up to the time of his death, Guy C. Irvine carried on a very large lumber business alone, and everything he touched turned into ready money. He was the first man of the hundreds of mill owners to introduce "gang saws" in the mills of this country. He built mill after mill and bought mill after mill until he owned 20 mills at one time. He was the wealthiest man on the Allegheny river, from its mouth at Pittsburg, to its source in the up-country mountains. For further information concerning this remarkable business man, turn to pages <del>132, 133, 134,</del> of "Old Times in Oildom."

---

## GEO. E. LANGDON.

Geo. E. Langdon, editor and proprietor of the Youngsville Enterprise, one of the representative young men of this section, never did anything of much account to the great oil business, but was born in Duke Center, McKean county, Pa., March 26, 1881, when the oil excitement was at its height. He can remember "Duke" in its palmy days when it was served by two railroads (but now it has none) and had a very large population, living in houses built upon blocks as was typical of oil country mushroom towns. He says that the "wheeze" of the old Duke Center pump station that run night and day for years still lingers in his ears.

He is the son of Rev. and Mrs. C. G. Langdon, now of Warren, Pa. His father was a rig builder and pipe line man. When George was but a small boy his father caught a hand between a walking beam and sampson post, and smashed that member, losing two fingers. The never took up oil work again, but entered the ministry.

Geo. E. Langdon entered the newspaper business at the age of nineteen years, when, in partnership with his father and a brother, J. P., now of Warren, they started the Warren County Record, at Sugar Grove, Pa. Afterward he and his brother were left to carry on the newspaper and printing business. In the spring of 1907, they moved their plant to Youngsville and founded the Youngsville Enterprise. In January, 1909, J. P. took up other work and left Geo. E. proprietor and editor of the Enterprise.

The Enterprise is the pride of Youngsville and one of the best papers in this section and is loyally supported by the people of the town and vicinity. Its mechanical equipment is probably one of the very best to be found in any country office, and includes one of the most complicated and remarkable machines now manufactured—a Lanston Monotype.

Mr. Langdon has a long life before him, and if nothing happens will make himself an influential citizen in the near future, and build up a lucrative business and an enviable reputation.

---

## JAMES ROY.

The following obituary of James Roy is reprinted from a Warren paper published at the time of his death. It is very appropriate.

### IN MEMORIAM.

Since our last issue Warren county has suffered a very heavy loss in the death of Mr. James Roy, of Glade township. He was born in Phelpstown, Ontario Co., N. Y., on the 14th of September, 1822. He came to this state in 1836, locating in Elk township. For many years he was one of the most prominent lumbermen in this section of the state.

In the various business enterprises which engaged his attention, farming, stock raising, oil producing or lumbering, he was ever known for unwavering honesty and integrity. He was not a member of a church but his life would put to shame that of many who are, judged by the text of the Apostle James:

"Pure religion and undefiled before God and the Father is this: To visit the fatherless and widows in their affliction and to keep himself unspotted from the world."

What he knew to be right he did, and had no use for questionable methods of acquiring wealth by taking advantage of the necessities of others.

His generosity was unbounded and his supreme happiness was in doing good.

He died on Friday afternoon surrounded by his two sons and five daughters. The survivors have the deepest sympathy of the community in their irreparable loss.

The following beautiful lines which appeared in print several years ago, are, we think, very appropriate to our late esteemed and benevolent fellow citizen, Mr. James Roy:

## WHAT WAS HIS CREED.

He left a load of anthracite
    In front of a poor widow's door,
When the deep snow, frozen and white,
    Wrap'd street and square, mountain and moor.

That was his deed;
    He did it well;
"What was his creed?"
    I cannot tell.

Blest "in his basket and his store,"
    In sitting down and rising up;
When more he got, he gave the more,
    Witholding not the crust and cup.

He took the lead
    In each good task;
"What was his creed?"
    I did not ask.

His charity was like the snow,
  Soft, white and silken in its fall;
Not like the noisy winds that blow
  From shivering trees and leaves; a pall

      For flower and weed,
        Dropping below.
      "What was his creed?"
        The poor may know.

He had great faith in loaves of bread
  For hungry people, young and old;
And "hope inspired kind words" he said,
  To him he sheltered from the cold.

      For he must feed
        As well as pray.
      "What was his creed?"
        I cannot say.

In words he did not put his trust,
  In faith his words he never writ;
He loved to share his cup and crust
  With all mankind who needed it.

      In time of need
        A friend was he,
      "What was his creed?"
        He told not me.

He put his trust in Heaven, and
  Worked ever on with hand and head;
And what he gave in charity
  Sweetened his sleep and daily bread.

      Let us take heed,
        For life is brief!
      "What was his creed?"
        "What his belief?"

## GLENN W. SCOFIELD.

The portrait herewith represents one of the best lawyers and statesmen that ever graced the nice little city of Warren. His political career commenced many years ago, when the voters sent him to represent them in the state councils at Harrisburg. He made himself felt in the legislative halls to such an extent that when he spoke all listened. He was a man of fine physique and had wonderful oratorical powers. He laid the foundation at Harrisburg for a successful political life. His great talents were ever after given to the people of the United State, his unequalled service to the great state of Wm. Penn only paved the way to more extended service of his beloved country. Term after term in congress was given to him by his admiring constituents until he was appointed one of the United States judges, which position he adorned up to the time of his death. Mr. Scofield was not one of the tricky kind of politicians. No spot or blemish ever appeared either in his private or public life. His constituents will endorse this statement. This is not written in the stereotyped phrase of laudation generally used in the praise of public servants, but it is solid fact. Judge Scofield has left behind him an unsullied record, that future generations will not be ashamed of. His wife was the daughter of Mr. Archibald Tanner, one of the pioneers of Warren. His old stone homestead stands in the very heart of Warren, surrounded by tall native pines, which will not very likely fall vicitims to the woodman's ax, while his son, Archie, and daughter inhabit this earth. It is but a few weeks since the judge's life partner, his wife, was laid to rest by his side, in beautiful Oakland cemetery.

## GEORGE H. LEONHART.

The photo on this page is a very good shadow of a born hotel man.

George H. Leonhart was born May 25th, 1842, near Warren, Pa., in Pinegrove township, and received his education in the Warren schools. He worked during vacations on his father's farm and in the lumber woods until 1860. He then went to Texas and stayed until 1861, then to St. Louis, New Orleans and Chicago. He remained in Chicago, Quincy, Milwaukee and LaSalle until 1865 when he came back to Warren and has remained there up to the present time.

While in Chicago he learned the art of cooking in a large restaurant. After arriving on his "old stamping grounds," at Warren, his thoughts naturally turned to the hotel business, which he has followed all these intervening years with marked success.

His family consists of a wife and two exemplary daughters which makes his home very pleasant.

For several years he owned and conducted the Exchange hotel, then purchased the Struthers house and moved in, renting the Exchange. Since taking possession of the Struthers hotel the rise in real estate and his adaptability as a "landlord" has put a large amount of "filthy lucre" to his credit.

George has, very recently, sold his furniture and rented the building to a young landlord named Gerow, of Tionesta, Pa., and will take a vacation from the hotel business for a time. No doubt he will feel like a cat in "a strange garret."

## A. E. AGRELIUS.

The picture here belongs to A. E. Agrelius, cashier of the Farmers State Bank, of Lindsborg, Kansas.

"Gene" Argelius, as he was familiarly named, was born of Swedish parents and raised on a farm about two miles from Youngsville. He received a common education at a country school and left this town a penniless sawmill hand thirty-three years ago.   After reaching Lindsborg he began the real estate business and soon found himself possessor of money enough to organize the "Farmers' State Bank of Lindsborg, Kansas." He was elected cashier and still holds that position up to the present time.   Mr. Agrelius was one of the organizers of the "Kansas Bankers Association," in 1887, and helped to frame legislation in financial matters, being one of the pioneers in the movement for guaranty of deposits by legal enactment. He was a charter member of the state Temperance Union and was one of the supporters of the prohibitory amendment to the state constitution, which has driven saloons from the state. Mr. Agrelius has held many offices and has been city treasurer for the last twenty years.   He is also a director in a $150,000 manufacturing corporation.   He took a very active part in the organization of Bethany college, of Lindsborg and the musical societies which have a national reputation for the rendition of "Handel's Messiah" given annually for the past twenty-eight years.

In addition to all this he and his estimable wife have reared and educated a regular Roosevelt family of five boys and three girls.   Surely, A. E. Agrelius is entitled to a high seat among the self-made men shown in the biographical sketches in this book.

## JOHN D. ROCKEFELLER.

Who has not seen the this picture? I wonder if there is a man, woman or child, in this broad land of ours, that has not seen the picture of the greatest "oil man" and greatest organizer on the globe, and the richest man of all the billions beneath the shining sun.

I am more than ever surprised that whole books of alleged "history" should be written in trying to make him out, as one of the meanest men in the country. I am not one of those that could see any truth in these bad reports. I am a stranger to him. I never saw the man, but I have seen thousands of men that were working for him, and his company, and I never heard one word of fault found in him by any of his employees, nor has there ever been a strike among his men. It was all praise, praise, praise; I speak with personal knowledge. I have organized 475 insurance lodges, within the last 35 years, all in the oil region, or nearby; thousands of Standard Oil Company workers have became members of my lodges, and all with one accord praise John D. Rockefeller and the Standard Oil Company as a whole. Is not this unparelleled—just think of it! A man at the head of 70,000 employees, and not one of them finding fault with him. Could any but a Christian, from childhood up to old age, show a better record. The fact that he—of his own accord—when but 16 years of age, saved the old First Baptist church, of Cleveland, O., from being sold, on a debt of $2,000) shows in what channel his mind ran. The boy appointed himself as solicitor and raised the money by subscription. Two years after this, at the age of 18, he was elected as one of the trustees of this same church. Then when the boy reached manhood and became immensely wealthy, he gave millions, upon millions to the cause of Christian education. Dear reader, how many men can you think of who would have piled up these millions to help hasten the day that would make them a billionaire (as Mr. Rockefeller will be, if he lives a few years more, and don't give his untold millions, all to the cause of Christianity, and —rating the sufferings of humanity—as he has been doing). Many a well meaning man would have put out these millions on interest, and let them help to shorten the time coming to the billionaire mark. But few men in this wicked world of ours but would prefer the title of being the only billionaire on this earthly ball to the title of being the largest giver to the cause of Christianity.

Now reader, I think that you think, by this time, that Mr. Rockefeller is paying me for this space in my book. I want to tell you that he knows nothing about this, and no other person but myself knows that I am scribling this. I am writing this as no vindivation of anyone. I have always thought deeply on this subject, and was filled with wonder, why so many people will abuse a man who has done so much good, and no harm, to them. Perhaps "the green eyed monster"—jealousy—has something to do with it. Some say that it (the Standard) is a great combine, and combines are very wicked things. The old saying is, "Many men makes light work." It is a plain question to the mind of any fair thinking man, or woman, that if not the Standard combine, people would be paying three or four times as much for refined oil, today (by each using his little pile of cash independently of all others), than they are now paying.

We all know that no man, individually, could have spent the millions in bringing the business up to the point of perfection, that the Standard Oil combination has brought it to. No one man in the United States had money enough to do it. And look at the millions of money saved by the company bringing order out of chaos. Years ago when a big well was struck in new territory, down went the price of oil, taking all but the strongest operators down with it. One well worth a few thousand dollars would cause many millions of dollars loss. Now since the Standard has spent millions in investigating, and experimenting, and figuring, no flucuations up and down takes place and when the oil is run the cash for it is ready instead of taking paper promises ahead six or eight months, and many times the payee would not last as long as the promise and all was gone; and all this was done by courage and fearlessness. It took both, to spend so many millions when the company might wake up, any morning, and learn that the production had ceased. No one knew to a certainty, that there was any oil to be found, beyond the banks of Oil creek, and it seems to my weak vision almost a miracle, that John D. Rockefeller, always chose the right man to fill the almost uncountable positions of his great company. Who ever heard of an employee being "bounced" by the Standard Oil Company. It is wonderful, indeed, that one man's head can contain such an unlimited amount of discernment His lieutenants were always wisely chosen. And now, as I write, I pick up the Oil City Daily Derrick, and learn that "yesterday John D. Rockefeller contributed to the straving millions in China, through the Red Cross, $5,000." How many hearts, both Christian, and heathen, with swell with thanks to "the richest man in the world." While this $5,000 worth of "the bread of life" is indeed saving the lives of those that are at the point of death, by starvation. Is John D. Rocekefeller worthy of praise or censure? It will not puzzle the brain of any woman or man to answer this question.

And now, to end this brief mention of the most successful man on God's footstool, I will say that to me, it looks little short of a miracle for any man to choose exactly the right men to help organize this company (which is the wonder of the whole world), and not make one mistake. It looks like inspiration to select such men to found the structure and carry it to its unprecedented success, as William Rockefeller (his brother), Henry M. Flagler, John D. Archibold, Henry H. Rogers, Charles Pratt, Hon. John L. McKinney, Hon J. C. McKinney, C. N. Payne, and many others that I could mention if my book was large enough.

## EDWARD WALKER

This cut is an excellent likeness of Mr. Edward Walker, one of Warren's old and successful business men and prominent and respected citizens. From an oil pumper to one of the largest if not the largest manufacturers of ice cream in the State of Pennsylvania explains, briefly of the strides forward Mr. Walker has made and his arrival at the business goal of life.

Pumping oil was interesting but it did not appeal to Mr. Walker as the vocation he desired. He branched off into the printing business and with S. E. Walker, his brother, present publisher of the Warren Evening Times, operated a job office for a short time. And S. E. Walker, his brother, present publisher of the Warren ren Evening Mirror, for it was so merged in 1882. Mr. Walker, the subject of this sketch, guiding its destinies for many years as publisher and proprietor.

In Jamestown, Chautauqua county, N. Y., on the 21st day of April, 1856, Mr. Edward Walker was born. The mother dying in his infancy, he was taken to Delaware county and reared on the farm of his uncle. When a young man he came to Warren and has since made it his home. By hard work, a natural business ability, honest principles and a pleasing personality, Mr. Walker rose to the top rung of the ladder of business success. And he started at the bottom, too.

In a small house in the rear of his home, Mr. Walker launched his ice cream business. As the volume of trade grew, he expanded the plant by tearing down an old barn and erecting a commodious factory. In 1904 the factory was destroyed by fire. This was discouraging but it did not deter Mr. Walker from his outlined onward march. Purchasing property on Union street which included a building erected for

the suspended factory, he opened the factory which has grown,
through Mr. Walker's executive ability, into the largest
producer of ice cream in this section. The question of a fresh
cream supply than bobbed up and became a knotty problem.
Mr. Walker met this condition with characteristic wisdom and
energy by purchasing the Foster farm, which is located on the
Warren-Jamestown traction line at Riverside and adjoins the
Prendergast farm in Chautauqua county. A creamery was
located on this farm, now known as the Walker farm. Mr.
Walker then, extensively known as an expert manufacturer of
ice cream, became associated with Jamestown, N. Y., parties
and the Jamestown Ice Cream Company was organized and is
now one of the largest factories in New York State. Mr.
Walker is president of that concern. This venture which
proved a very successful one, again resurrected the cream
supply problem and it was met squarely and unhesitatingly
as before by purchasing the Sugar Grove Canning Company's
plant and installing therein a creamery and condensed milk
plant which is without doubt the finest in Western Pennsylvania. The creameries, condensed milk plants and ice cream
factory here, together with his outside interests, makes Mr.
Walker one of the biggest dealers in this line of business in
this part of the country.

His factory in Warren is a handsome, three-story, brick
building, supplied with all the latest devices and machinery.
Many important pieces of equipment came from the fertile
mind of Mr. Walker himself, who has many good inventions
to his credit, among these being a brine freezer which was invented in 1900.

The Walker Ice Cream Company, of Warren, of which
corporation Edward Walker is president, supplies all the important trade centers with sweet cream, condensed milk and ice
cream.

## LEWIS KRAEER.

Lewis Kraeer, of Sheffield, Pa., was born December 10th, 1845, in Washington county, Pa. He attended the country school until he was 16 years of age, and then enlisted in the 13th Regiment Cavalry, Co. E, and went to war. He was captured by the Confederates in the battle of Winchester and taken to Libby prison, but was exchanged at the expiration of 17 days. About this time his father became blind and he was honorably discharged. This was in the summer of 1864, and he returned to his home in Washington county.

Mr. Kraeer was employed about three months as brakeman and fireman on the P., C. & St. L. R. R., and then went to the oil field at Smith's Ferry on the Ohio river, with only three cents to his name. He served some time dressing tools and drilling and then took a contract to drill a well. Oil was selling at $8.00 a barrel, but before the rig was completed it dropped to 25 cents. Throwing up his contract, he went to Parker's Landing and went to work by the day dressing tools and drilling. He took what money he had accumulated and started in business for himself, getting nothing but dry holes. Not dismayed, however, he persevered, and in 1875 luck began to come his way. Up to the present time he has drilled with uninterrupted success in Butler, Warren, McKean, Forest, Elk, Cameron, Lycoming, Fayette and Tioga counties, Pa., and Allegany county, N. Y. He also had a number of wells in Ohio and Indiana. Altogether our subject has drilled about 500 wells. He was a large property holder in Ohio but has sold most of it. He also owned land in Indiana but disposed of it. At the present time he is a stockholder in the Pure Oil Company.

Mr. Kraeer has always believed that oil and gas could be found in paying quantities at a greater depth than had hitherto been drilled. In 1909 he started a test well at Lower Sheffield, hoping to find the Medina sand. The well is located about 1,350 feet above sea level.

The following is log of what is known as the "Kraeer Deep Well:" Casing, 280 feet; Clarendon sand, 1,079 feet; some oil in this sand which is 20 feet through; some showing of gas at 1,160 feet, not paying quantities. Cooper or Sheffield sand at 1,392 feet; gas at 2,330 feet, not paying; a sand at 2,700 feet, 35 feet thick; a sand at 3.3600 feet, 15 feet thick; 600 feet of black shale; 150 feet of limestone, then 90 feet of shale, followed by 390 of limestone. At a depth of 4,905 feet, salt in a solid form for 95 feet; at 5,000 feet, a mixture of sand and slate was run into, which continued to a depth of 5,250 feet; the well began caving, a lining of 4½-inch casing was put in, 5,250 feet; after drilling about 30 feet, the casing parted and dripped, and the well was plugged. This is the deepest well ever drilled in Northeastern oil fields, and in fact but one deeper well has been drilled in the Eastern field.

Our subject is a Democrat with Independent tendencies. In 1910, Mr. Kraeer was candidate for representative in State Legislature of Pennsylvania, but was defeated. He takes his defeat in a Bryan way.

He has traveled through England, Scotland, and France, having made two trips to those countries.

Mr. Kraeer was married August 30, 1866 to Miss Hepay Baker, of Washington county, Pa. Ten children were born to them. Of these five are living: Samuel, Edward, Caroline, Alda and Oliver. His second wife, whom he married in 1890, was Miss Flora Kelley, of Tidioute, Pa. They have two children, Lois and Donald.

Our subject is a member of the Odd Fellows and Wanda Club, of Sheffield. He is a member of the United Presbyterian church and takes an active interest in the furtherance of Christian work. Mr. Kraeer's love for home is among his shining traits, and his devotion to his family makes him a man worthy of the highest esteem.

## JAMES B. BORLAND.

James B. Borland, managing editor of the Franklin Evening News and president of the company which publishes it, is a native of Lawrence county, but practically all of his life has been spent in Franklin. While his newspaper does not date back to the earliest days of the oil industry, it has been associated more or less with the business, particularly with the refining and manufacturing branch.

In his early youth Mr. Borland displayed an aptitude for the printing business. In 1875, when he was only 14 years of age, he and J. A. Morrison bought a small hand press and printed cards on a small scale, continuing in that business for about a year. In 1877 Mr. Borland and C. L. Griffin, now a Franklin merchant, published the Venango Star, a monthly newspaper. Later he and J. Ross Barackman published the High School Monthly, and after that passed out of existence Mr. Borland assisted in the publication of the French Creek Daily, a small boys' daily. It was while he worked on this paper that he decided to start a daily that was more pretentious. And so, on February 18, 1878, the Evening News was launched by him, Barackman and James B. Muse, now editor of the Democratic Vindicator at Tionesta. In a short time Barackman dropped out and his place was taken by Alex. G. McElhinney. The News was about the size of a small handbill, but it met with popular favor and continued to exist, though it passed through many financial storms.

Mr. Borland has had numerous partners in the enterprise, but he has been associated with the paper since the day of its first publication. It is now published by a corporation and is housed in what is conceded to be the finest newspaper building in any small city in the country.

The Evening News is distinguished from the fact that it is perhaps the only boys' daily, that ever reached the proportions of a real newspaper, at least one the size and influence of the News.

---

## SAMUEL PETERSON.

This picture represents one of the most remarkable self-made men in this part of the country. Samuel Peterson was born in Denmark and when but 17 years old came to this country without capital or friends. He attended school in this country until he could talk "United States," and when 22 years of age he commenced the manufacture of handles a n d spokes in a diminitive little building at Irvineton, Pa. His business increased quite fast and it soon became necessary to look for more room. He then in the year of 1882 built a large and commodious factory at Warren, Pa., with all the modern conveniences. The business seemingly continued coming his way and he was obliged to build two more large buildings at Warren. He also built handle factories at other places, one at Titusville, Pa., one at Cochranton, Pa., and in the spring and summer of 1911 he built another at Campbell, Mo., this facilitates taken care of a large and growing business. He carries a very large stock of both rough and finished materials and ships his goods to nearly all the states of the Union. Mr. Peterson has of late years invested a large amount of money in real estate and stock in other concerns. He is a director in the Jefferson County Gas Co. and the Citizens National Bank. He lives in one of the finest residences in Warren. He is also some of a farmer having purchased four of the best farms in the fertile valley of Broken Straw between Youngsville and Pittsfield and fitted them up with buildings, stock and machinery of all descriptions. There are many wealthy men in Warren, a majority of them having made their wealth by speculation, but Mr. Peterson has made his money by close attention to all the details of a growing industry.

## HENRY R. ROUSE.

The portrait of this little sketch is put here in remembrance of one of the most remarkable men that ever made a home in Warren County. Henry R. Rouse was born at Westfield, Chautauqua County, N. Y., the ninth of October, 1823. He was the son of Samuel D. and Sarah Rouse. He received a good academic education in his native town, chiefly by his own exertions. He grew up in indigent circumstances. His diligence, honesty and kindness won the esteem and help of his teachers, most of whom remitted his tuition fees, but in after years he paid all with interest. He, before reaching his majority, migrated across the State line and reached on foot Warren, landing among the Penemites with only one dollar left in his pocket. Finally he brought up at

Tidioute and taught school one term with great success. Lumber was money those days, and he took part of his wages in shingles. This laid the foundation for a large fortune. When about 19 years of age he became a citizen of Enterprise, Southwest Township, Warren County, Pa., where he remained until the time of his death. At Enterprise he soon made himself felt in the business world. He bought fine tracts of pine and hemlock timber, built a large saw mill and cleared the best farm in the vicinity. The people of this county was not slow to recognize his good qualities, and they sent him to the State Legislature, where he proved himself to be a full equal of many older men with many years experience in legislative matters. When the oil business was in its infancy he was quick to take hold of some of the best territory on Oil Creek. But this wealth caused his extremely sudden death. Just when he began to realize that he was one of God's favored few, he was called hence, and the manner of his death had been unheard of up to that eventful moment. He drilled a well on one of his leased farms at Rouseville, a new oil town named in his honor, and when the pay was reached a tremendous flow of oil and gas went skyward with a roar that filled the valley of Oil Creek. At that time the tremendous force of this now natural blessing was not understood and a large crowd of men gathered around the great curiosity and some one was smoking that most useless of all useless things, a dirty cigar, and when the gas came in contact with that little roll of tobacco leaves the greatest explosion of the whole oil region took place. Many men were killed instantly, many were maimed and scared for the balance of their life. Mr. Rouse was hurled to the ground unconscious, but soon recovered an upright position and ran with oil saturated and flaming clothes, but soon became exhausted and fell to the ground. Two men picked him up and carried him from the flames. This greatest of oil country holocausts took place April 17, 1861.

Although suffering excruciating pain he was brought back to consciousness, in a short time, and wonderful to state, he realized that he was in a dying condition and proceeded to make his will, inside of two hours after the accident took place.

Here is a copy of his will, which reads as if he had spent days and weeks on it in place of pain racked hours:

In the name of God, Amen, I, Henry R. Rouse, being as I believe near my last moments, but sound in mind, do make this my last will and testament:

1—My executors to be George H. Dimmick, Samuel D. Rouse and Samuel Z. Brown.

2—I bequeath to my father, Samuel D. Rouse, five hundred dollars per year during his life time.

3—Rouse & Mitchell hold the notes of A. Skinner and Allen Wright for twenty-five hundred dollars. My half I bequeath to them. They are having hard enough times without having to pay the note.

4—All the leases of Rouse & Mitchell and Rouse, Mitchell & Brown I want to have their leases at one-half the oil, and I bequeath to them all my share of said rents over the one-half the products of the wells, as now stipulated, to be paid in their respective leases.

5—I bequeath to George H. Dimmick two thousand dollars for the use of himself and his mother to be paid out of the residue when my estate is settled up.

6—To John Mitchell I bequeath my black mare.

7—I have the Sheriff's Deed of the store and dwelling house occupied by Thomas Moreau. I bequeath said property to his two youngest children, Eva and Maggie, their father to have the use of it until they come of age.

8—I bequeath the residue of my estate after making some other bequests to the Commissioners of Warren county, the interest of it to be expended on the roads of said county.

9—I have a little namesake, Harry Rouse, in East Granby, Conn. I bequeath him five hundred dollars. I cannot think of his name. His mother is the daughter of Joel C. Rouse-Viets.

10—David H. Taylor I bequeath to him five hundred dollars.

12—I bequeath to my aunt, Clara C. Hart, five hundred dollars.

13—I bequeath to Myron Waters five hundred dollars to be paid when my estate is settled up.

14—I also bequeath five hundred dollars to my hired boy, Myron Dunham, to be paid when my estate is settled up.

15—I wish to change the object of the bequest contained in No. 8 so as to give the benefit of one-half of it to the poor of Warren county. It is given in trust to the County Commissioners for that purpose.

16—To Almedia Arnold I bequeath two hundred dollars.

17—To Joel C. Rouse, of Saratoga, N. Y., I bequeath three hundred dollars.

18—I bequeath to Mrs. Moreau, wife of Thomas Moreau, three hundred dollars.

19—Two gentlemen carried me out of the fire. I bequeath to them each one hundred dollars.

20—Let my funeral be without display. No funeral sermon to be preached. Bury me by the side of my mother at Westfield.

21—I have a beautiful picture, an engraving, in Hershfield's store at Pittsburg. I bequeath it to William Hearst, of Meadville.

22—I bequeath my library to my father.

23—I bequeath my wardrobe to Mrs. Thomas Moreau. I have nothing more to add at present. I authorize all who are here present to witness the foregoing as my last will and testament.

In testimony that the foregoing is the last will and testament of Henry R. Rouse

## SILAS E. WALKER.

Silas E. Walker, publisher and owner of the Warren Evening a n d Weekly Times, practically a lifelong resident of Warren, Pa., and numbered among that city's respected and prominent residents, has struggled step by step up the rugged, steep path of life toward that goal coveted by all men—business success. That he reached the top is due to the predominating composition in his makeup—perseverance, coupled with honest, upright and straightforward qualities and a pleasing personality. From laborer to contractor; from part owner of a job printing office to the owner of the leading daily paper in Warren—this in a nutshell chronicles the strides Silas E. Walker made in realizing ambitions.

Silas E. Walker was born near Deposit, Delaware county, New York, and came to Warren in 1868. He was then 16 years of age. For several years he followed the plastering trade. He heard the "call of petroleum" and branched off into the oil business. This was in 1876 when the first petroleum strike was made in this vicinity. For a year he labored as an oil pumper and then went to Bradford, Pa. Following a year's stay in that city he returned to this locality and settled in Clarendon, engaged in the oil drilling business as a contractor and was very successful. Mr. Walker thought there was a good opening for him in the meat business and opened a shop with George W. Cogswell as his partner. He subsequently disposed of his meat interests and returned to plastering and masonry and prospered as a contractor in those lines.

It was in 1893 that Mr. Walker entered the newspaper business. He launched the daily and weekly Democrat, selling out in 1900 during which year he started the Warren Evening Times. In 1901 Mr. Walker rebought the Democrat and closed its life. It was hard sledding with the Times and the upward route was beset with difficulties, but one by one they were overcome. The Times kept its head "above water" and slowly grew in circulation and prestige, in the present, 1911, Mr. Walker adding to his equipment a perfecting press capable of printing twelve pages at one operation.

Silas E. Walker has been a moving spirit in politics as long as he has been a booster for Warren and Warren county and that has been always. As a Democrat he has labored continually for his chosen party and is recognized as one of the leaders of this party in this section. Mr. Walker served as deputy revenue collector under the administration of Grover Cleveland, was one of the presidential electors chosen eight years ago. Mr. Walker served as constable in Warren at one time, also.

Mr. Walker is active in lodge affairs, never allowing the opportunity to slip by of attending meetings of the organizations he belongs to, when possible to participate.

Summing up his life in a few words he has been a sterling citizen, a clean, scrupulous officer holder and a shrewd, successful man of business.

## MANLEY W. BOVEE.

Manley W. Bovee was born in Eagle Township, Waukesha County, Wisconsin, February 25, 1849. Went to Pennsylvania in February, 1869, and did his first work in the oil business on the Wood farm near Petroleum Center pumping for Willis Irwin and Milton Stewart.

Worked near Fagundas a short time in 1870 and then went to McCray Hill where he worked for the same concern. Was married to Mrs. Elizabeth W. McCool, August 29, 1871. Have four children, all boys.

In the fall of 1872 moved to Clarion County, working near Turkey City until June, 1873, at which time he and his cousin, Frank A. Bovee opened a store at Pickwick, a new town started there at that time. They ran the store until 1880. During this time they got into the oil business being compelled to take old wells and every other thing too numerous to mention in payment of accounts. They soon had wells at Triangle and Shippenville and a lot of junk which they shipped to McKean County and drilled on the Barse tract their first wells that paid.

They closed out their grocery business in 1880 and from that time devoted all of their time to producing oil, owning properties in Warren, Forest, Venango and Butler counties.

Mr. Bovee in 1888 was elected county chairman of the Democratic party, and in 1890 was nominated for the Senate, his opponent being W. R. Crawford. Uncle Billy beat him nicely.

In the fall of 1892 his name was placed on the ticket for Assembly. Mr. John Hunter who had been nominated at the convention withdrawing. There was no show for an election as his opponent, the Hon. C. C. Thompson, who was very popular.

Was nominated for the Assembly in 1898, his opponent being Hon. Ed. Parshall. Mr. Bovee made a fight this time but Mr. Parshall won out by 84 votes, a Republican majority of 2,000 being reduced to those figures.

Mr. Bovee has taken an active interest in lodge affairs belonging to the Ancient Order of United Workmen since March, 1873, now one of the old members. He is a member of the I. O. O. F. of Grand Valley, Pa., the Knights of the Maccabees, and for twenty years has taken an active part in the Grange. He was master of the Pomona Grange for four years of Warren County, Pa.

Has been located at Bartlesville for six years.

When Mr. Bovee left Grand Valley and took up his residence in Bartlesville, Grand Valley, Warren County, Pa., lost one of its brightest citizens, and Bartlesville gained accordingly. He belongs to many lodges and is as much at home in one as any other. He will take any office in any lodge that he belongs to and perform its duties from the start as well as if he had always filled the chair of all of them. In fact he seems to possess all the gifts that nature showers upon mortal man. He is competent to successfully fill any office within the gift of the people, and the only reason that he has not been one of our law makers is that he belongs to a minority party.

Forest Furniture Factory, Youngsville, Pa.

## FOREST FURNITURE FACTORY.

Here is the picture of the Forest Furniture Factory of Youngsville, Pa. It is one of the great money makers of the above named borough. Its four stories is packed with the finest and latest style machinery. The location is directly in the forks of the Lake Shore and Pennsylvania Railroads, a very desirable location. Lumber is shipped in and furniture shipped out with no horse power required. If the Lord had made the lay of the land with a view to the building of just such an industrial building, it would not be excelled as a location for the purpose for which it was built.

Fire protection is perfect, as the deep blue waters of the Broken Straw creek flows gently by, and in easy reach if ever needed. The furniture made here is of the latest style and best make. When once used by dealers there is no more use for traveling salesmen. Dealers send orders after a trial, without solicitation. Orders are lying around the office in great piles unfilled. The superintendent has just called in three salesmen to save being swamped with business.

Amel Sagadahl is the very efficient superintendent, and likewise an inventor of new machinery used in the manufacture of furniture. He has secured a half dozen new patents within the last two years that are much appreciated by manufacturers at large. The Forest factory now has nearly 10,000 square feet of floor surface, room for 200 men, and in the near future a new addition will be added. More room is a real necessity to meet the growth of the business.

The officers of the company are as follows: President, Amel Sagadahl; secretary and treasurer, Arthur Briggs; superintendent, Amel Sagadahl; bookkeeper, F. H. Hokinson; directors, Amel Sagadahl, F. E. Sherman, Jamestown, N. Y.; Wilson McGrew, Pittsfield, Pa.; Edwin Swanson and W. J. Mead.

## JAMES D. WOODARD.

James D. Woodard was born in Youngsville, Pa., October 11, 1861, and when but a mere youth commenced to learn the tailor's trade with Charles Anderson of this place. He prospered from the start. After a few years he transferred his business to Erie, Pa., and after a successful period of business he became a useful citizen of Warren, Pa. By this move Erie was a loser and Warren a gainer. For the last twenty-five years Warren has had the benefit of his business genius. He prospered from his first investment. Everybody recollects the Woodard & Lessor Clothing Store, managed successfully by Mr. Woodard as senior partner. After a few years Mr. Woodard became sole owner and carried on the business with marked success until he sold out the clothing business and became a large stockholder in the Warren Street Railway which interest he still retains at the present time and now holds the important office of secretary of the company. Mr. Woodard does not tie himself down to one business interest alone, but is connected with many that goes to make Warren the most beautiful city of its size found anywhere in the United States. In addition to helping organize the Warren road, he is one of the main stockholders in the Warren & Jamestown Street Railway and was the main mover in this excellent enterprise. And as James D. Woodard is of a makeup that cannot lie down on his laurels on "easy street" and take a well earned rest, he has recently built one of the best equipped theaters found in Warren or any other town, and "just to keep his hand in" he has recently bought the Humphry House property at Jamestown, N. Y., and will soon build a play house that will set the pattern for that flourishing city of the lake.

He has now within the past month taken his family to the big hotel to make their home in the fast growing Chautauqua County city of Jamestown, N. Y. Since becoming an Empire State resident, he has made many up-to-date improvements on this far famed hotel. Nothing is left undone that goes to make a first class stopping place for the best class of hotel patrons, and with all departments rivaling the first class city hotels the charge is no higher than the average country hotel charges. In fact Mr. Woodard has improved the house from top to bottom without regard to cost, and best of all, he has made his riches by close, intelligent attention to honest business. No wild speculation has entered into his business. His mature judgment has always been his sure helper. As "Jim" bought the heart of the city, we expect to hear that he has bought the whole circle around him ere many years.

## JOHN W. AGREELIUS.

This is a picture of one of the self-made men of borough of Youngsville. By his strict attention to honest business, during his whole life, he has earned that title. He was born in Sweden, 74 years ago, and came to this country when 12 years of age. On his arrival in this country he made his home with the family of Joseph Mead, on Mathews Run, for one year. At the age of 21 years he struck out for himself and commenced the business of peddling wooden pumps all around this part of the country. He was very successful at that business. When he had saved up a sufficient pile of cash he built a shingle mill and was an adept at the manufacture of shingles. He, after several years of success at that business, was overtaken by a fire, with but a small amount of insurance, and the devouring element laid his little fortune low. But, nothing daunted, he soon rebuilt his shingle mill with a stave and basket manufactory added. Then he built the best brick store building in town, filled it with goods of different kinds, and was soon on the road to mercantile success. He has continued the selling of different kinds of goods up to the present time.

When a young man he formed the acquaintance of Miss Sarah Jane Dexyou, of Russellsburgh, and took her as a life partner, and lived many happy years with her. The couple reared four children, three girls and one boy. Alice is a Mrs. Siggins, of Meadville; Grace is a Mrs. Rhodes, of Corry, and Blanche is Mrs. Jobs, of Erie. Three highly cultured young ladies, well mated, and happy. The son is a druggist of more than ordinary ability. When graduating at Buffalo he stood at the head of his class of 50 at both junior and senior examinations. The only time that feat has been done (the same student taking both premiums) at Buffalo was when Ray V. Agreelius done it, and Ray is now superintendent of his father's big store and "is a chip off the old block" as far as strict attention to business is concerned.

John W. Agreelius has been a useful citizen. He has been a School Director, Postmaster, Trustee of the M. E. church for many years. He was a Trustee 27 years ago and President of the Board when the first brick church was built in town, and last year the old church was torn down and a larger and new one built, and as a coincidence Mr. Agreelius was, and now is, President of the Board of Trustees. He, for many years, has been the competent teacher of Bible class No. 1 and is the best Bible scholar in the M. E. Sunday school. His wife died last year and a good Christian church worker went to her Heavenly reward. To temper his lonesomeness, to a certain degree, John makes monthly visits to his three married daughters at Erie, Corry and Meadville. With all this he keeps a quiet eye on his many kinds of business, and things pass off with no drawback. If John W. Agreelius is not a self-made man, Warren county don't contain one.

## JOHN WILLIAM WAITZ.

John William Waitz, of Oil City, Pa., son of John and Louisa (Melitz) Waitz, was born August 13th, 1858, at Albany, N. Y. His father moved from Erie to Oil City, Pa., in the palmy days of the oil business, and there spent the last days of his life, dying in 1882, at the age of 64 years.

Our subject attended the common schools at Oil City and Rouseville until he was fifteen years of age, when he went to Erie, Pa., and served as clerk in the grocery store of French & McKnight for three years; has always been studious and technical and is a self-made man.

When Johnny Steele, or "Coal Oil Johnny," was winning fame as a prodigal by spending the large income from the wells on the farm now owned by our subject, Mr. Waitz was a small boy at Rouseville, and he has grown up among the derricks of this region, gaining thereby a practical knowledge of the business, which has enabled him to prosper to such a large extent. From boyhood Mr. Waitz has always been a close student of oleaginous events, and upon general principles there are but few better posted men in the business. This thorough knowledge of the industry, together with an indomitable will, push, energy and enterprise, enabled him, in assuming control of the famous Steele farm, when about 20 years of age and has since turned every available resource to the best possible advantage. The old farm, which had grown into a barren waste by years of neglect, was soon transformed into a pleasing and sightly place. The old wells, too, which had gone to rack and were barely making sufficient production to cover the cost of operating them, were renovated, put in first-class order, and by a systematized method of operation the old producers were made to yield a handsome production.

View of the John W. Waitz Farm

With characteristic conservativeness he drilled quite a large number of new wells, all, or nearly all, of which proved paying investments. Mr. Waitz at present has 80 producing wells on the Steele farm, and it is safe to say that he will take out more money in oil than there was in the halcyon days of "Coal Oil Johnny." Mr. Waitz has since added to his producing area by the purchase of the west side of both the Archie and John Buchanan farms, and which lay adjacent to the original Steele farm. This, too, proved good territory, and on which he has in operation 50 producing wells, making in the aggregate 130 wells. These give a handsome production and is considered one of the best paying properties along the placid waters of historic Oil Creek.

His ventures in the Raymilton field and other localities in Venango county have likewise proved to be successful, and to him belongs the honor of discovering the northern extension of the Raymilton field. He is also interested in various manufacturing concerns in Venango county, has mining interests in Arizona and old Mexico.

In 1870, when his father moved from Oil City to Rouseville, Johnny Steele had already squandered his fortune and was employed as baggage master at the Rouseville depot; and when our subject, a boy of 14 years of age, went about the depot, little did he think that some day he would be the owner of the Johnny Steele farm and 250 oil wells.

Mr. Waitz is mechanically inclined. When but 18 years of age, he conceived the idea of pumping oil wells by compressed air. A large amount of experimenting had been done in the way of raising fluid by compressed air, the fluid being raised by the spray, in the proportion of about ten parts of air to one of fluid; Mr. Waitz's idea was to raise the fluid in a solid column, upon the theory that if a cubic foot of air was supplied it would raise a cubic foot of oil. From this idea he has originated the plant for flowing oil by use of compressed air now in operation on his property on the Steele farm. Among the leading features of this system is that whereby the air is compressed through the cylinder of an air compressor from one well to another which gives the air compressor the benefit of the back air pressure from the wells as they are flowed, thereby reducing the horse power required, the air being supplied from well to well, or from one group of wells to another until all the wells on an oil farm have been daily discharged of fluid. The air lines to the various wells, can, if desired, be conducted underground, so that the land can be tilled and utilized as farming land.

Mr. Waitz is a man who always makes himself familiar with the details of his various enterprises, and is guided largely by his own judgment. His hobby being to do all work in a practical way, he has ever utilized his ideas to that end.

**Birthplace of "Coal Oil Johnny"**

Politically, Mr. Waitz is an Independent Republican, and has taken quite an interest in politics, and is a thirty-second degree Mason.

Mr. Waitz was married in 1889 to Myrtle M. Neill, of Oil City, and to them one son, William Neill Waitz, has been born.

He is a member of the Presbyterian church, and is a liberal contributor to charitable organizations. He has been quite a traveler, having been very generally over the United States, Europe and South America.

His advice to young men is: "Be studious and persevering, and do not waste your earnings and time in frivolity; protect your standing; be self-reliant and be careful in your selection of associates." Personally Mr. Waitz is a man of rare personal charm and strict business integrity.

A few facts about this world-renowned farm will be somewhat interesting to readers of the present day.

The farm was formerly owned by a Mrs. McClintock, a widow. She adopted Johnny Steele when he was but a child. She was burned to death by lighting a fire in a stove with coal oil—the very thing that made the farm famous. The old farm house is still in good shape, and is now occupied by Mr. Waitz's teamster, and the office in which Johnny done his business is now being used as a chicken coop. Quite a change from the palmy days of "Coal Oil Johnny."

The writer of this had the pleasure of attending the first installation of Mr. Waitz in the Masonic Lodge at Rouseville when he first entered the oil business.

# CONTENTS

| | Page |
|---|---|
| Hauling Oil on Sleds | 7 |
| Staging Before Railroads Were a Blessing to Oil City | 9 |
| Oil Creek Pond "Fresh" | 12 |
| Pithole Hotel and Livery Charges | 14 |
| General Burnside's Railroad | 16 |
| James S. McCray | 19 |
| The Grandins and J. B. White | 24 |
| Narrow Escape From Being a Bloated Bondholder | 27 |
| The Lumber Business in Parker City | 29 |
| John Galey and the Robinsons | 33 |
| Parker City | 36 |
| Oil City Sixty Years Ago | 39 |
| Jack McCray | 43 |
| A Greedy Landlord | 46 |
| When Oil City Was a Shanty Town | 53 |
| High Standard Officials Who Are Natives of Brokenstraw Valley | 56 |
| Big Things Which Started in Western Pennsylvania | 60 |
| Could Not Give His Rocky Hillside Away | 63 |
| A Public Spirited and Successful Editor | 68 |
| Something About Gas | 72 |
| Youngsville's Prospects of Oil and Gas | 75 |
| Bad Oil Speculation | 80 |
| H. P. Kinnear and the I. O. O. F. | 83 |
| Oil Region Inhabitants | 88 |
| Pickpockets | 92 |
| Old Time Lumbermen | 95 |
| New Times in Oildom | 100 |
| Old Time Oil Tanks | 104 |
| Starving Animals | 110 |
| Old Time Quadrille Band | 114 |
| Churches in the Old Times | 118 |
| God Bless the Swedes | 123 |
| Youngsville's Founders and Business Men | 129 |
| New Times in Oildom | 137 |
| "Dunc" Karns and "Tom" King | 141 |

## CONTENTS—(CONTINUED)

Warren's Big Men ............................................... 145
West Virginia Experiences ..................................... 151
Rambling Recollections of the Last Fifty Years in the Oil and
    Lumber Country ............................................. 158
Interesting Letters to the Author.............................. 164

### BIOGRAPHICAL SKETCHES.

Gen. Charles Miller ........................................... 167
Hon. O. C. Allen .............................................. 168
Hon. John L. McKinney ......................................... 169
Hon. Chas. W. Stone ........................................... 171
Hon. W. M. Lindsey ............................................ 172
C. N. Payne ................................................... 173
Frank M. Knapp ................................................ 174
Capt. H. H. Cumings ........................................... 175
Hon. J. C. McKinney ........................................... 176
Hon. R. E. Dickinson .......................................... 177
A. J. Hazeltine ............................................... 178
Hon. J. B. White .............................................. 179
Cyrus A. Cornen ............................................... 181
E. B. Grandin ................................................. 186
George W. Dinsmoor ............................................ 187
E. O. Emerson ................................................. 190
A. E. Agrelius ................................................ 182
George C. Priestley ........................................... 191
McKinney's Cornet Band ........................................ 195
N. P. Wheeler ................................................. 196
Joseph A. Schofield ........................................... 197
Youngsville's Fire Department ................................. 198
John C. Dinsmoor .............................................. 200
Lansing Ditmars Wetmore ....................................... 202
Lewis Emery, Jr................................................ 204
Levi Smith .................................................... 209
Guy C. Irvine ................................................. 213
Geo. E. Langdon ............................................... 214
James Roy ..................................................... 215
Glenn W. Scofield ............................................. 218
George H. Leonhart ............................................ 219
A. E. Agrelius ................................................ 220
John D. Rockefeller ........................................... 221
Edward Walker ................................................. 224

Lewis Kraeer ......................................................226
James B. Borland ...............................................228
Samuel Peterson ................................................229
Henry R. Rouse ................................................230
Silas E. Walker ................................................234
Manley W. Bovee ..............................................236
Forest Furniture Factory .......................................239
James D. Woodard .............................................240
John W. Agreelius .............................................241
John William Waitz ...........................................243

FOURTH EDITION, COPYRIGHT 1912, BY GEO. W. BROWN.

Metalmark Books is a joint imprint of The Pennsylvania State University
Press and the Office of Digital Scholarly Publishing at The Pennsylvania State
University Libraries. The facsimile editions published under this
imprint are reproductions of out-of-print, public domain works that hold
a significant place in Pennsylvania's rich literary and cultural past.
Metalmark editions are primarily reproduced from the University Libraries' extensive
Pennsylvania collections and in cooperation with other
state libraries. These volumes are available to the public for viewing online
and can be ordered as print-on-demand paperbacks.

LIBRARY OF CONGRESS CATALOGING-IN-PUBLICATION DATA

Brown, George W. (George Washington), 1828–1916, author.
Old times in oildom / George W. Brown.
pages    cm
Summary: "The memoirs and stories of George W. Brown, who was deeply
involved in the oil industry in Pennsylvania in the late nineteenth and early twen-
tieth centuries. First published in 1911 by the Derrick Publishing Company"
—Provided by publisher.
ISBN 978-0-271-06699-8 (pbk. : alk. paper)
1. Oil Creek Valley (Crawford County and Venango County, Pa.)—History.
2. Oil City (Pa.)—History.
3. Petroleum—Pennsylvania—History.
4. Brown, George W. (George Washington), 1828–1916.
I. Title.

F157.O3B83 2015
974.8'97—dc23
2015008605

Printed in the United States of America
Reprinted by The Pennsylvania State University Press, 2015
University Park, PA 16802-1003

The University Libraries at Penn State and the Penn State University Press,
through the Office of Digital Scholarly Publishing, produced this volume to
preserve the informational content of the original. In compliance with current
copyright law, this reprint edition uses digital technology and is printed on paper
that complies with the permanent Paper Standard issued by the
National Information Standards Organization (ANSI Z39.48–1992).